I0793610

IMAGES
of America

GRAFTON

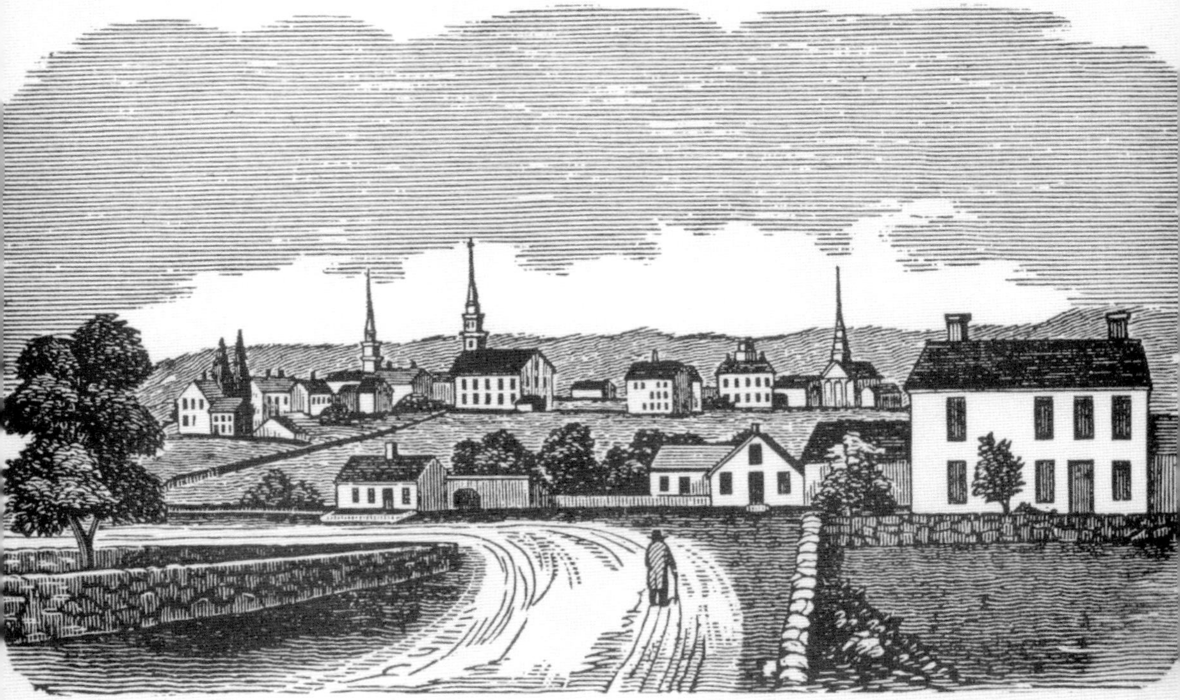

GRAFTON AS IT WAS IN 1839, FROM OLD UPTON ROAD

In this 1839 woodcut, a man strolls down Old Upton Road in the direction of Grafton Center. In the distance, three church steeples and the Grafton Inn with its belvedere can be seen. This street, once called Nipmuc Road, was the original route into Grafton and followed an Indian trail from Mendon. The population of Grafton at that time was about 3,000. (Courtesy of the Grafton Historical Society.)

On the Cover: Helen Warren poses as Miss Liberty at a fall festival on Grafton Common around 1910. The celebration featured music, food, and activities for both children and adults. The Lyman School Band, at right, entertained the crowd. Children were given tools and materials to make bluebird houses while their parents listened to patriotic speeches. (Courtesy of the Grafton Historical Society.)

IMAGES
of America

GRAFTON

Linda Marean Casey
and the Grafton Historical Society

ARCADIA
PUBLISHING

ISBN 978-1-4671-1611-4

Published by Arcadia Publishing
Charleston, South Carolina

Printed in the United States of America

Library of Congress Control Number: 2015951810

For all general information, please contact Arcadia Publishing:
Telephone 843-853-2070
Fax 843-853-0044
E-mail sales@arcadiapublishing.com
For customer service and orders:
Toll-Free 1-888-313-2665

Visit us on the Internet at www.arcadiapublishing.com

Dedicated to all those who believe that local history matters

Contents

ACKNOWLEDGMENTS

We are indebted to many people for helping make this book possible. It has truly been a team effort. First, we must acknowledge our debt to the many volunteers of the Grafton Historical Society who have collected, preserved, and organized photographs since the society's beginning in 1964. A special thank you to the society's more recent "Friday Volunteers," who, for over five years, met weekly to sort the artifacts, newspaper clippings, and photographs that have provided rich material for this book. Members of this group who deserve special mention include Nancy and Jean Deschenes (now deceased), Barbara Bryant, Jane Nozzolillo, Ralph Michniewicz, and Joseph Schilke. Joseph Morin, our youngest member and gone too soon, deserves special mention for reminding us that youth are our most important audience. We are very grateful to the hardworking teams from each section of Grafton who solicited photographs and stories for this publication. Jacqueline Davison and Elizabeth Stinson, along with June Lufkin and Jane Lewis, made up the North Grafton team. Elizabeth Weeks led the team for South Grafton, which included Helen Blazis, Rachel Costello, Kathy Aberizk, Ronald Klocek, and Stephen Gosselin. Special thanks go to Mary O'Hara for advising on Grafton Center and providing editorial help and to Rob Aberg for technical assistance with the photographs. We are deeply indebted to the many families who so generously searched through their family albums to find photographs to share with us. Thank you to our editor, Liz Gurley, for her patience and guidance and to Daniel Casey, Thomas Casey, and Carolyn Jakubiak for their support and encouragement throughout this process. Without the help of all of these individuals, this project would not have been possible. Thank you all.

Unless otherwise noted, all images appear courtesy of the Grafton Historical Society. Courtesy lines have been included for those photographs that were acquired from private family collections.

Introduction

Situated on a frontier pathway and near a network of rivers and streams, the land that became Grafton was an attractive site for both Native Americans and English settlers. At the time of the first European contact, the area was inhabited by the Hassanamisco Indians, a clan of the Nipmuc tribe. The territory was sparsely populated, and the tribe was semi-migratory. In the spring and summer, the native women tended the fields, while the men fished and hunted. In the fall, women harvested crops, and the men engaged in war or diplomacy. During the winter, the tribes moved to sheltered valleys, returning to the village in the spring for planting.

The frontier pathway through Grafton was traveled by Thomas Hooker in 1636 on his journey to Connecticut, where he established the city of Hartford. By the 1640s, the Reverend John Eliot, a missionary from the Boston area, was actively preaching Christianity to the native population in central Massachusetts. Eliot established a series of villages of Christianized natives referred to as "praying Indians." Grafton was the third such village and was named Hassanamesit, meaning "place of small stones."

King Philip's War, an uprising by the native population in 1675, proved fatal to the praying Indian villages. The natives were divided in their loyalties, and the English did not trust them. For the duration of the hostilities, the natives were imprisoned on Deer Island in Boston Harbor, where most perished from starvation or exposure. The uprising was defeated in 1676, but 25 years passed before the few remaining Nipmuc families returned to claim their land at Hassanamesit.

By the early 1700s, the colony of Massachusetts had experienced a great influx of new settlers, mostly farmers. Land in central Massachusetts was attractive farmland. The Willard family, whose grandsons became famous clockmakers, had settled here by 1716. In 1718, Elisha Johnson was permitted to purchase a tract of land on condition that he build and maintain bridges over the Blackstone River. A few other settlers were permitted to purchase land, and by 1728 nine English families had established homes here.

In 1724, a group of 40 investors, mostly farmers, asked to purchase 7,500 acres of land from the Nipmucs. The Massachusetts General Court approved the transaction in 1728, and the governor named the new town Grafton after the Duke of Grafton, grandson of King Charles II. Although most of the remaining Nipmuc land was eventually sold, Grafton boasts a Native American reservation on Brigham Hill with approximately four acres of land that has never passed out of tribal ownership.

Grafton was a farming community from its beginning and remained so for almost 250 years. Rivers were dammed to supply waterpower to local sawmills, gristmills, and blacksmith shops. Small villages grew up near the dams. Eventually clusters of villages became identified as Grafton Center, North Grafton, and South Grafton.

Grafton Center was the earliest village to be settled. The original purchasers of land built their houses and farms around the meetinghouse. Other small villages near Grafton Center included Kitville, near the dam at Silver Lake, where tools were made, and Centerville, situated at a dam site along the Quinsigamond River at the base of Brigham Hill.

North Grafton developed as a result of dams and mills along the Quinsigamond River in the north end of town. One village there was called New England Village, named for the New England Manufacturing Company that owned a mill in the area. A secondary village, called The Depot, formed in the mid-1800s as a result of the Boston & Albany Railroad passing through North Grafton.

South Grafton developed during the first quarter of the 19th century, when industrialization moved up the Blackstone River from Rhode Island. Textile mills and the mill villages associated with them were established at three sites on the river, creating Farnumsville, Saundersville, and Fisherville.

From the earliest times, local townspeople identified more readily with their villages than with the town of Grafton. By the late 20th century, though, these village loyalties had begun to fade, primarily due to a unified high school and improved transportation that expanded people's experience.

This book captures the sense of village life that has characterized much of Grafton's history. These photographs show the essence of each of those villages, as well as the forces that have unified those villages to become one town.

One

Hassanamesit

Grafton is home to the Hassanamisco Reservation, an historic site with approximately four acres of land that has never been owned or lived on by nonnative people. The reservation is part of the original 8,000-acre Hassanamesit Plantation of praying Indians, established by the Reverend John Eliot, a Puritan missionary. A Grafton Indian, James the Printer, aided Eliot by helping to translate the Bible into the Indian language.

The center of that early Hassanamesit settlement is thought to be located on Keith Hill in present-day Grafton, where a church was reported to have been built in 1671. Between 2003 and 2014, the Fiske Center for Archeological Research excavated that site hoping to identify the early village location. Its work uncovered the home of Sarah Boston, a descendant of the original praying Indians.

King Philip's War, an uprising of natives in 1675, ended the praying Indian towns, and the natives of Hassanamesit Plantation were dispersed. In 1698, a few native families returned to claim their land. The sale of land to English investors in 1728 left the Nipmucs only 1,200 acres. Corrupt practices and financial misfortunes resulted in the loss of most of this land, so that by 1861, they owned only the small reservation tract.

The reservation, on the eastern slope of Brigham Hill, is the location of an 1801 building known as the Homestead. During the early 20th century, the Cisco family resided there and became tribal leaders and stewards of the reservation. James Lemuel Cisco (1846–1931) became chief of the Hassanamisco in the 1920s. He was succeeded by his son Samuel and later by his daughter Sarah Cisco Sullivan, also known as Princess Sweet Flower. Sarah lived on the reservation all her life, serving as hostess of the Indian fairs and educating local young people about Indian culture. Her daughter Zara Cisco Brough, known as Princess White Flower, also held the title of chief of the Nipmuc tribe and can trace her ancestry back to James the Printer.

Annual tribal gatherings at the reservation began in the 1920s and have continued into the present day. Renamed the Annual Hassanamisco Indian Fair, the event engages the public in tribal ceremonies. The Homestead is no longer used as a residence, but it continues to be the focus of Nipmuc cultural activities. The reservation is maintained by the Nipmuc Nation Tribal Council.

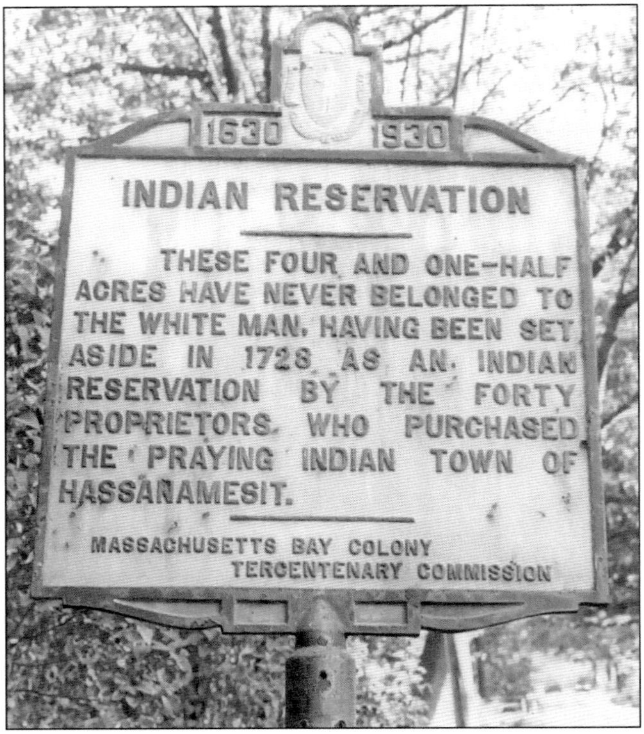

This sign identifying the Hassanamisco Reservation was erected by the Massachusetts Tercentenary Committee in 1938 on the 300th anniversary of the founding of Massachusetts Bay Colony. Grafton is unique in having two other signs: one signifying the Thomas Hooker trail that passed through Grafton and one near Grafton Common designating the early native village of Hassanamesit.

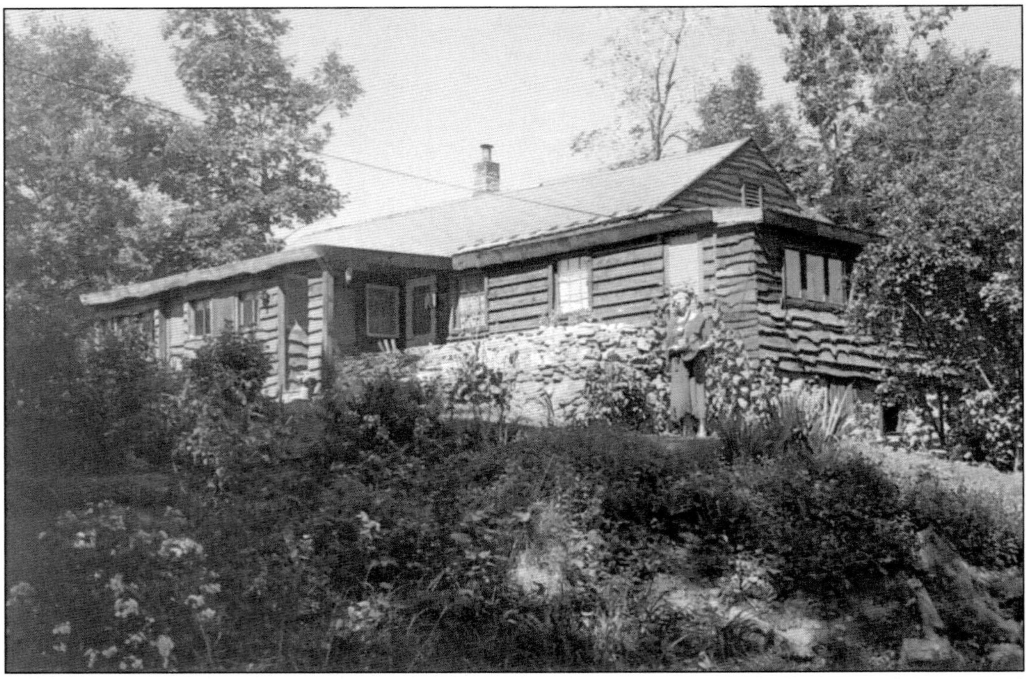

The Hassanamisco Reservation, located on the eastern slope of Brigham Hill, is part of the original 8,000-acre Hassanamesit Plantation of praying Indians established by the Reverend John Eliot, a Puritan missionary. This homestead is the only building on the present-day reservation, parts of which date from 1801. During the 20th century, the Cisco family resided there and served as tribal leaders and stewards of the reservation.

Princess White Flower (1919–1988), chief of the Nipmuc tribe, lived at and presided over the reservation for many years. She was a direct descendant of a line of chiefs and traced her lineage to James the Printer, a Nipmuc who helped translate the Bible into the Indian language. Princess White Flower was president of an electrical and ecological consulting company, a draftsperson, a technical writer, and a fashion designer.

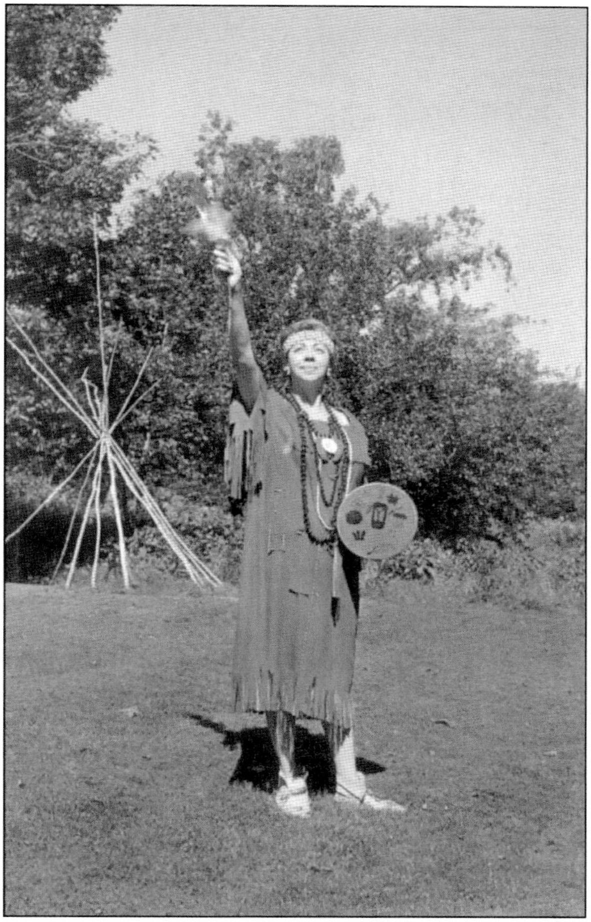

Annual tribal gatherings at the reservation began in the 1920s and have continued to the present day. The Annual Hassanamisco Indian Fair engages the public in tribal ceremonies. The reservation today is maintained by the Nipmuc Nation Tribal Council and continues to be the focus of Nipmuc cultural activities.

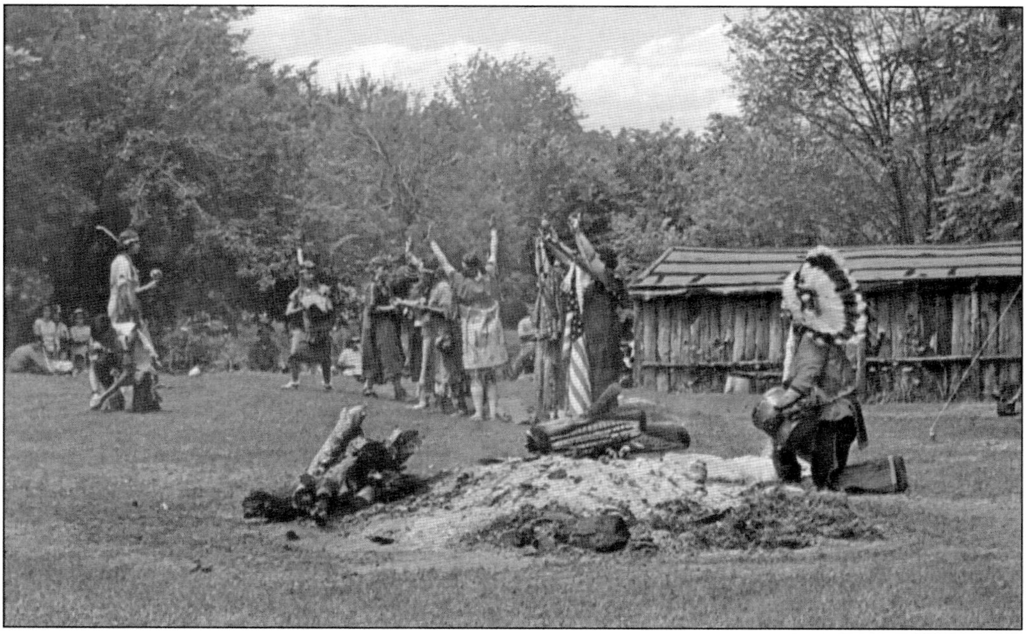

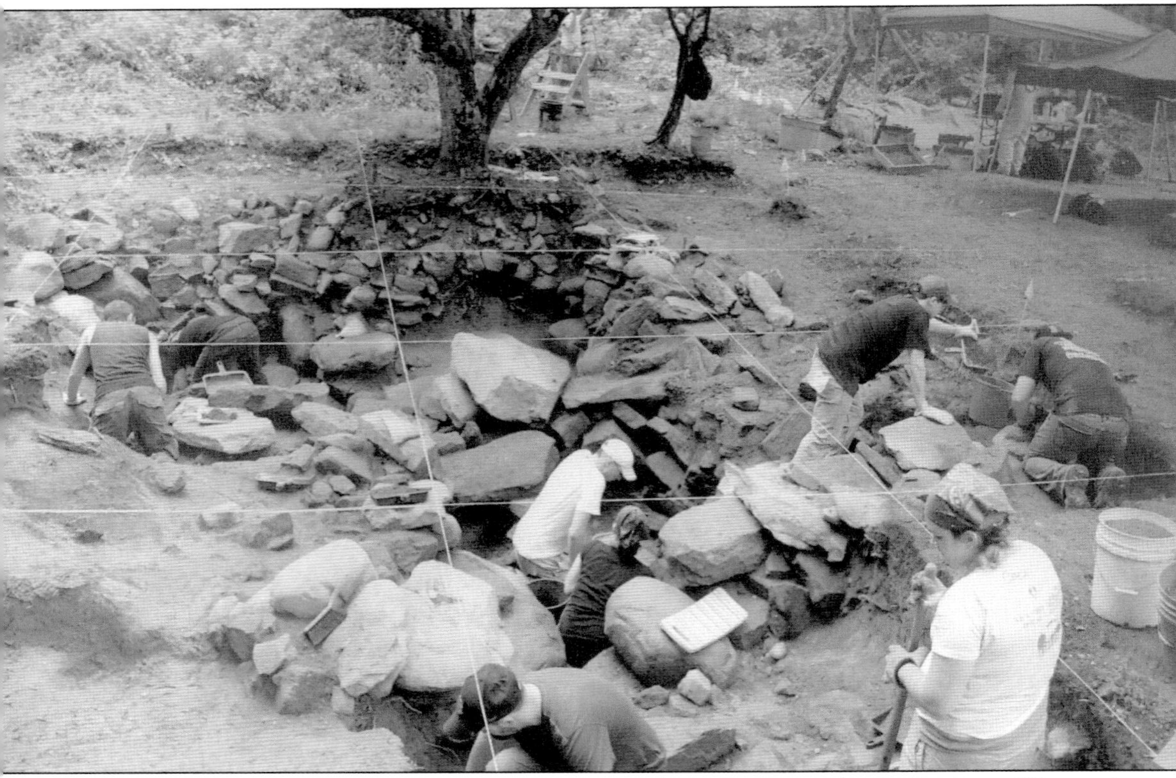

Between 2003 and 2014, faculty and students from the Fiske Center for Archeological Research at the University of Massachusetts at Boston excavated a site on Keith Hill hoping to identify the early praying Indian village established by the Reverend John Eliot in 1660. Their work uncovered the home of Sarah Boston, a Nipmuc who lived there in the early 1800s. It is believed that the homestead at this site dates from an earlier time, when it was the home of Sarah and Peter Muckamaug, whose family was part of the original Hassanamesit Plantation and who lived on this property after King Philip's War (1675–1676). (Courtesy of Heather Law Pezzarossi, Fiske Center, UMass Boston.)

Two

FARMING

Grafton was a farming community at its founding and remained so for almost 250 years. The Willard family, the first English family to settle in Hassanamesit, established a farm in the north end in 1716. All but one of the original Grafton investors were farmers, and after purchasing land from the Nipmucs in 1728, they divided the town into many large farms. Most of these became family farms and were handed down from generation to generation. Farm supply businesses flourished. By the mid-20th century, there were poultry farms, piggeries, turkey farms, vegetable farms, and many dairy farms.

In 1901, Grafton State Hospital was established as a therapeutic farm colony for "chronic insane" patients. A dairy farm was put into operation in 1905, and the farm expanded in 1912 to include a piggery, a poultry plant, vegetable gardens, and an orchard. The hospital operated one of the many large farms in Grafton.

With the development of local manufacturing and the growth of the villages, local farmers provided food for mill workers as well as for their families. When the local farmers could not supply enough food for the fast-growing mill populations, the North Grafton mill established its own farm to help meet the demand.

Grafton has a long history of orcharding, as well. The Nipmucs grew apples and other fruits before the English settlers came to the Grafton area. Orchards were cultivated well into the 20th century in all sections of Grafton. In Grafton Center, the Mortimer Peach Farm on Keith Hill became Fiske Farms Orchards, one of the largest growers of apples in New England. In The Depot section of North Grafton, orchards dotted the landscape. In the 20th century, Stearns Davenport established Creeper Hill Orchard and reclaimed 60 vintage varieties of apples. Orchards bearing a variety of fruits grew in many places in South Grafton.

Grafton retained its rural aspect for almost 250 years. By the 1960s, improved transportation and refrigeration made it possible to ship food from areas of the country that could grow food more cheaply and more efficiently. Over the next 50 years, most of the farms disappeared from all three sections of Grafton.

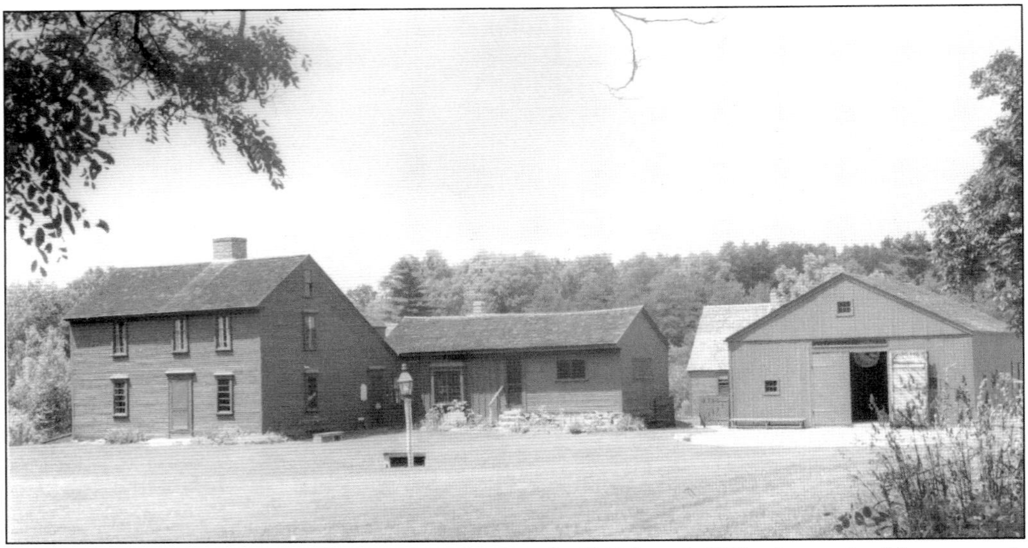

The Willards were the first family to settle in Grafton. In 1716, Joseph Willard moved to Hassanamesit with his wife, Martha. He was one of the original petitioners for the purchase of the Nipmuc land. The farm included a clock shop, where their grandsons learned the trade. Benjamin, Simon, Ephraim, and Aaron Willard are renowned as premier American clock makers. The farm is now the Willard House and Clock Museum.

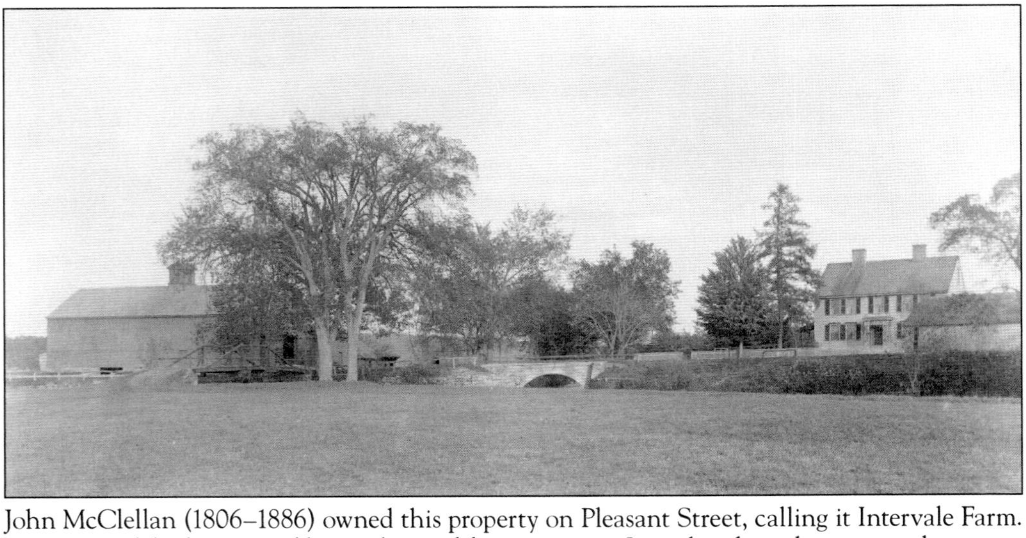

John McClellan (1806–1886) owned this property on Pleasant Street, calling it Intervale Farm. It was one of the largest and best cultivated farms in town. In earlier days, the area was known as Leland's Landing because the farm was situated across from a boat landing where the Blackstone Canal joined the Blackstone River.

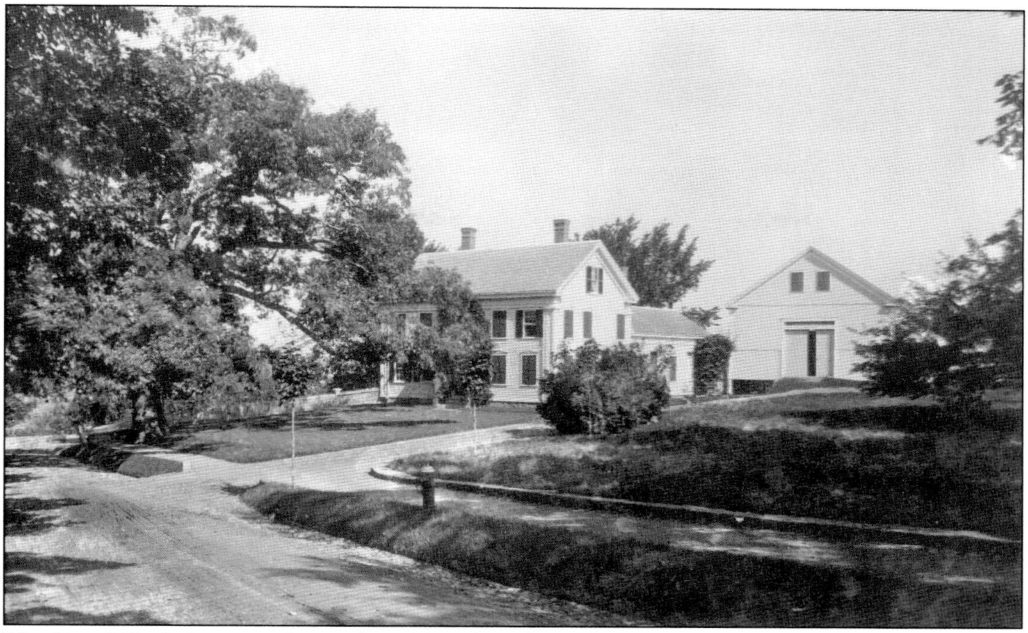

The Royal Keith farm was located at 23 Keith Hill Road. Keith (1769–1857) was one of Grafton's early manufacturers of ready-made shoes. After apprenticing in Boston, he manufactured coarse, hand-sewn work shoes, which he sold in Boston, Providence, New York, and in the South for slaves. During the embargo of 1812, when shipping by sea was impossible, he drove a team of horses overland to Richmond to deliver shoes.

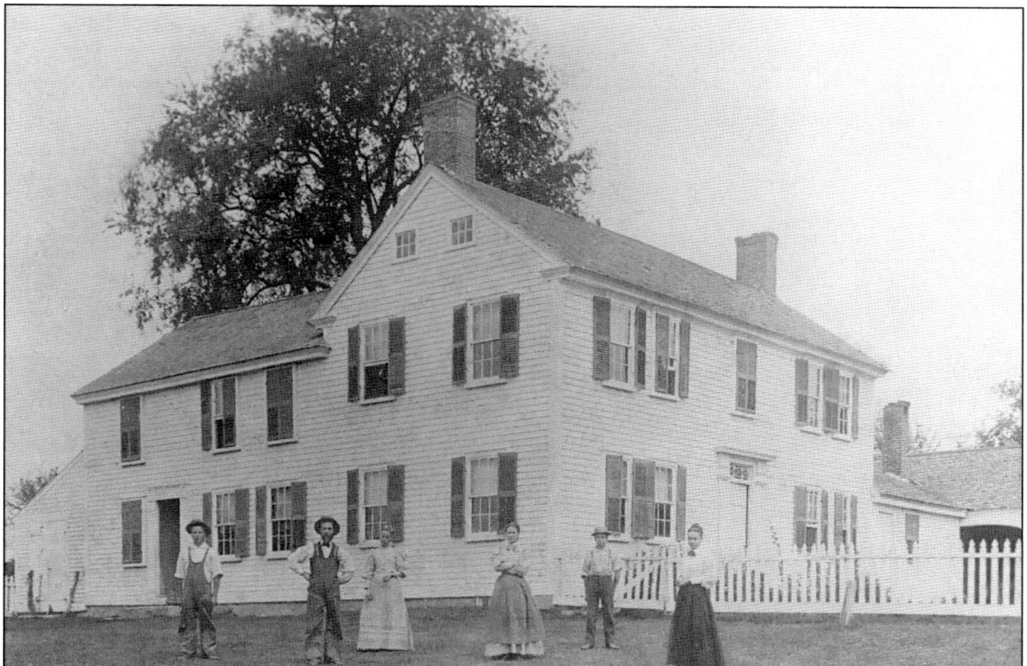

The Bannister farm was located on Providence Road and was owned by the Leland family for over a century. Henry L. Bannister (1835–1904) purchased it in 1878, and it remained in his family throughout most of the 20th century. His grandson Henry Hartness ran it as a dairy farm.

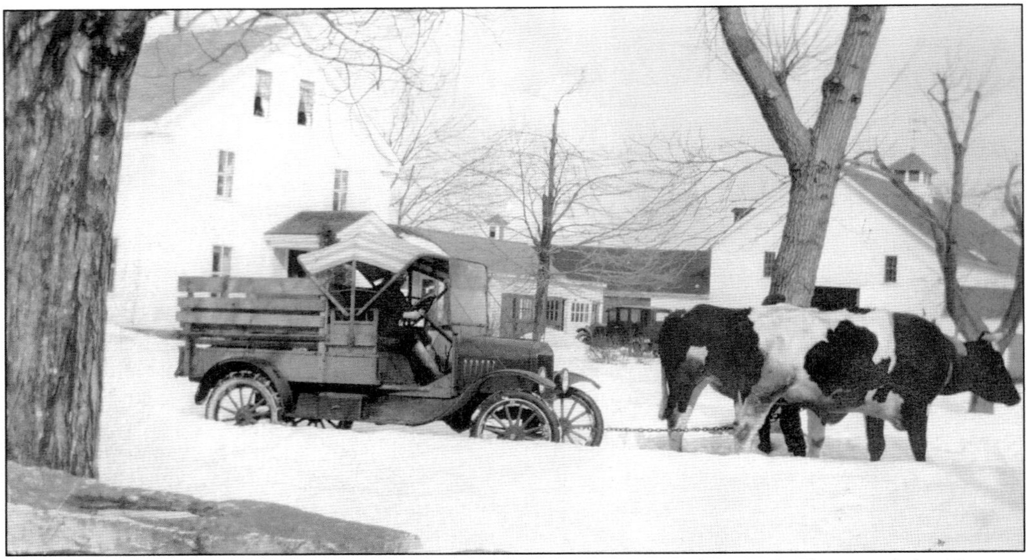

The Prescott farm, also called Misco Farm, on Old Upton Road, was the home of the Francis Prescott family during the first half of the 20th century. Prescott represented Grafton in the state legislature. This photograph was taken during the winter of 1920. The Pease family now owns the farm. (Courtesy of William Fiske.)

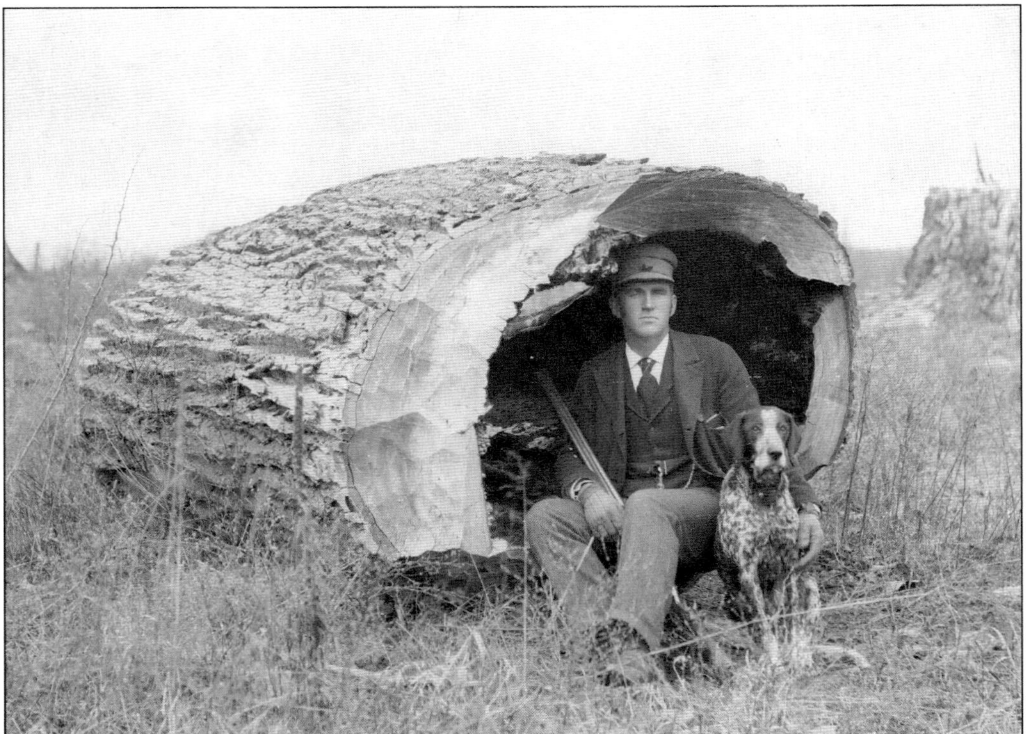

Sumner Leonard poses with his dog beneath a large log. The many farms and orchards in Grafton attracted wild fowl, rabbits, and herds of deer, making Grafton a good place for hunting.

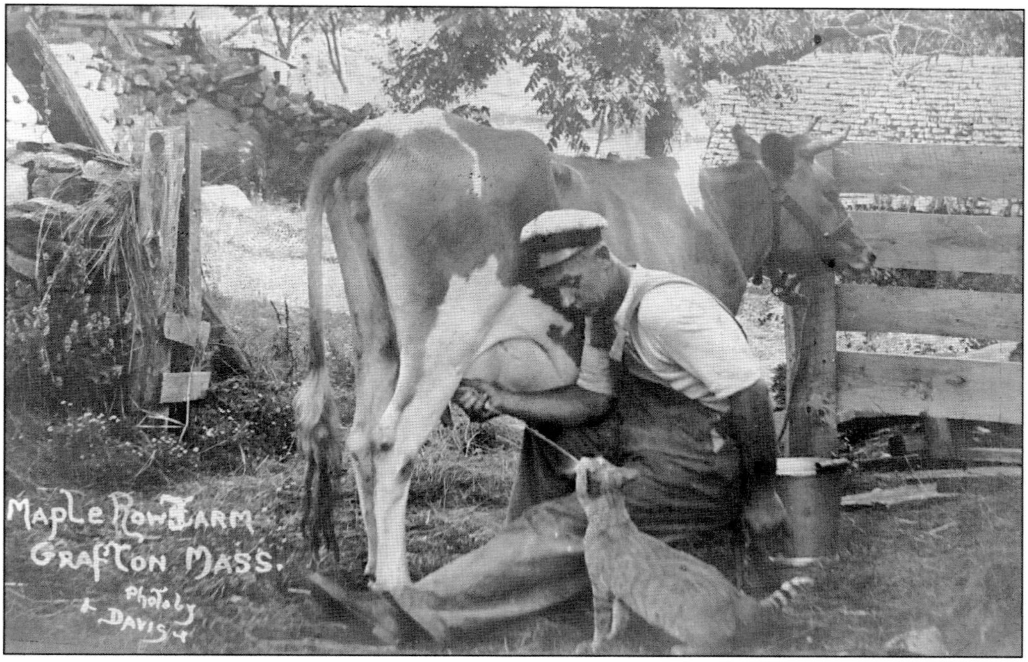

Roland J. Axtell of Maple Row Farm milks his cow and feeds his cat in this photograph from around 1910. The Axtell farm, established by Thomas Axtell around 1735 on land purchased from the Nipmucs, was located at the junction of North Street and Institute Road. Axtell descendants owned the farm until the mid-20th century. (Courtesy of Donald Clark.)

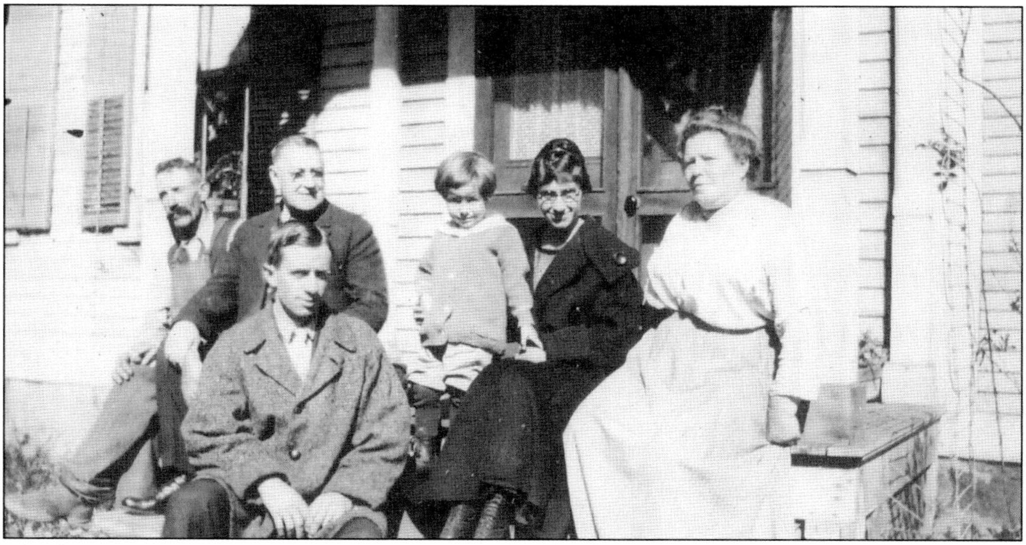

The farm manager's family is chatting on the steps of Grafton's "poor farm." In Colonial days, Grafton provided for its poor by boarding them with private families at the town's expense. In 1834, the town purchased a farm on Brigham Hill to care for the indigent. Later, the poor farm was moved to the site of the present-day Wyman-Gordon Company. Tramps were also fed and sheltered here.

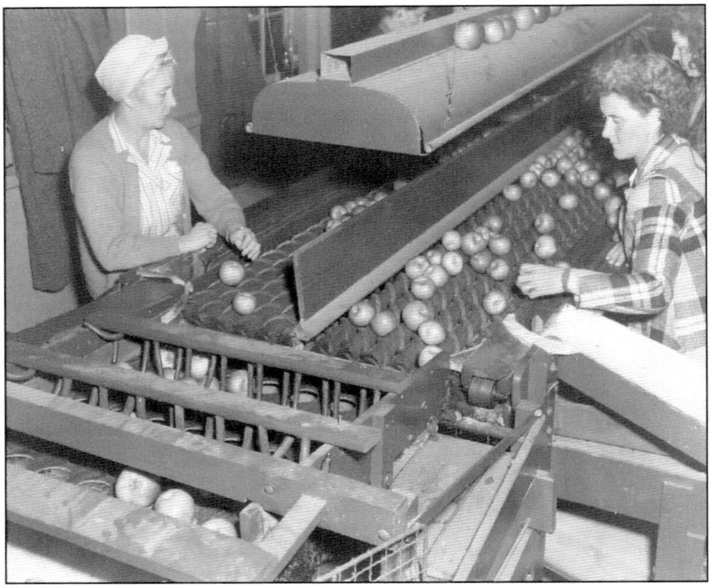

In 1920, Daniel and William Fiske bought the Mortimer Peach Farm on the summit of Keith Hill. By 1938, their business, Fiske Farms Orchards, was one of the largest apple producers in New England with more than 18,000 trees. The orchard produced apples, peaches, and pears. By the 1940s, conveyors were used to sort the apples. In 1954, the farm was divided into house lots and sold. (Courtesy of William Fiske.)

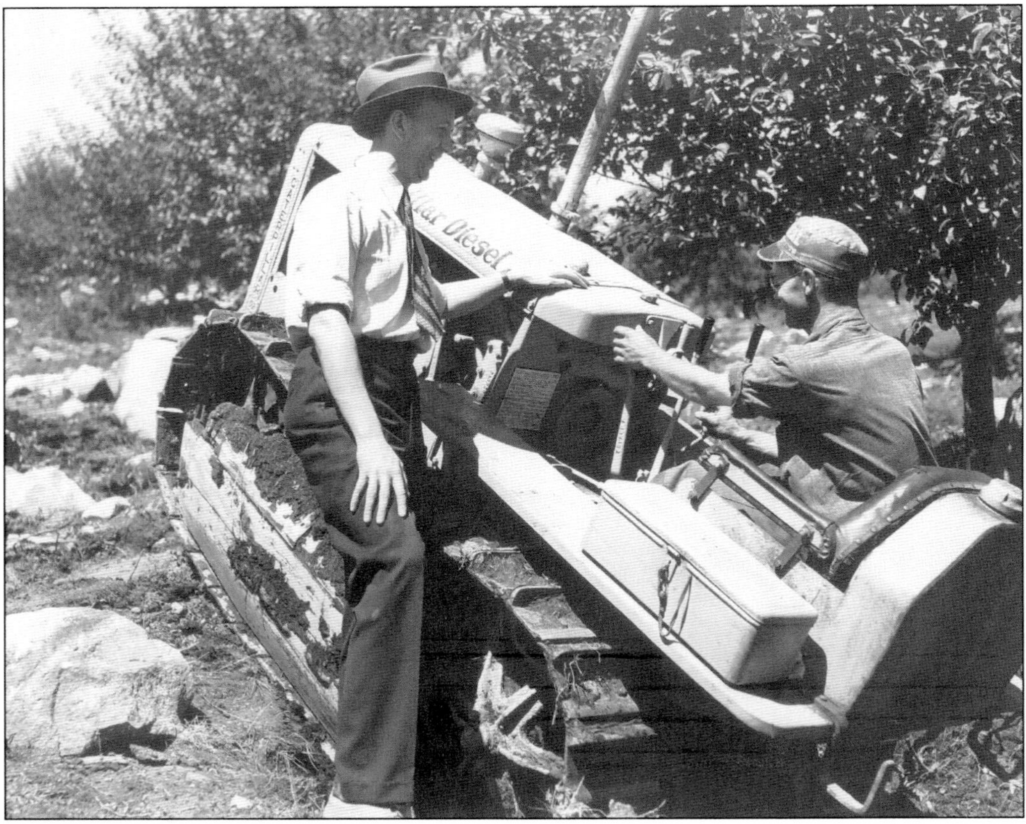

In 1938, the Caterpillar Tractor Company introduced a small diesel tractor. The Fiske enterprise used this machinery to expand its productive acreage by removing large boulders from the area. During the 1938 hurricane, 6,000 apple trees were uprooted or split. Through sheer determination and hard work, Daniel Fiske and his crew salvaged 5,000 trees by replanting them or wiring them back together. The company was producing again by the next year. (Courtesy of William Fiske.)

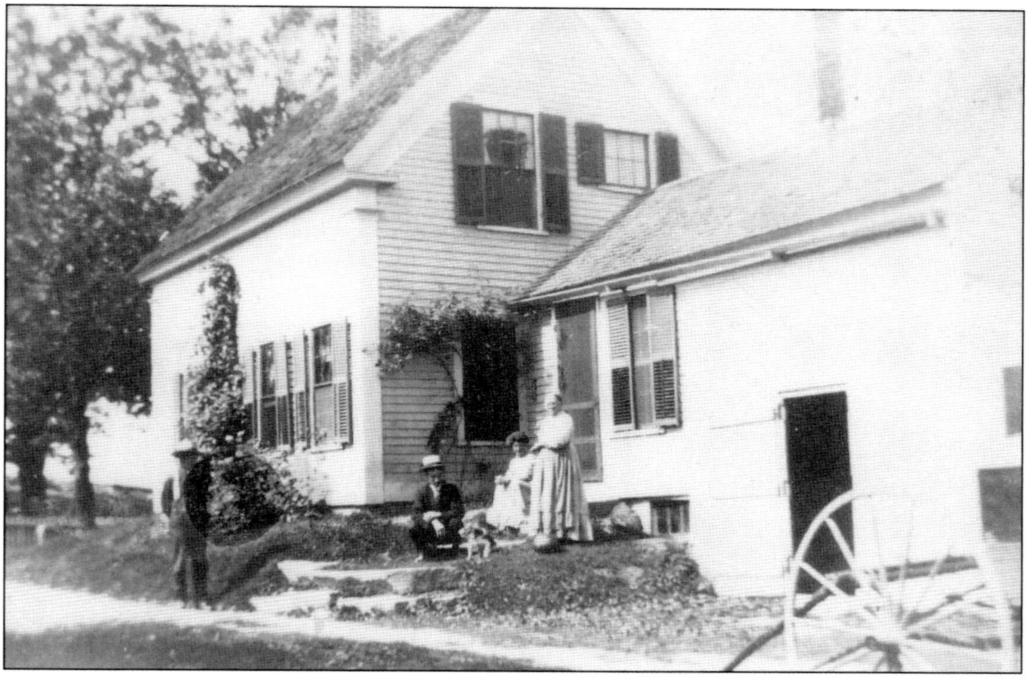

The Pratt farm at 140 North Street is pictured around 1900 with the family posing in front. In addition to operating his dairy farm, William L. Pratt was a meat inspector for the county, traveling to local slaughterhouses to inspect and stamp meat products. (Courtesy of Carolynne Grimley.)

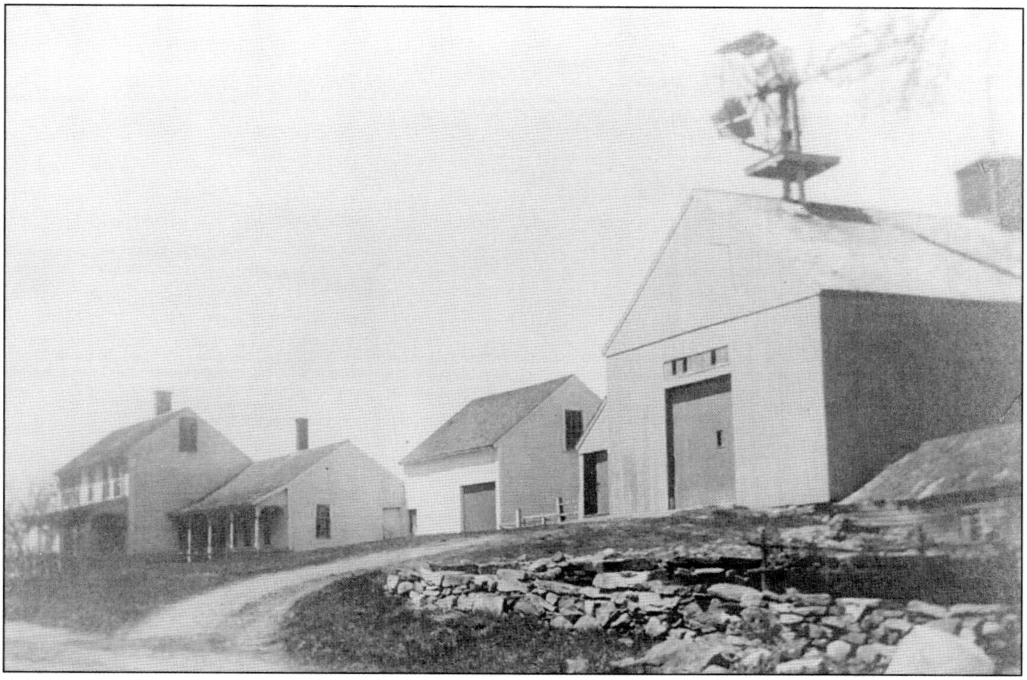

The Houlden farm on Wesson Road was established by Col. John Goulding (1726–1791), who cleared and cultivated this farm from the wilderness in the mid-1700s. He later established a tannery here. The business and farm were taken over by his son Ephraim. Although the business disappeared, the farm remained in the Goulding family until the late 1800s. (Courtesy of Ruth Houlden.)

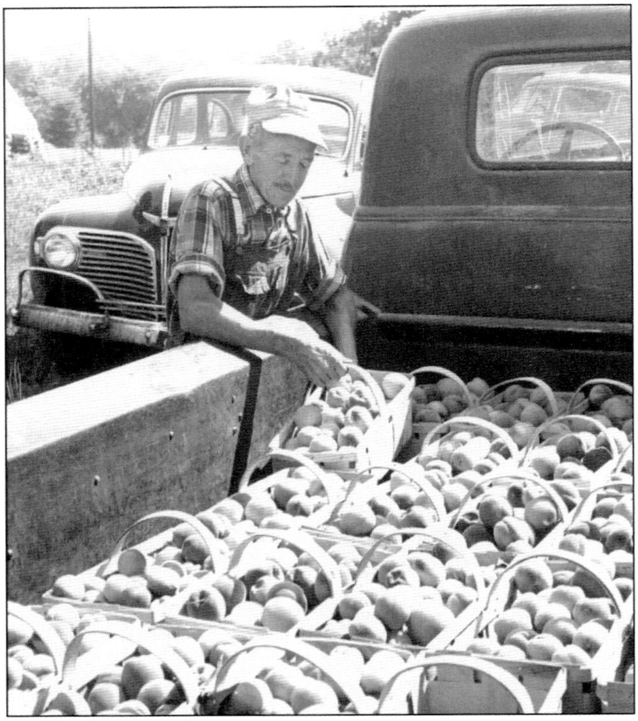

Stearns Lothrop Davenport (1885–1973) places a basket of peaches in the back of his pickup truck. Davenport, a horticulturalist and owner of Creeper Hill Orchard, grew a wide variety of fruits, including peaches, pears, currents, berries, hazelnuts, and apples. He developed several new varieties of apple, including the Davey and the Jean, and reclaimed 60 vintage apple varieties. Tower Hill Botanical Garden maintains the Davenport vintage apple tree collection. (Courtesy of Amy Callihan.)

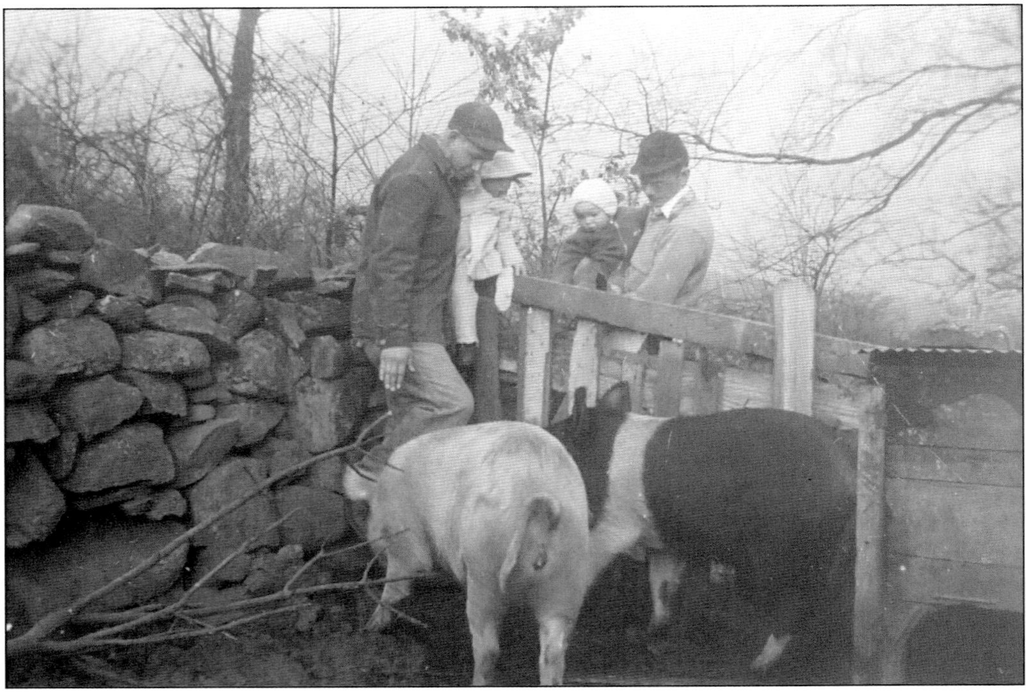

Charles Corey (left), holding son Charles Jr., and Bernard Corey (right), holding Carolynne Corey, visit pigs at the family farm on North Street. Charles Corey raised mink on the farm until noise from airplanes flying to Grafton Airport disturbed the animals and ended the business. Corey and his wife, Florence, also cultivated and sold pansies commercially from the farm, and in the 1950s they raised chickens and horses. (Courtesy of Carolynne Grimley.)

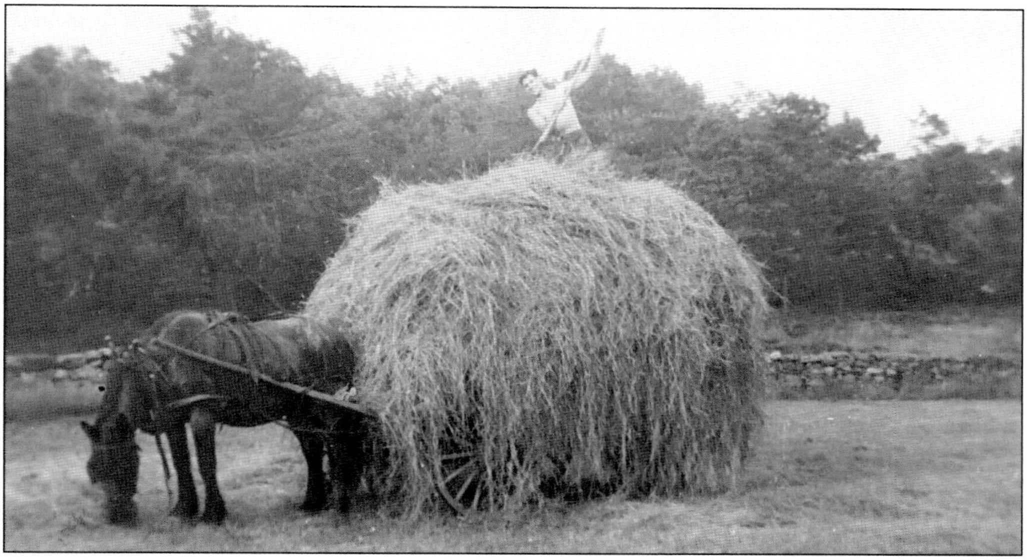

George Lemoine works on a hay wagon at the Mularczyk farm in South Grafton. This Farnumsville farm, located across from the Fairview Cemetery, was owned by Anthony and Amelia Mularczyk. Amelia worked at the Wuskanut Mill, as well as assisting on the farm, growing flowers, and canning fruits and vegetables. (Courtesy of Nancy Lemoine.)

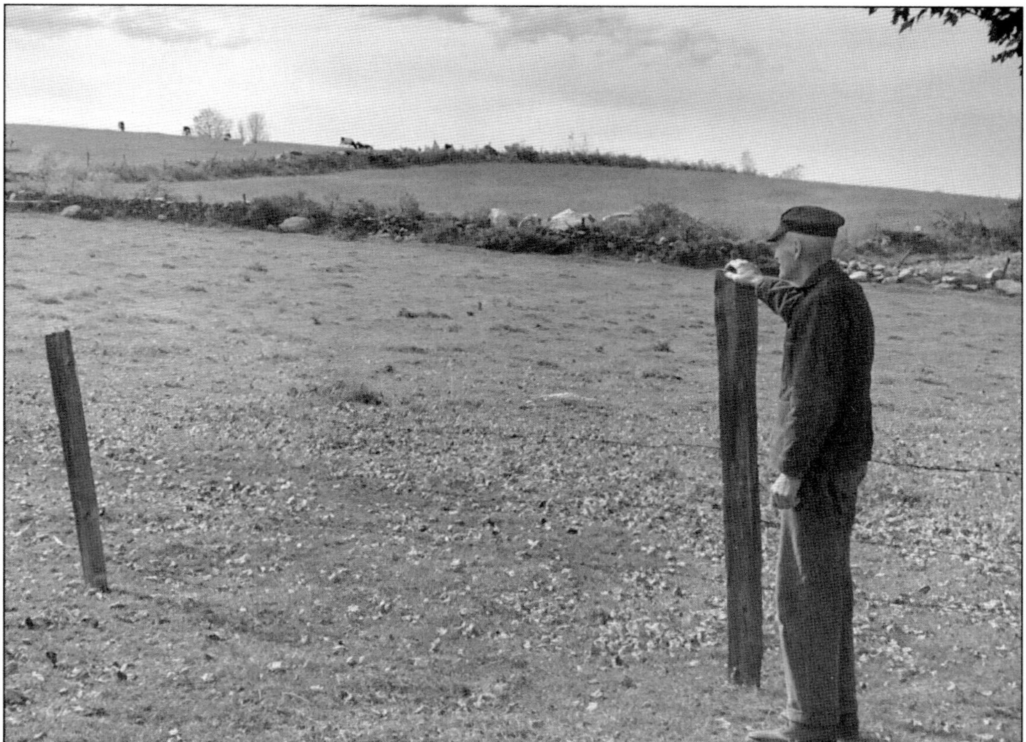

Avery J. Elvidge looks out over his family farm on Potter Hill. His acreage on the top of Potter Hill occupied the site of one of the earliest Grafton farms—that of Ezekial Brigham (1723–1788). In the late 19th century, it was owned by Rufus B. Potter, for whom the hill was named. It was later acquired by the Elvidge family.

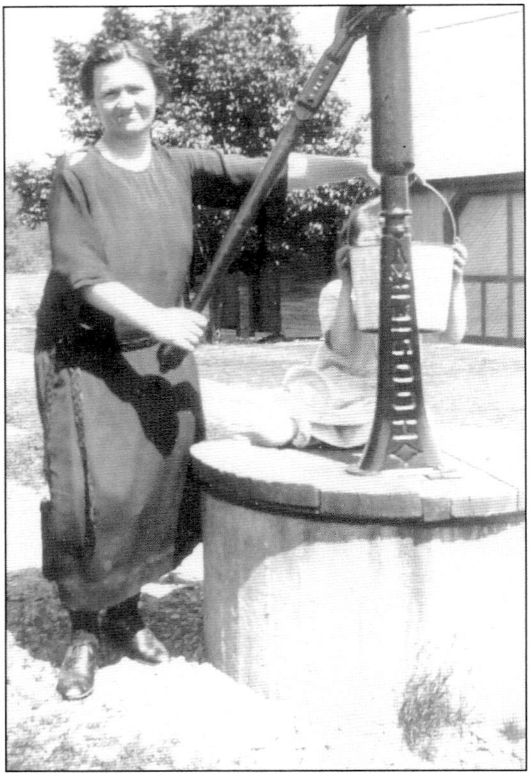

Olimpia Such raises the hand pump at the Such farm in Farnumsville. Joseph and Olimpia Such raised cows, pigs, and chickens, as well as fruits and vegetables at their farm on Providence Road. Olimpia did much of the farm work while her husband worked at the mills. She was the only woman to serve on the building committee for the Polish National Home in the 1930s. (Courtesy of Nancy Lemoine.)

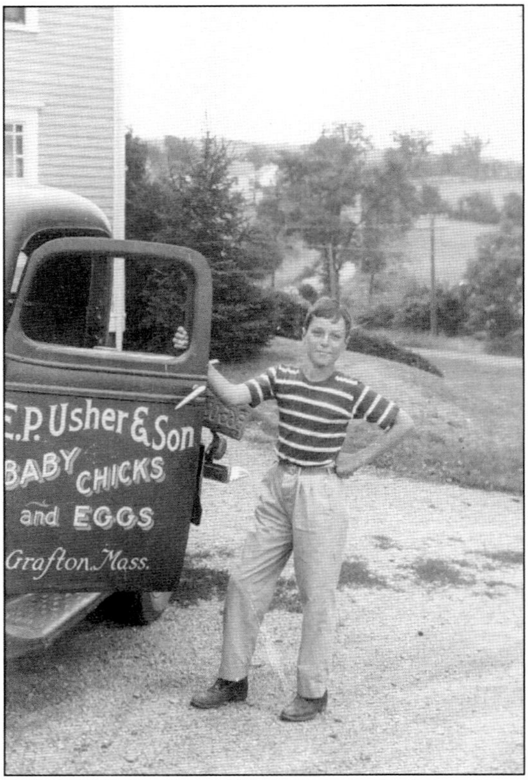

Gordon Usher stands proudly beside the family truck. The Usher family raised poultry at 2 Bruce Street, property they owned from the late 1880s to the late 1900s. This property was sold to Joseph and Simon Bruce in 1788 by the Guardians of the Grafton Indians. The ravine below the house is called Bruce Hollow.

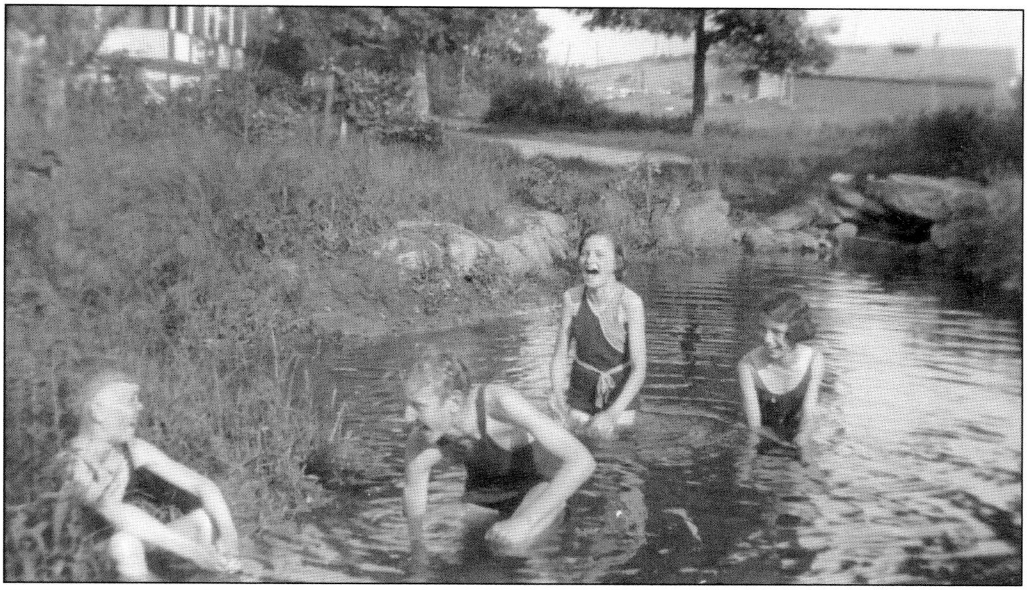

Children swim in the pond on a sunny summer afternoon at the Mularczyk farm. Every farm had a pond to provide water for the livestock. The girl standing at center is Sophie Mularczyk, and the boy second from left is Walter Nadolink. (Courtesy of Nancy Lemoine.)

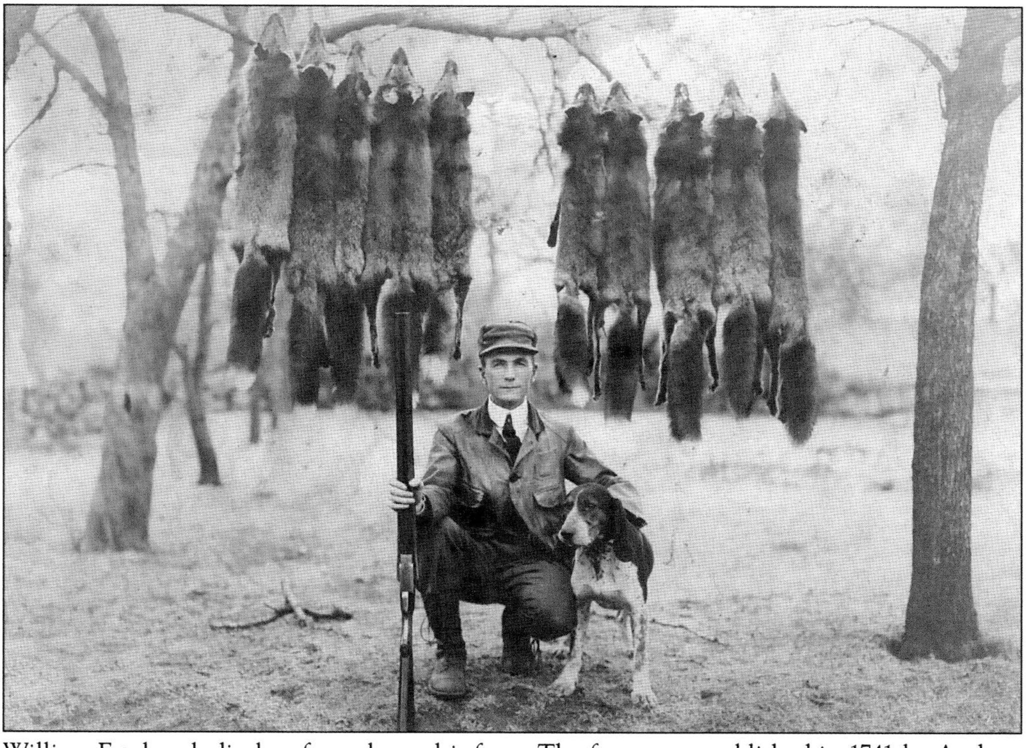

William Estabrook displays fox pelts on his farm. The farm was established in 1741 by Andrew Adams, who raised livestock and chickens—and as a sideline, manufactured wooden pipes made from white cedar. After the Civil War, the farm was owned by Edwin Estabrook, who grew fruits and vegetables. In 1918, he sold out to his son-in-law Leroy Knowlton, who turned to dairying. The Knowlton family still owns the farm.

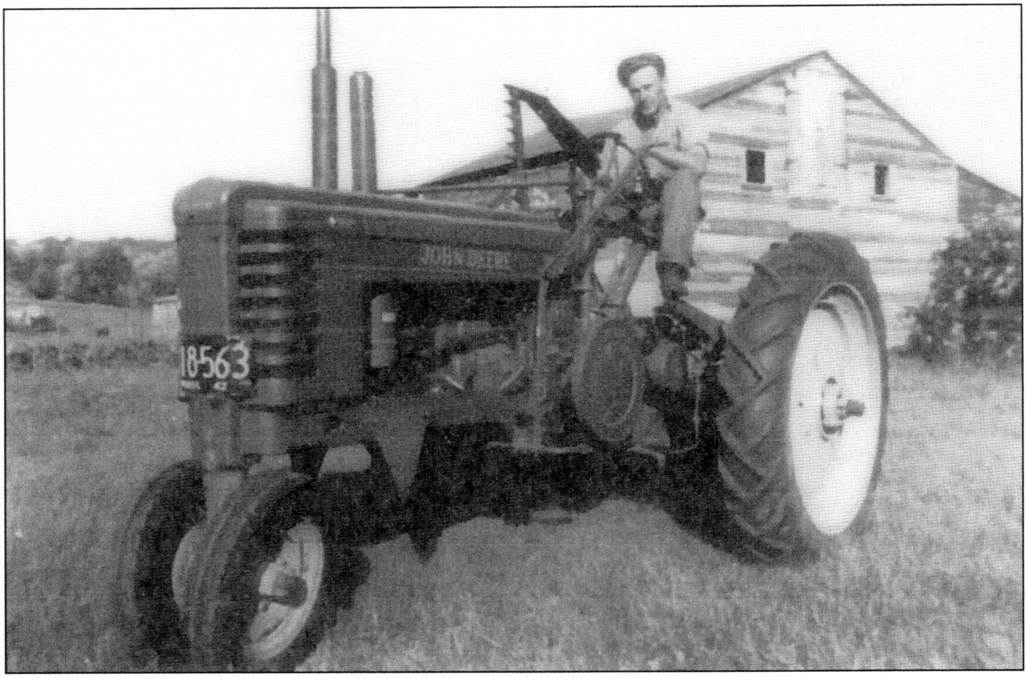

Mitchell Tomkiewicz (above) sits on his tractor at the Tomkiewicz farm (seen below) in 1948. Tomkiewicz was one of the first farmers in the area to purchase a tractor to cultivate his fields. His parents, John and Isabella Tomkiewicz, came to Farnumsville from Poland in 1920. They established one of the first dairy farms in the area and delivered milk to all of the South Grafton villages. They also raised chickens and pigs and bred milk cows. Mitchell and his wife, Esther, later took over the farm and in the early 1940s began growing corn and selling from a roadside stand. The stalks were chopped up and used to feed the cattle during the winter months. The farm flourished as a dairy until 1964, when it was converted to raising of beef cattle. (Courtesy of Eileen Flynn.)

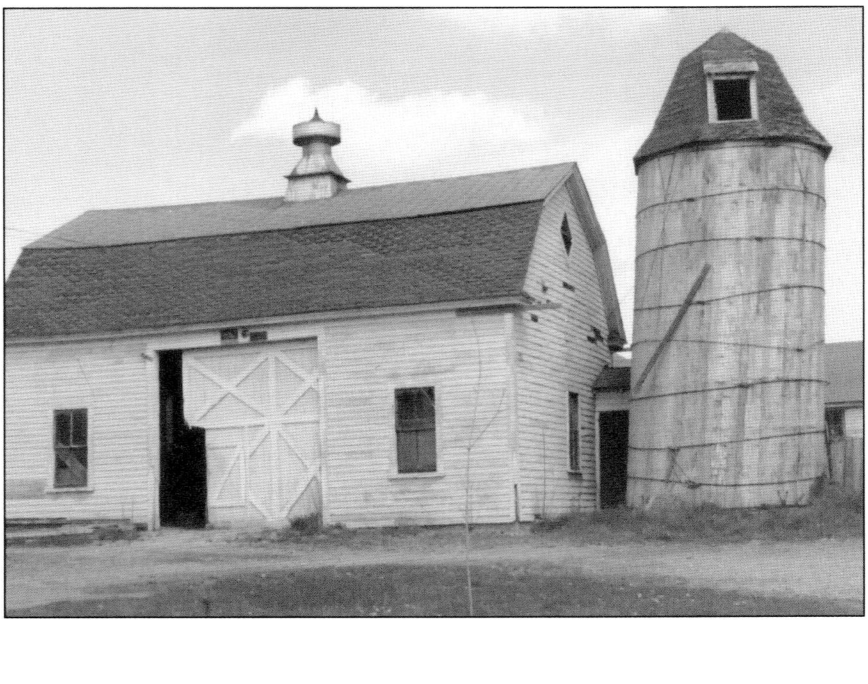

Three

Grafton Center

Grafton Center was the section of town settled earliest. In 1724, a group of 40 investors petitioned the Massachusetts General Court to purchase 7,500 acres of Nipmuc land. A price of 2,500 English pounds was determined to be fair. The contract was approved in 1728 with the requirement that the purchasers build a schoolhouse, a meetinghouse for public worship, and hire a schoolteacher and a minister. The meetinghouse was built on the town common in 1730. The schoolhouse was built the following year near the site of the present Baptist church. In 1735, the town was officially incorporated and renamed Grafton for the Duke of Grafton, a grandson to King Charles II.

Choosing a dam site was one of the top priorities for the early settlers who needed waterpower for sawmills and gristmills. The first dam was established on the Quinsigamond River, at the bottom of Brigham Hill. A village grew up around a mill built there and became known as Centerville. Another dam was established on Misco Brook near the Upton line, forming Silver Lake, where the small village of Kitville developed.

Many small businesses were established around the town common to meet local needs. In the early 1800s, Royal Keith, a local man who had apprenticed in Boston, initiated a business in ready-made shoes. Other local businessmen followed, and within 25 years, Grafton became a regional leader in shoe and boot production, as well as leather tanning and currying. Eventually, three-story shoe factories were constructed around the common. In 1837, approximately 900 men and 500 women made almost 700,000 pairs of shoes and 18,000 pairs of boots. Grafton shoe makers specialized in "brogans," work shoes of simple construction, purchased by laborers and plantation owners for their slaves. Shoes and boots were made in every corner of Grafton Center, including the basements of the Grafton Town House and the Baptist church. On North Street alone there were 10 factories, most related to the shoe industry. After the Civil War, when the industry moved to the South and West for cheaper labor, the shoe factories were disassembled, and the area around the common was developed into a residential area of fine homes.

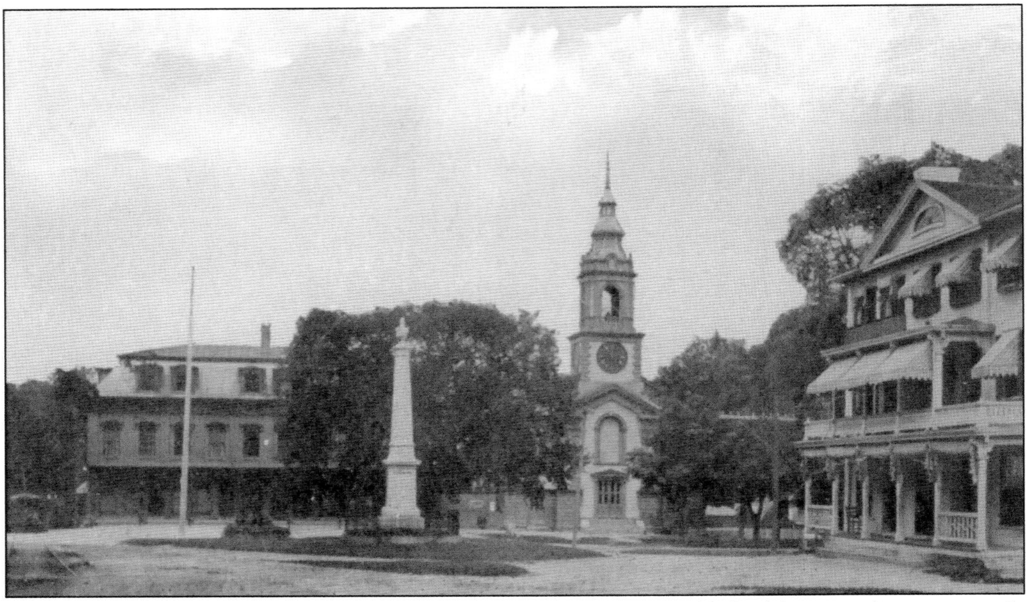

The original investors who purchased the Nipmuc land in 1728 established farms in the countryside but set aside four acres at the town center for a meetinghouse and a school. Much of that land is now Grafton Common and this Central Square. Over the years, businesses, banks, and shops were built around the park, creating the picturesque Grafton Common Historic District. The district includes the town common and all the buildings that surround it.

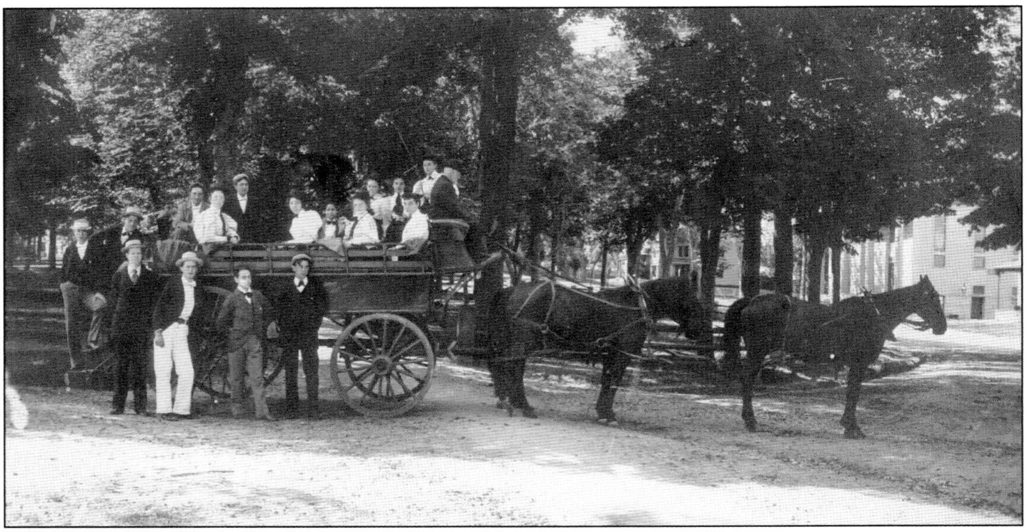

A group of young people on a horse-drawn wagon congregates at Grafton Common around 1900. By this time, the trees planted in 1845 had grown large and the common was dense. Originally the site of the meetinghouse, by 1900 it had evolved as the center of community activities, such as parades, festivals, fundraisers, and concerts. Today, it continues to be the site of a wide variety of community events.

This daguerreotype is the earliest known view of Grafton. It shows the Evangelical Congregational Church and newly planted trees on Grafton Common. Based on the size of the trees, the photograph is believed to date from 1845, when Silas Forbush, a local shoe entrepreneur, redesigned and replanted the common to appeal to Victorian tastes. He planted trees, added fences with granite posts, and installed wrought iron arches with hanging lanterns.

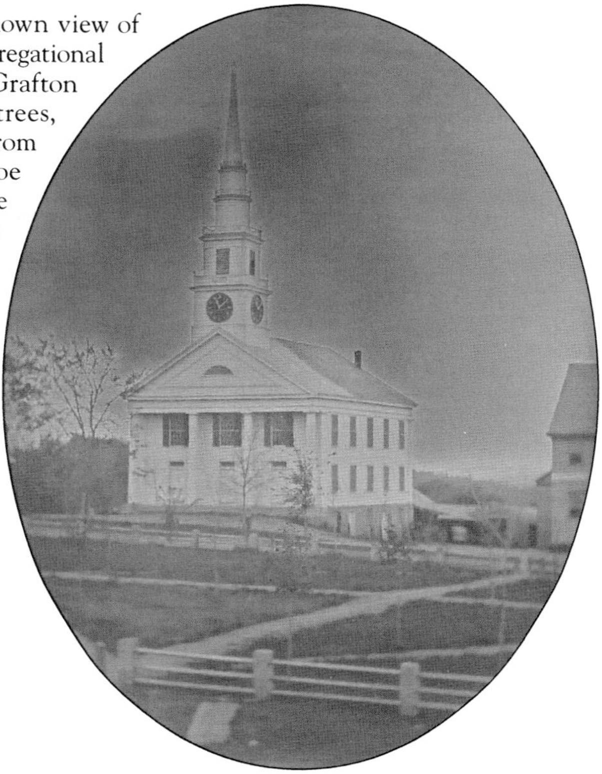

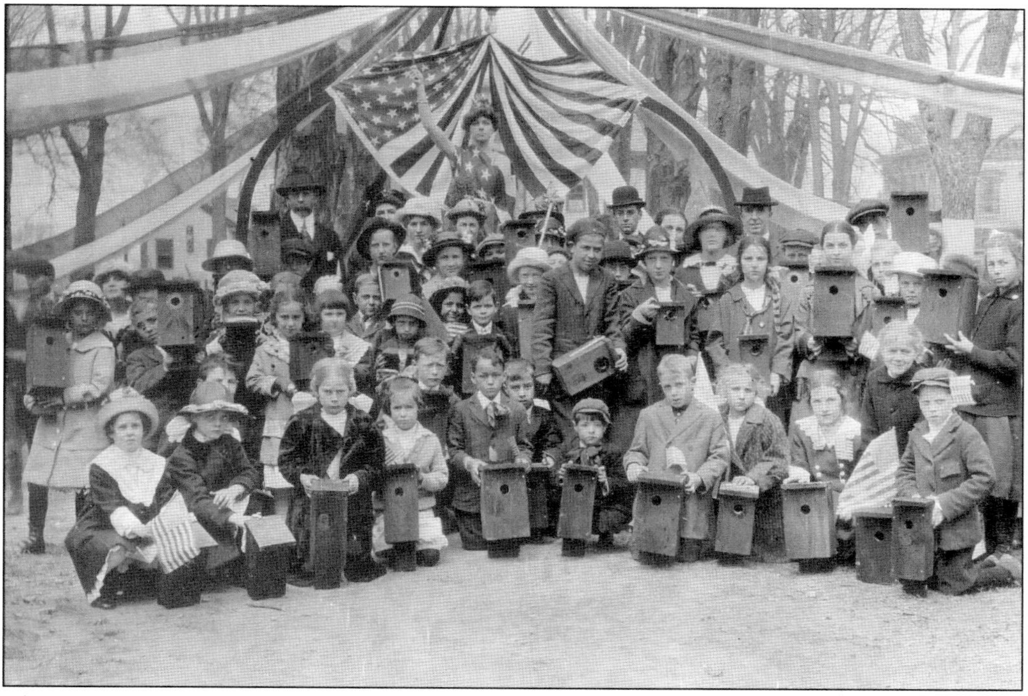

This fall celebration held around 1910 featured Helen Warren as Miss Liberty. She poses on Grafton Common with children who proudly display birdhouses they have just constructed. The wrought iron arches over the path can be seen in this photograph.

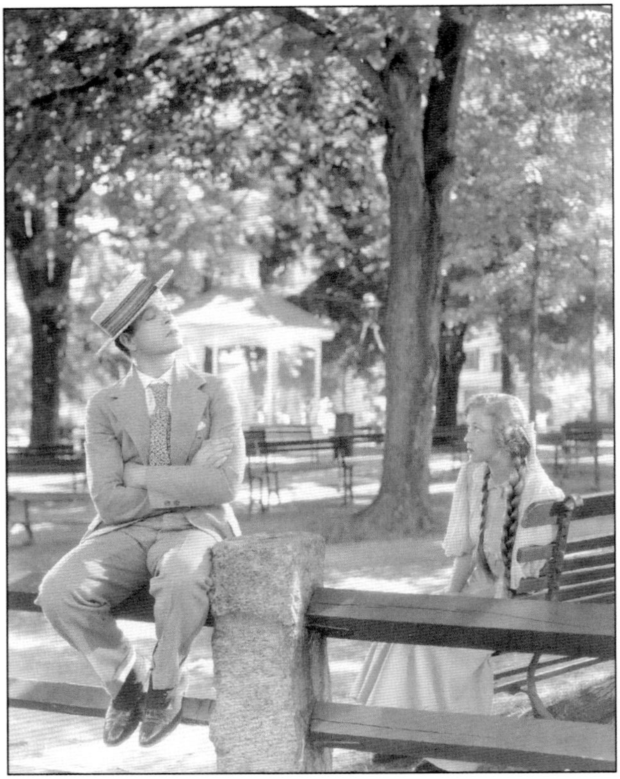

The bandstand at the center of Grafton Common is a reminder of a time when Hollywood came to town, bringing lights, cameras, and movie stars. It was 1935, and the movie was *Ah, Wilderness!*, written by Eugene O'Neill. The movie featured Hollywood stars Eric Lindon and Cecelia Parker, seen here seated on the common (left). Local folks in period costumes (below) served as extras and were paid $3 per day. In the movie, the common was filmed as the site of a Fourth of July celebration. The bandstand was left as a thank-you to the town and has been maintained as the central feature of the Grafton Common Historic District.

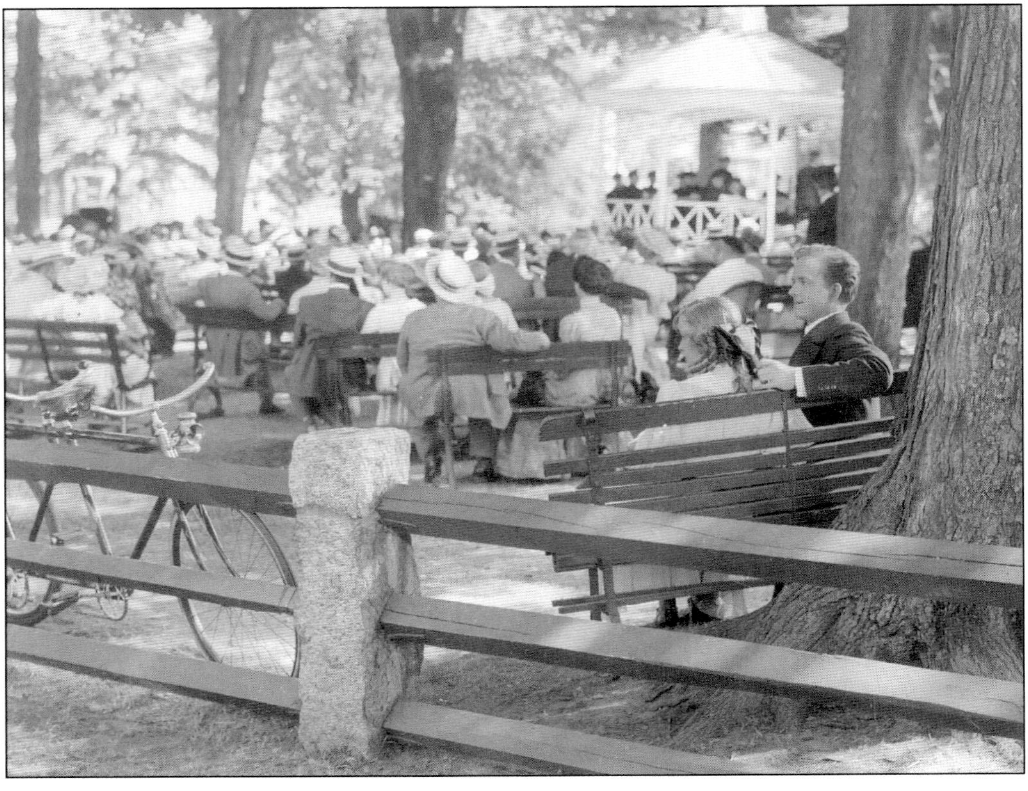

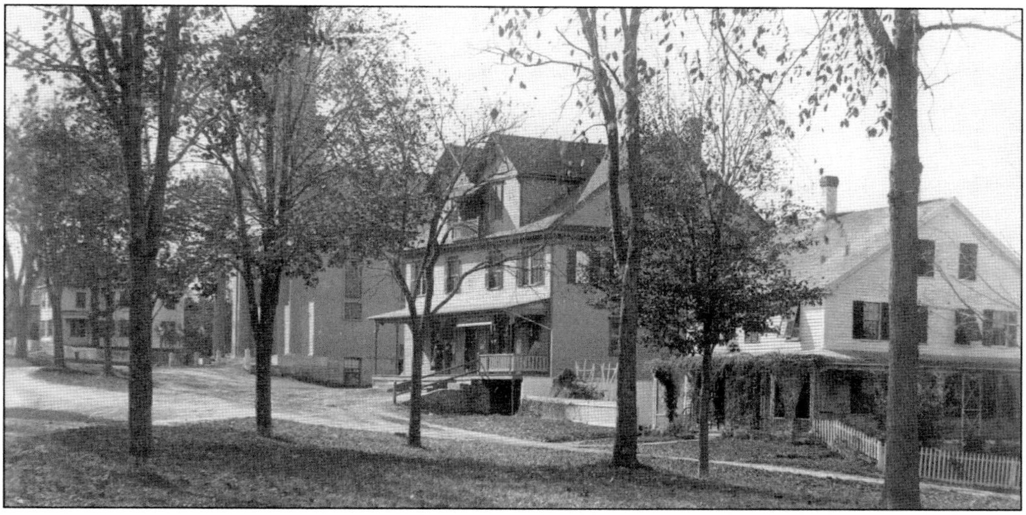

The Arcade Building (above), Grafton's original meetinghouse, was constructed on the common in 1731. It remained there until 1831 when a dispute arose within the original Puritan parish. The Congregationalists built a new church on the west side of the common, and the Unitarians constructed their church on north side. The old meetinghouse was sold, moved from the common, and transformed into a commercial building. In the late 1880s it was the site of Clarence Elliot's meat market. During the 1940s and early 1950s, it housed a First National Store (below), managed by Dick Greany, and a cobbler shop in the basement. The Parker family lived on the top floor. It was torn down in 1957 to make a parking lot for the church next door.

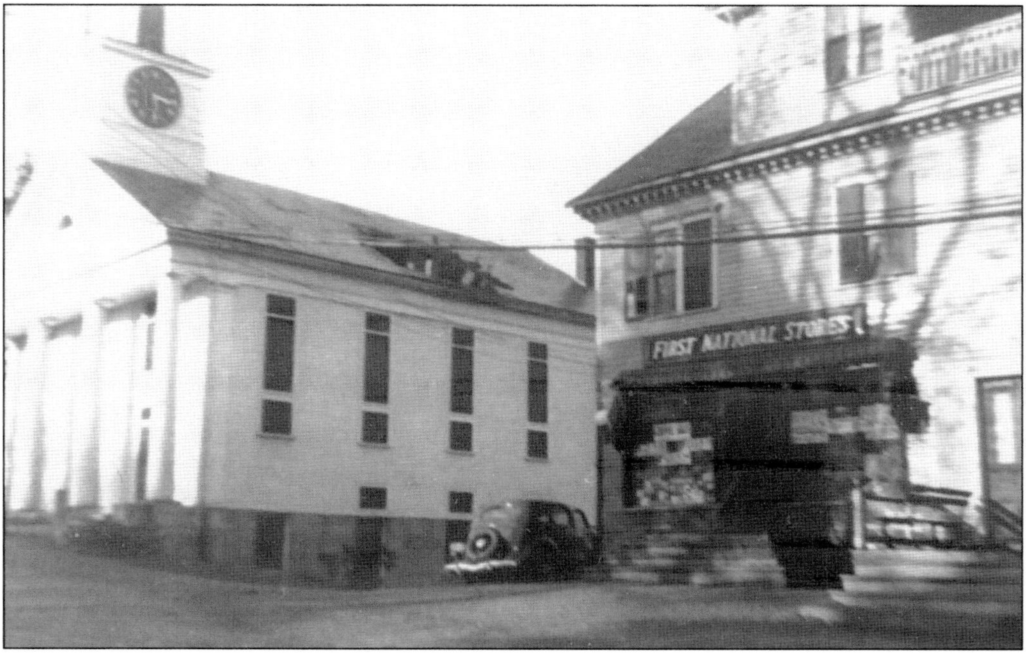

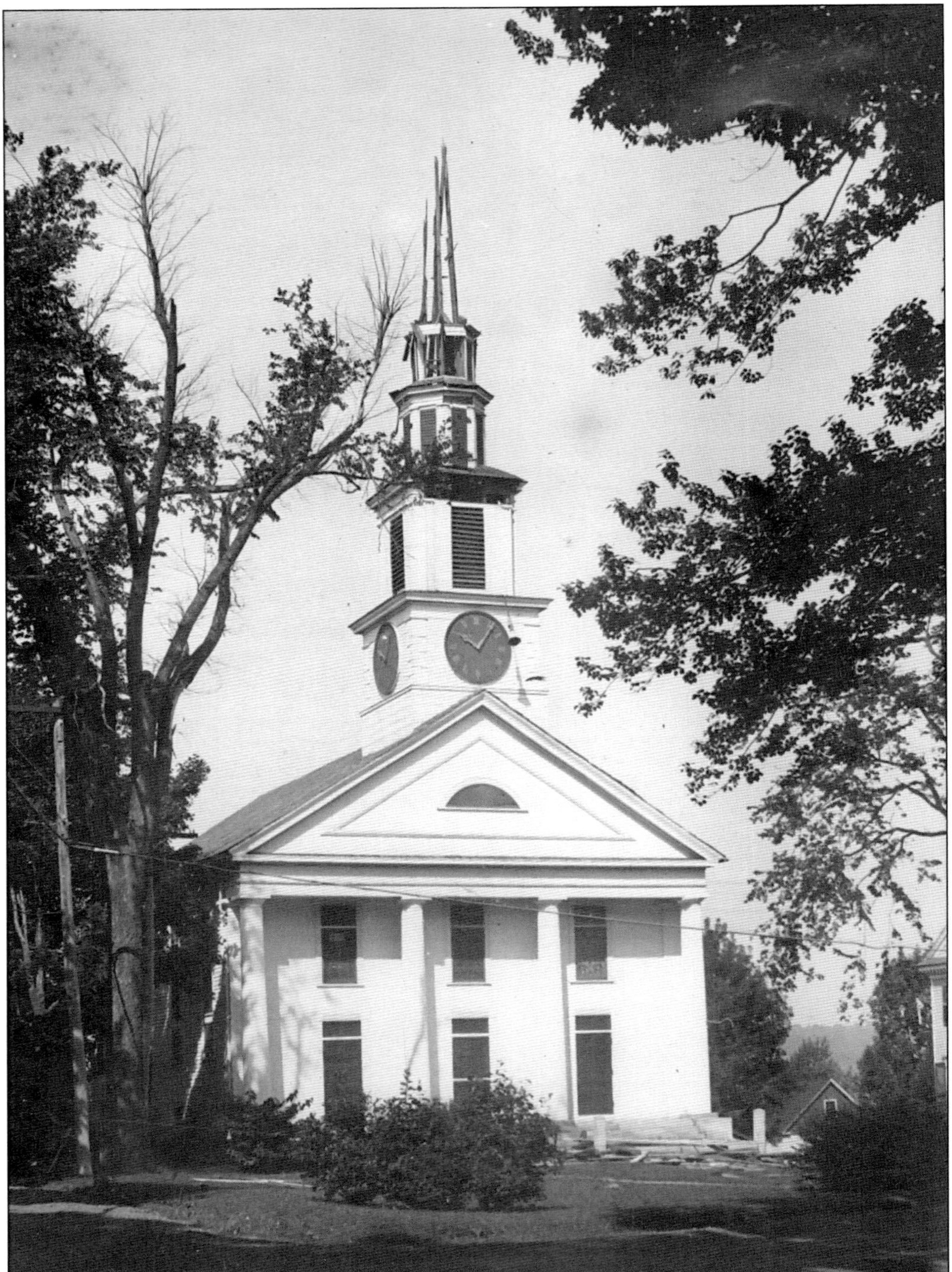

The first church in Grafton was organized in 1731 by a group of investors who built their meetinghouse on the town common. Following a series of religious disagreements, one faction constructed this building, the Evangelical Congregational Church, on the west side of the common in 1833. During the hurricane of 1938, the steeple, which houses a Willard clock, was toppled and plunged through the roof into the sanctuary. In this photograph, repairs are under way.

The Unitarian Universalist Society of Grafton was established in 1832 following a split with members of the original church. In 1862, the Unitarian church building, located on the north side of the common, was destroyed by fire and replaced by this structure. Although painted white for the last 100 years, the church is shown in this 1887 photograph painted two shades of brown.

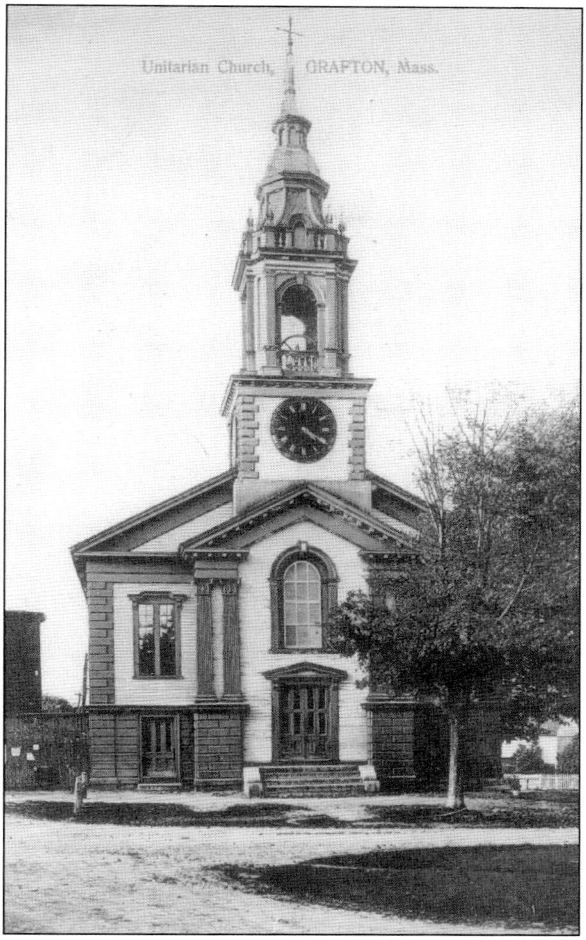

In the early 1830s, missionaries visited Grafton's Catholic families. A small chapel dedicated to St. Philip was eventually built on West Street. Gradually enlarged, it was made a parish in 1869. St. Philip Church was the mother church of St. James, St. Mary, Holy Angels, and Our Lady of Lourdes. In 1977, the growing parish family replaced this building with a modern structure.

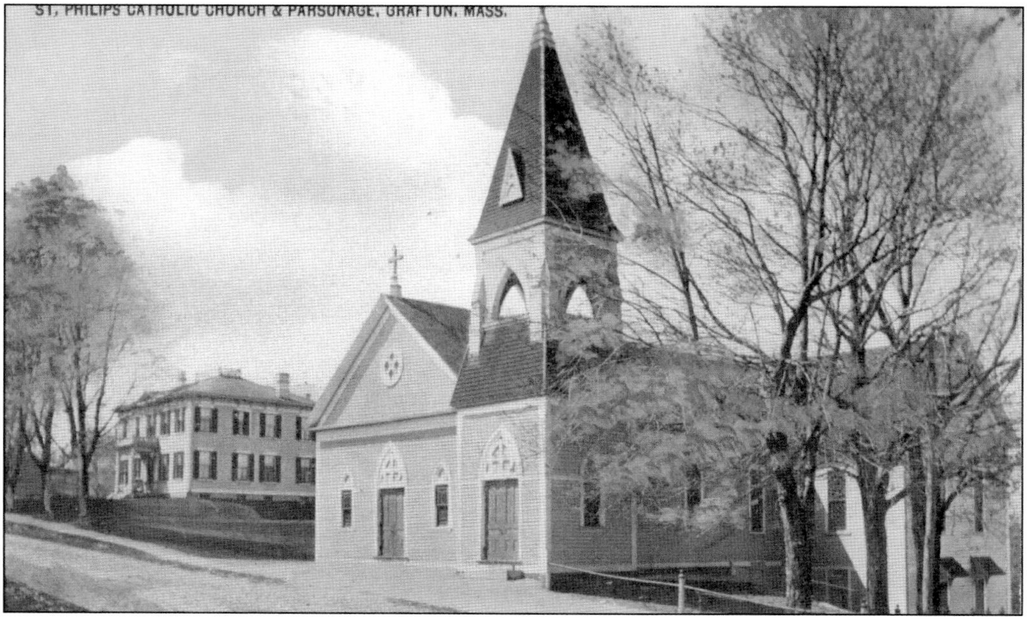

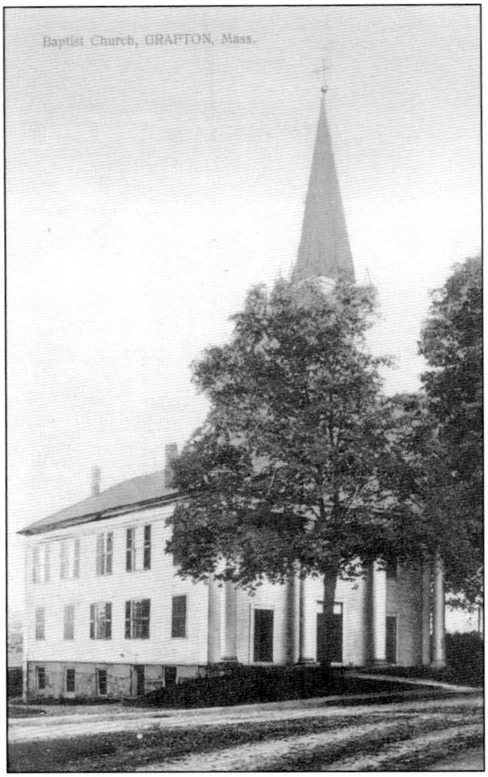

In 1800, the Grafton Baptist Church, with 15 members, purchased land beside a stream on Pleasant Street for $12. They erected a church there and baptized members near the stone bridge. In 1830, the present church was built at 1 South Street. In 1968, the town's two Baptist parishes joined to form the Baptist Church of Grafton. The Second Baptist Church building in North Grafton was sold and later torn down.

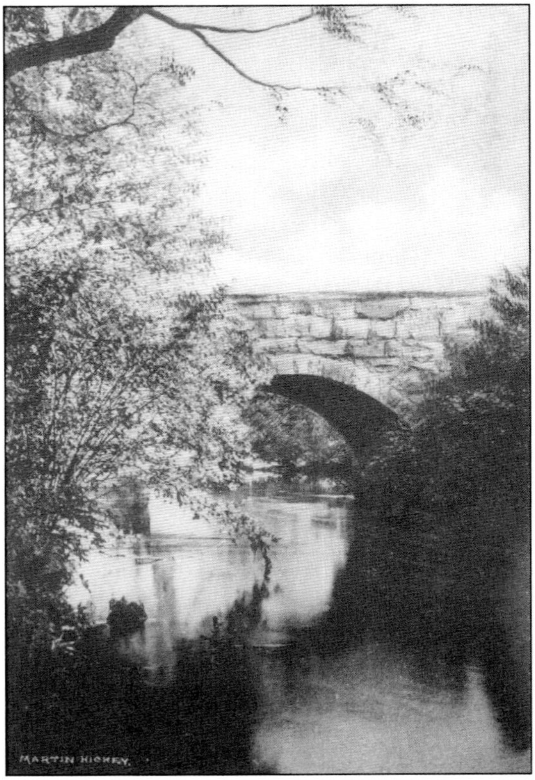

This stone arch bridge on Pleasant Street was the site of baptisms for the early Baptist Church. This bridge is one of three stone arch bridges built in Grafton during the second half of the 19th century. There is another on Pleasant Street in South Grafton and one over the Quinsigamond River in the New England Village area of North Grafton.

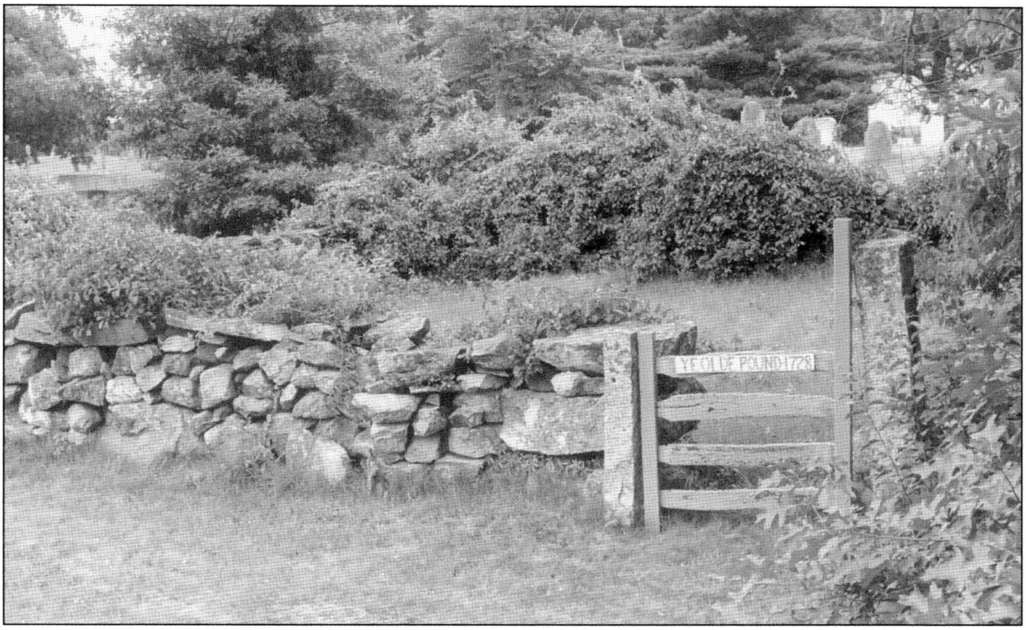

The old town animal pound is a stone enclosure located next to the Oak Street Cemetery. Because of a lack of strong fences in colonial Grafton, livestock could wander off their owner's lands and threaten nearby kitchen gardens. The community animal pound enclosed stray animals until their owners could claim them. Town records show that, as early as 1735, horses and swine were impounded here and their owners fined.

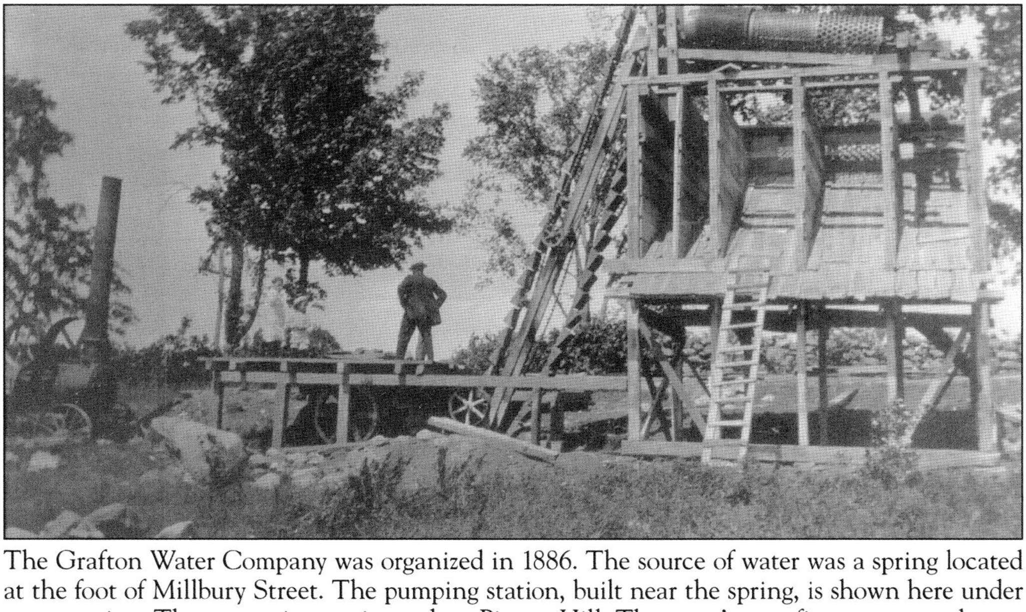

The Grafton Water Company was organized in 1886. The source of water was a spring located at the foot of Millbury Street. The pumping station, built near the spring, is shown here under construction. The reservoir was situated on Pigeon Hill. The town's very first water supply was an aqueduct that brought water from a spring on Keith Hill to residents.

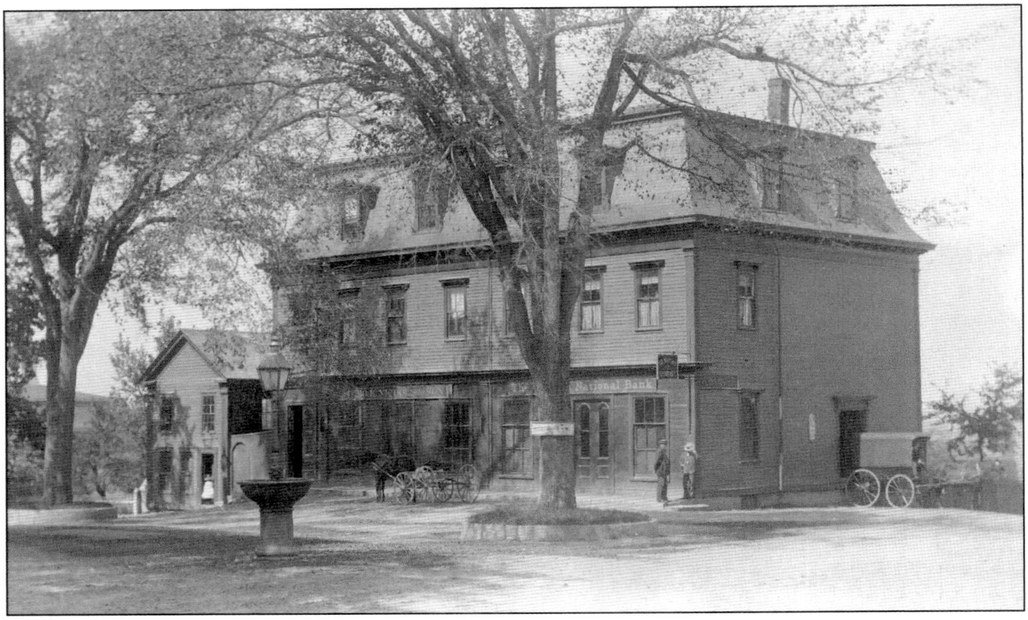

This building at 2 Grafton Common (above) was constructed in 1806 by Jonathan Wheeler. It was called the "Green Store" because of its color and to differentiate it from the "White Store" at the other end of the common. In 1860, it was modernized by adding a mansard roof and creating a third level with a large hall. The men of the town gathered here to discuss politics and business. In the 1940s, it housed Tebo's Market (below), run by Charlie Tebo, and the Hilltop Spa, run by Phoebe Flynn. Tebo's Market boasted the best meat in town. The Hilltop Spa was where politics, business, and local gossip were processed and disseminated. The sale of cigarettes, magazines, comic books, ice cream sodas, and penny candy attracted a steady flow of customers.

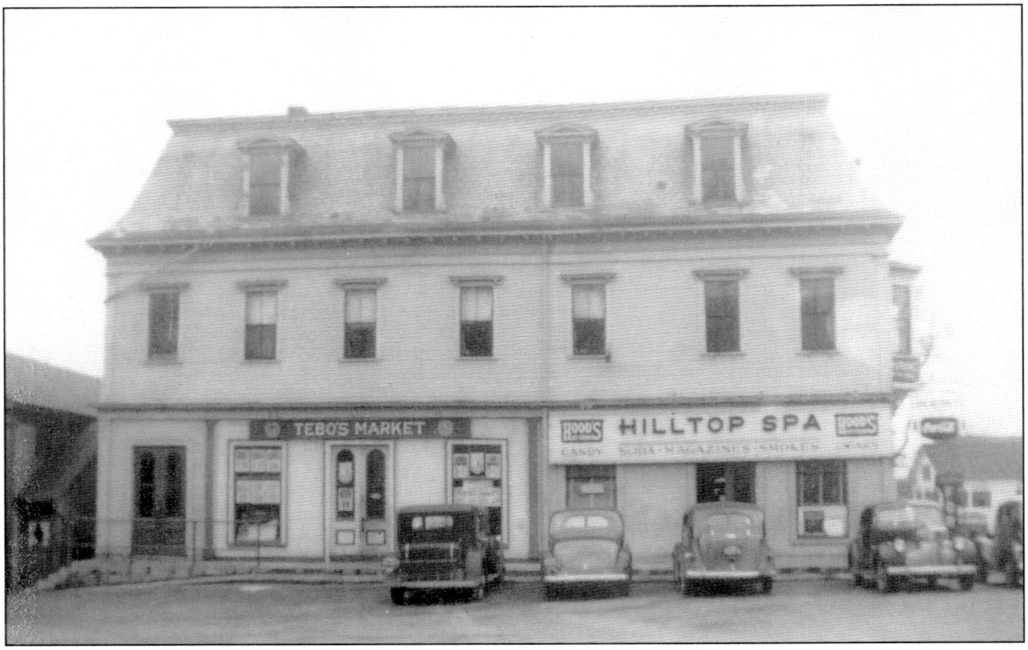

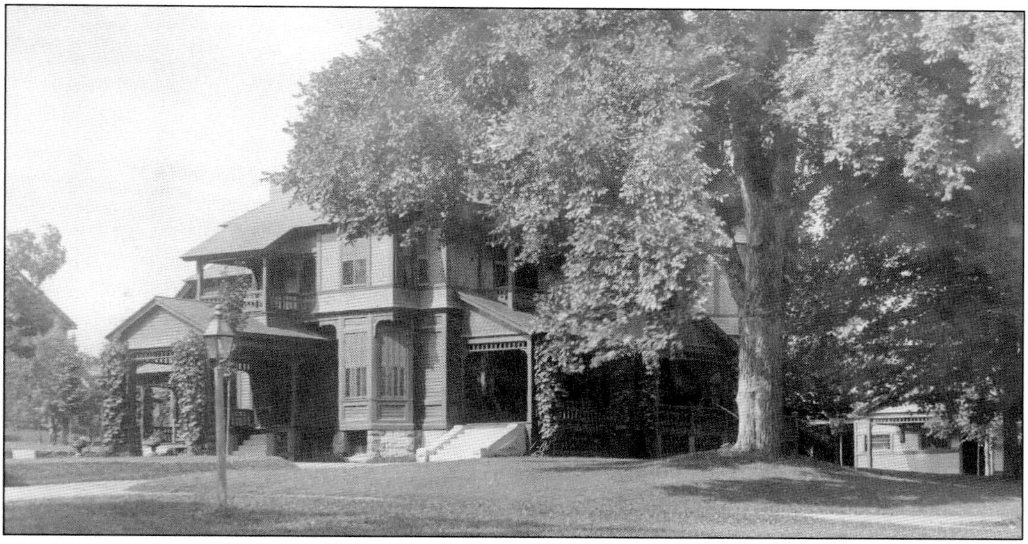

The Fisher Mansion, built in 1885 at the south end of the common by the owner of the Fisherville Mill, was considered to be the finest house in town. The three-story home of George Fisher and his wife, Ella, cost $20,000 to construct and had 20 rooms and 9 fireplaces. It had a reception hall, a library, a billiard room, and a conservatory. The Fishers spared no expense, using exotic woods throughout.

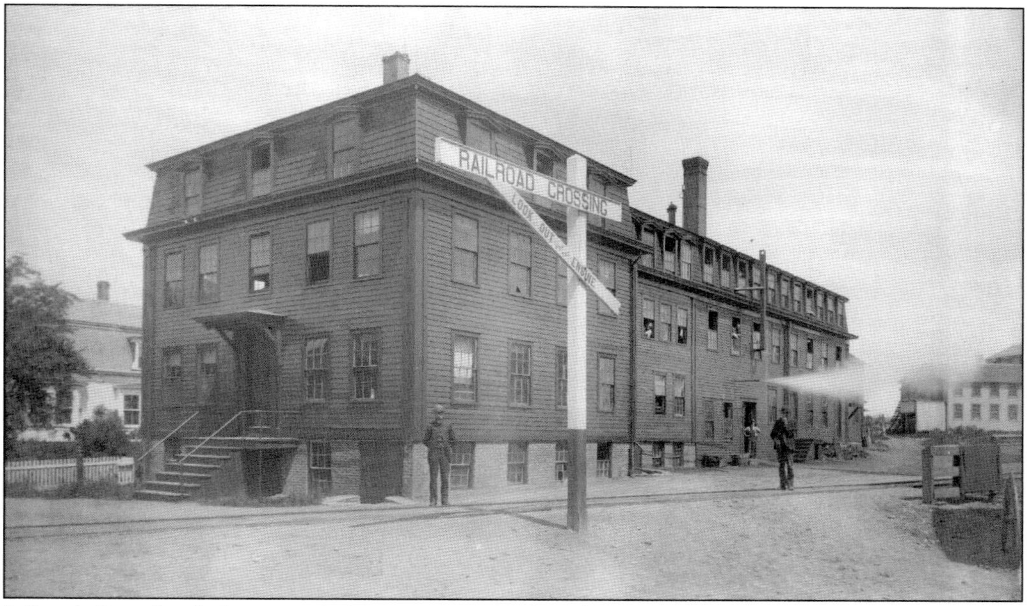

J. Frank Donahue's farm supply business operated in this building at 2 North Street during the first half of the 20th century. The building was originally Gibbs and Allen, a large shoe factory producing shoes and boots for men and boys, during the 19th century. The building was removed in the 1950s.

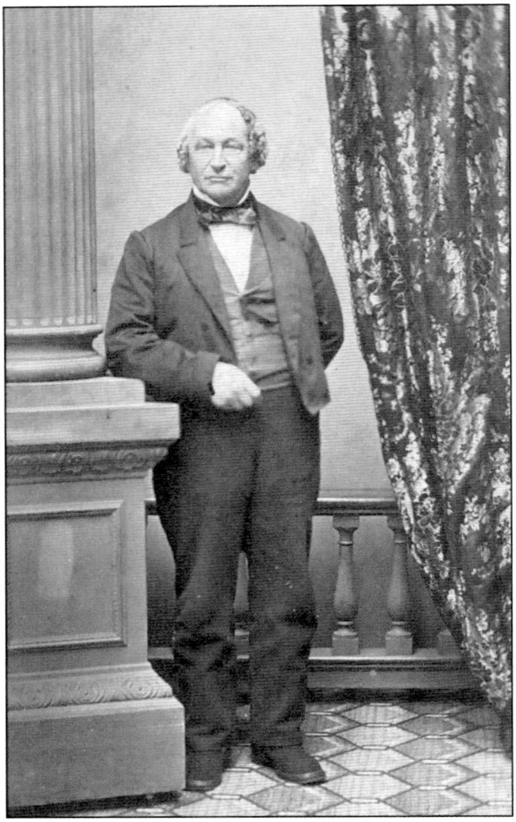

Capt. Jonathan Warren, an early shoe industry entrepreneur, began making shoes and boots at the age of 20 and continued successfully for 35 years. He was captain of the local militia, town treasurer, state legislator, and founder of the First National Bank. He accumulated much property and built the commercial building that became the Grafton Town House.

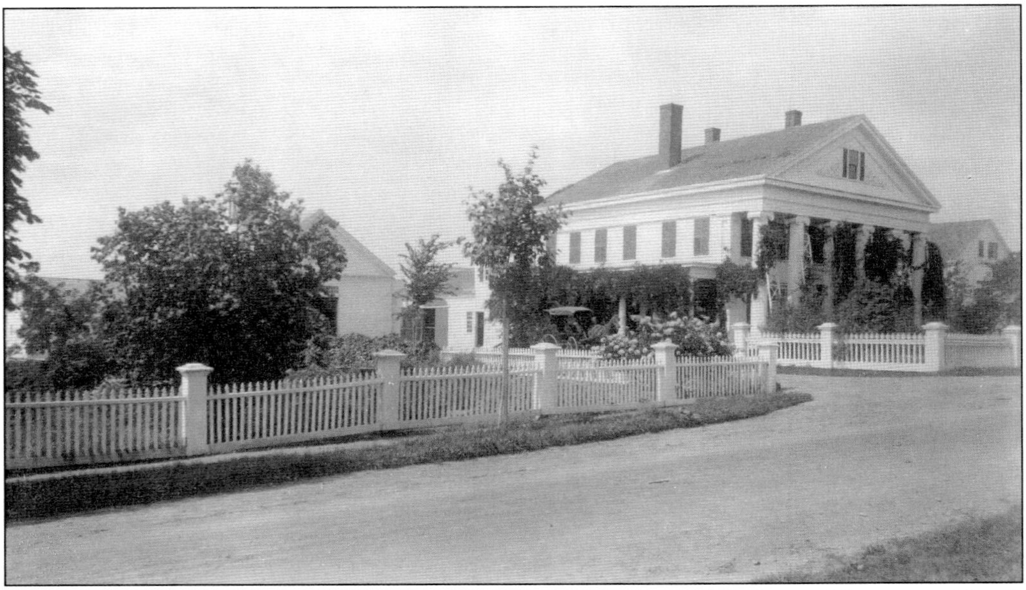

Built by Capt. Jonathan Warren for his family in 1827, this Greek Revival house on North Street reflects the success of the leather industry in Grafton. The Warren family home had a formal garden, a wagon house, and unique fencing along the front. The rear overlooks the Quinsigamond River Valley. The Warren family was active in Grafton business and government for several generations.

The Civil War monument was erected in 1867 to honor the 59 men from Grafton who died in the war. Eleven Grafton men died at Antietam; others were lost at Gettysburg, Fredericksburg, Cold Harbor, New Bern, and Andersonville. The raw marble for the monument was imported from Italy and a shed was built in the square where workmen carved the stone. The monument, including the dedication ceremony, cost $2,793.

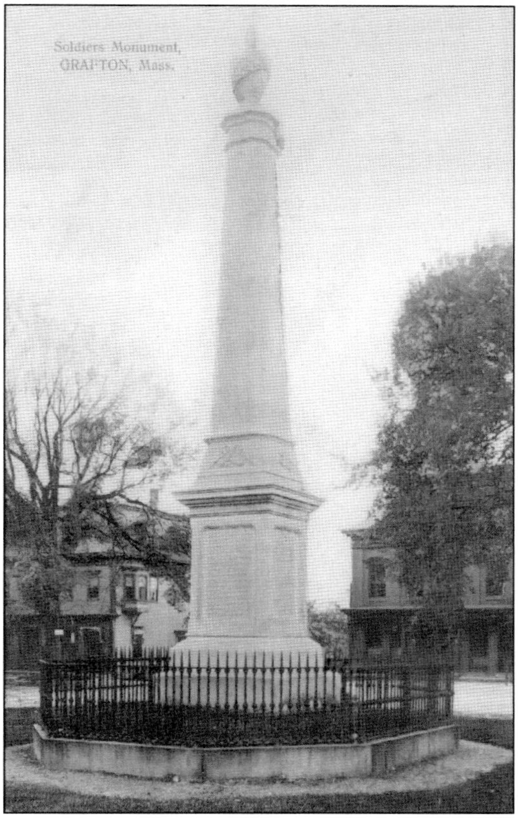

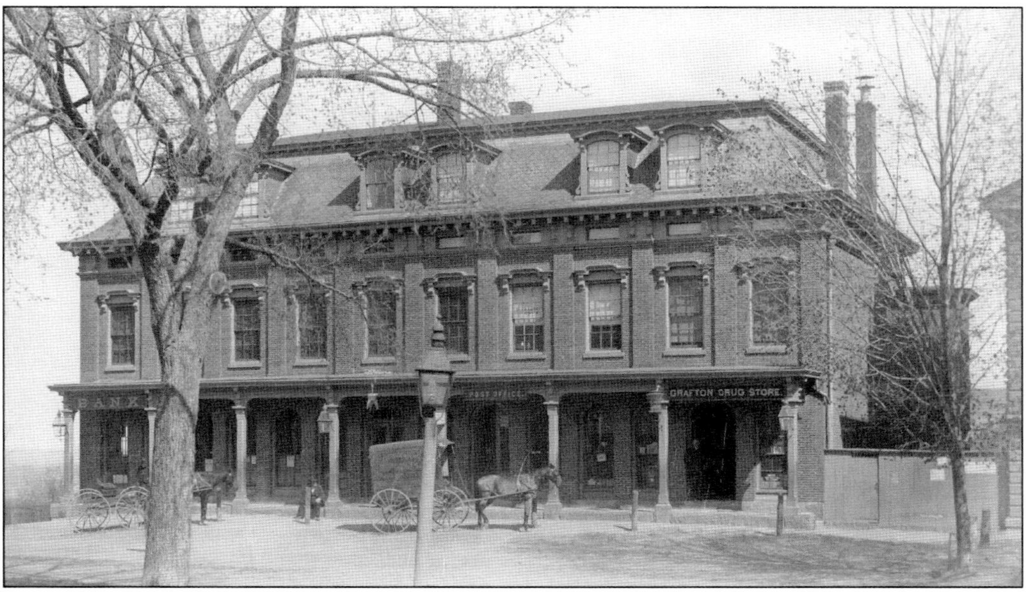

The Grafton Town House was constructed in 1850 by Capt. Jonathan Warren, who manufactured shoes in the basement and leased the rest of the building to other businesses. After it was destroyed by fire in 1862, Warren rebuilt it with a large hall on the second floor for town meetings. In 1885, the town bought the building for $17,000, and it served as the seat of government and the center of business and social events for over a century.

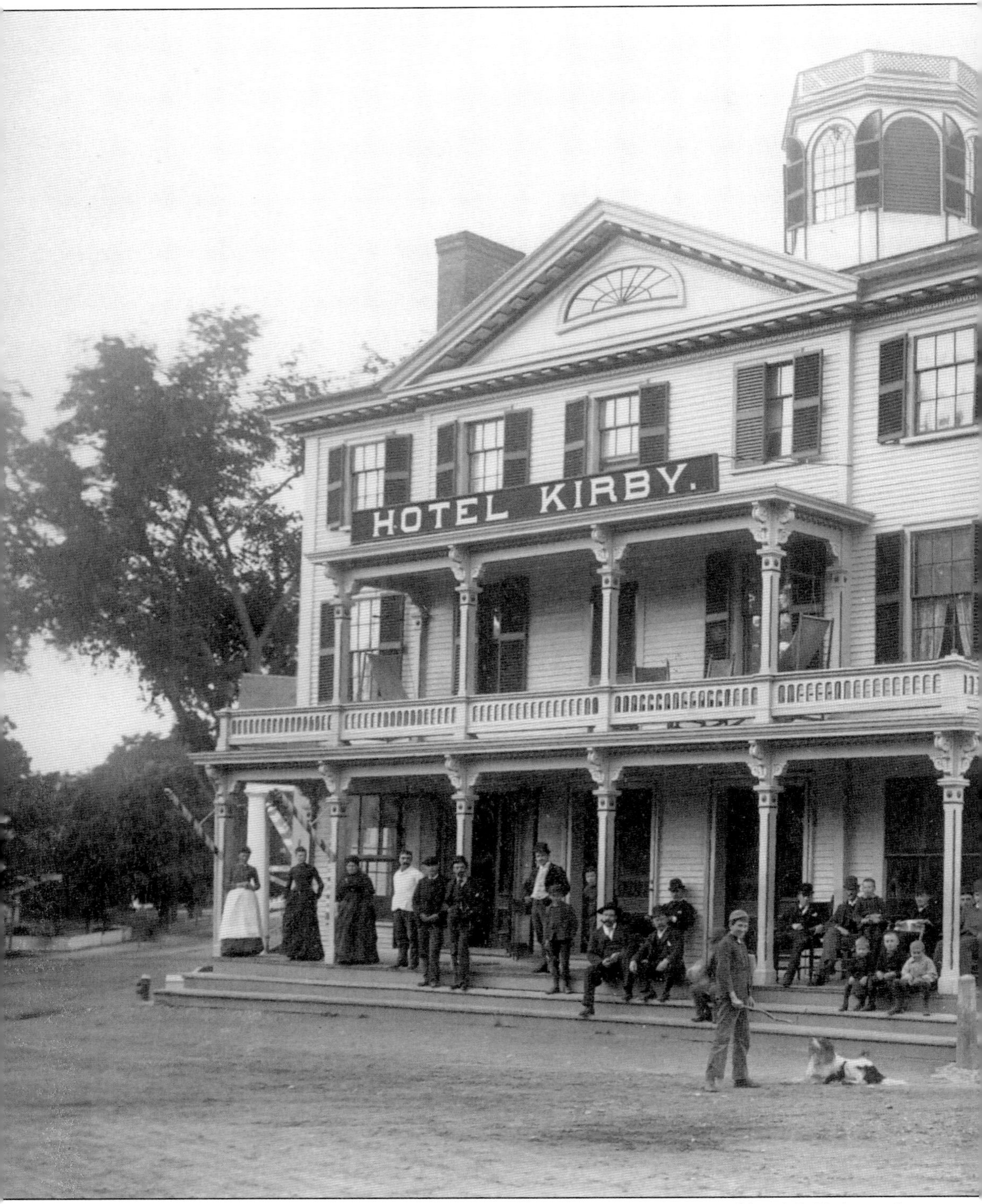

The Grafton Inn is shown as it appeared around 1895 when it was owned by A.J. Kirby and was called the Kirby Hotel. It offered 40 rooms, a horse stable, and a bountiful table. The inn has been in operation since it was constructed by Samuel Wood in 1805 and is the oldest building on Grafton Common. When Route 140 was the road to Cape Cod, the inn enjoyed a brisk business

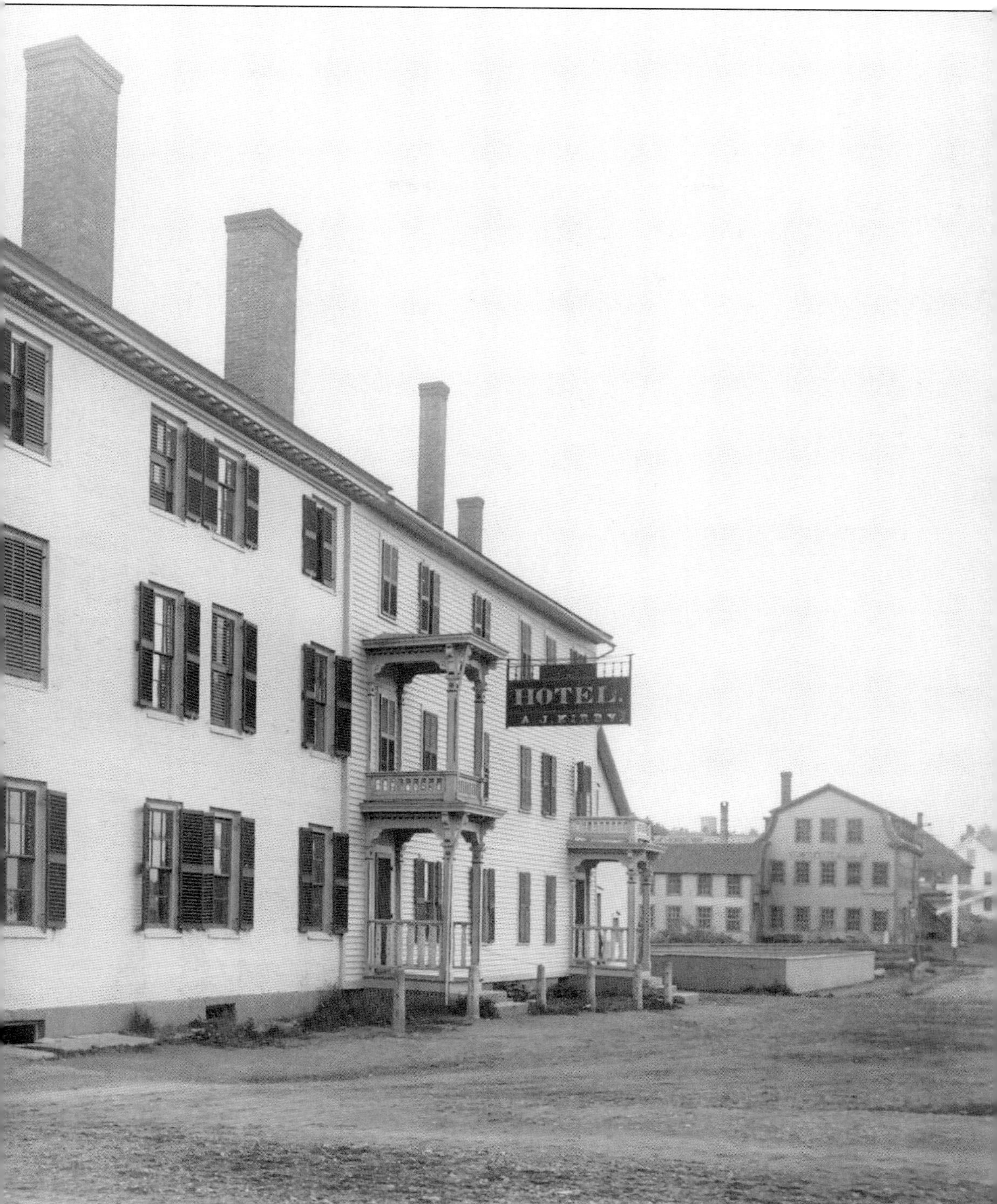

with vacationers. Porches were an important feature of many buildings in the late 1800s. Guests of the inn enjoyed sitting on the porch watching the bustle of activity around Grafton Common. This porch was removed in the 1980s when the inn was renovated.

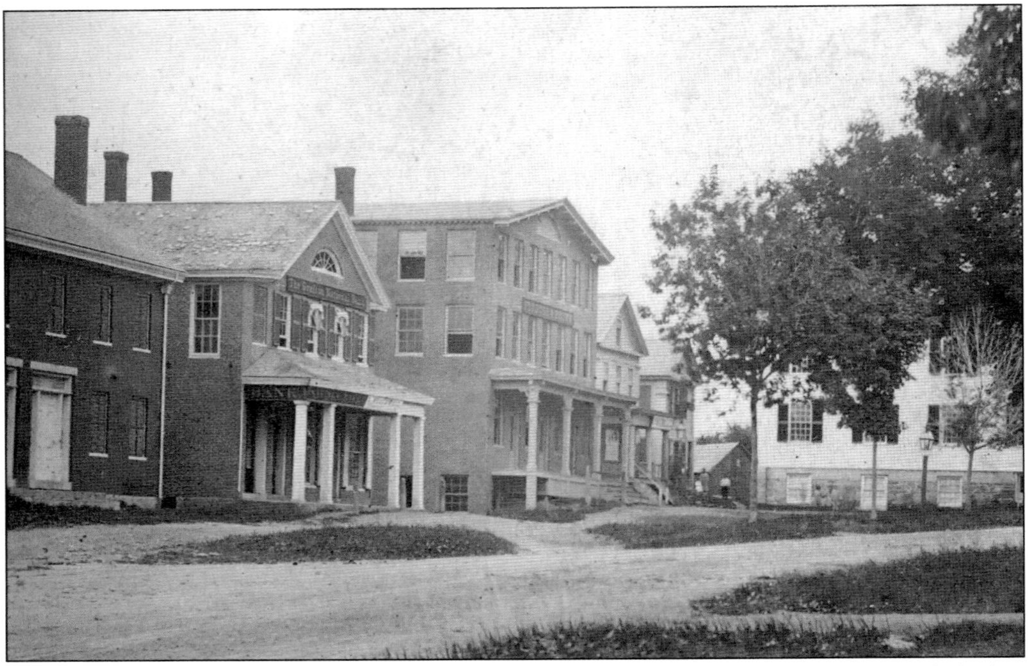

When the Grafton Public Library was constructed in 1927, three buildings were demolished to make room for it: Grafton National Bank, Forbush and Brown Shoe Company, and Stockwell's Tailor Shop, all shown here. The Baptist church is seen on the far right. As early as 1858, a private library had been established by the Grafton Lyceum. At that time, no fiction was permitted on the shelves.

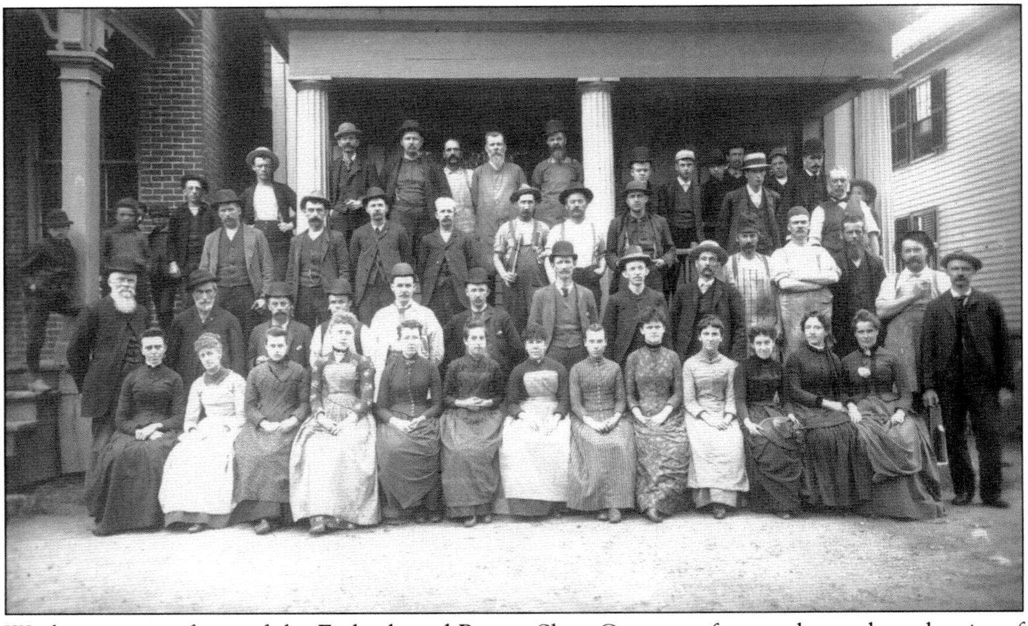

Workers pose in front of the Forbush and Brown Shoe Company factory, located on the site of the present library. In the early 1800s, Grafton Center became the site of a new industry: ready-made shoes. Many shoe factories, tanneries, currying shops, and shoe-related businesses sprang up, mostly along North and South Streets.

This bronze statue of Jerome Wheelock (1834–1902) stands at the south end of Grafton Common. Wheelock was born in Grafton and became a noted mechanical engineer. Before the age of 30, he invented a steam engine valve that revolutionized steam transportation. For this, he received international recognition. Funds from a Wheelock bequest were used to build the Grafton Public Library in 1927.

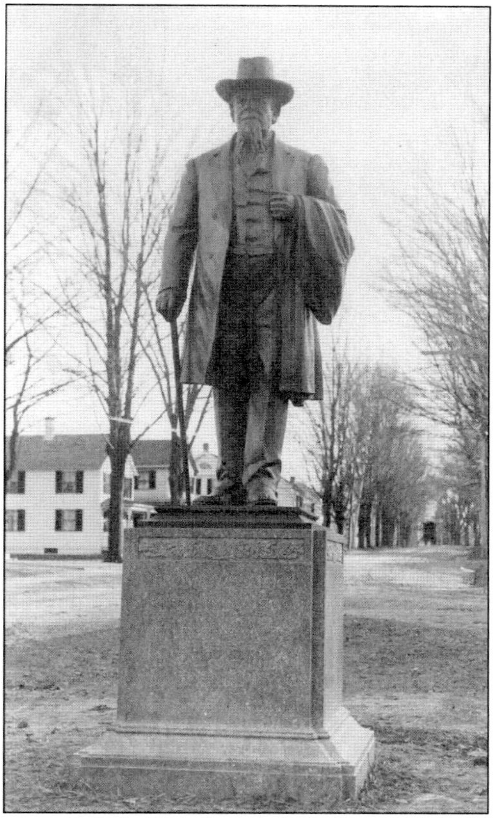

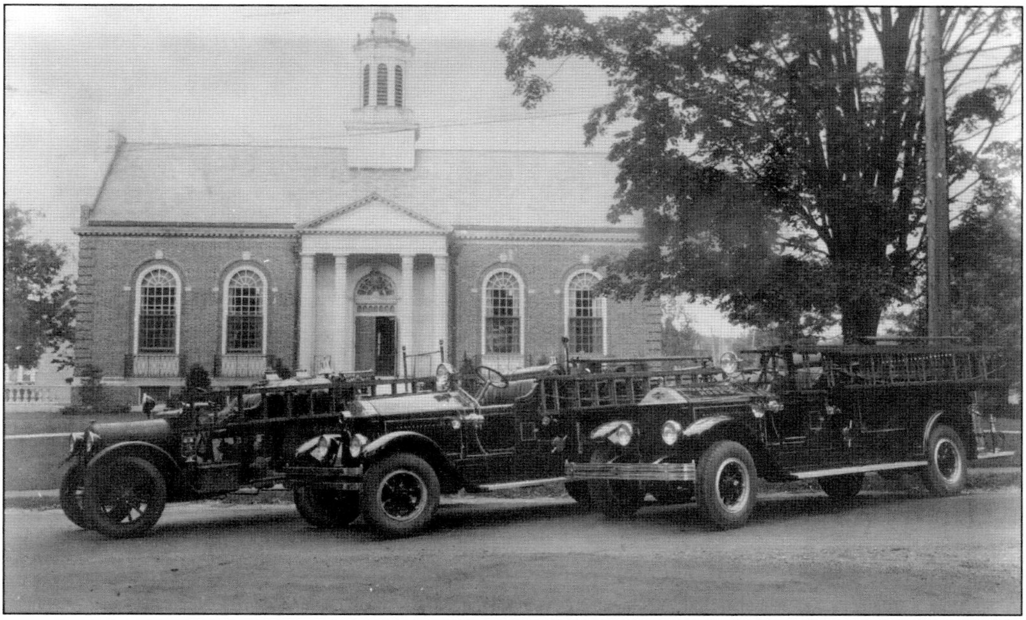

Three fire engines are on display in front of the Grafton Public Library around 1930. They represent Rescue Hose No. 1 from Grafton Center, Rescue Hose No. 2 from North Grafton, and Rescue Hose No. 3 from South Grafton. Musters were held in the nearby square, and the hose companies could compete for prizes given for speed in various firefighting techniques.

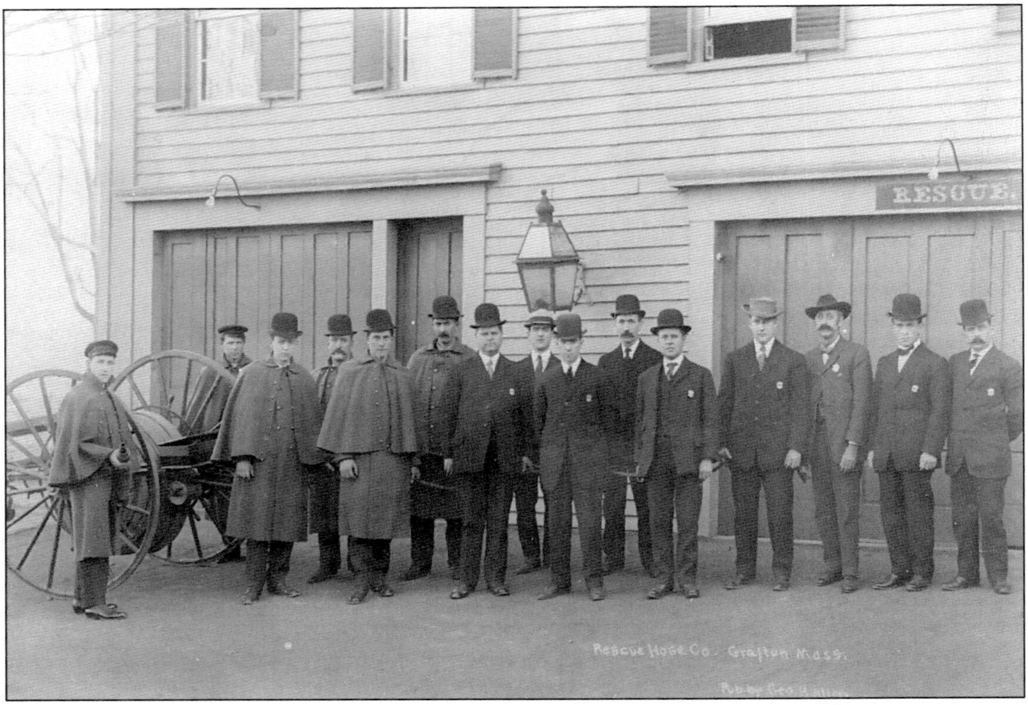

The Rescue Hose No. 1 was the fire company serving Grafton Center. Here, the company poses in front of the station with a horse-drawn pumper. The station was originally located on North Street, but in the 20th century, it was moved to a lot on Upton Road.

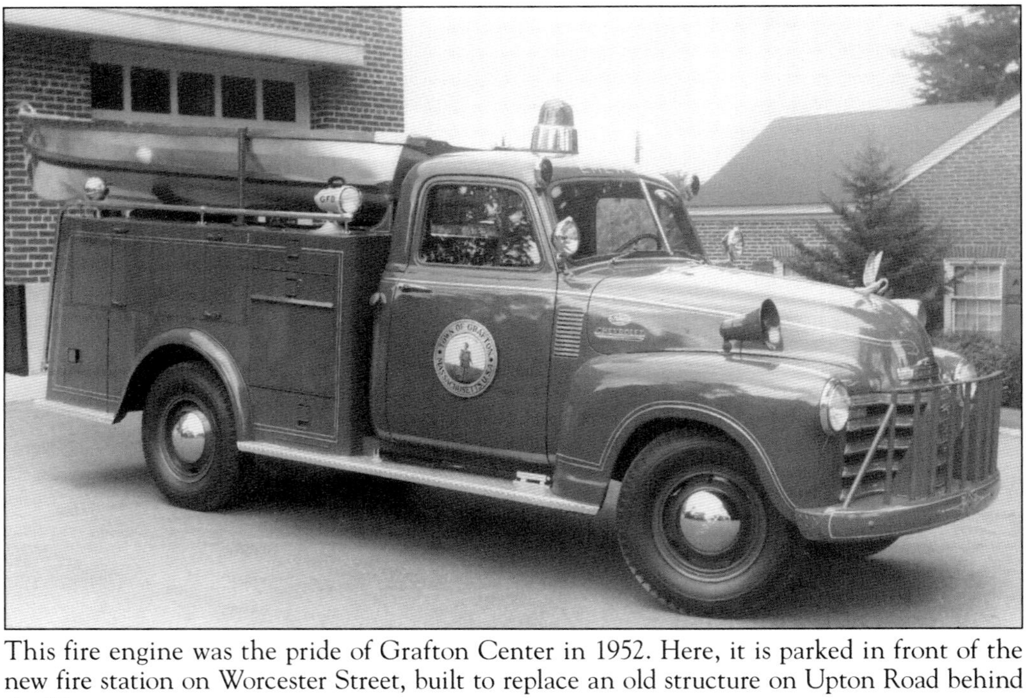

This fire engine was the pride of Grafton Center in 1952. Here, it is parked in front of the new fire station on Worcester Street, built to replace an old structure on Upton Road behind the library.

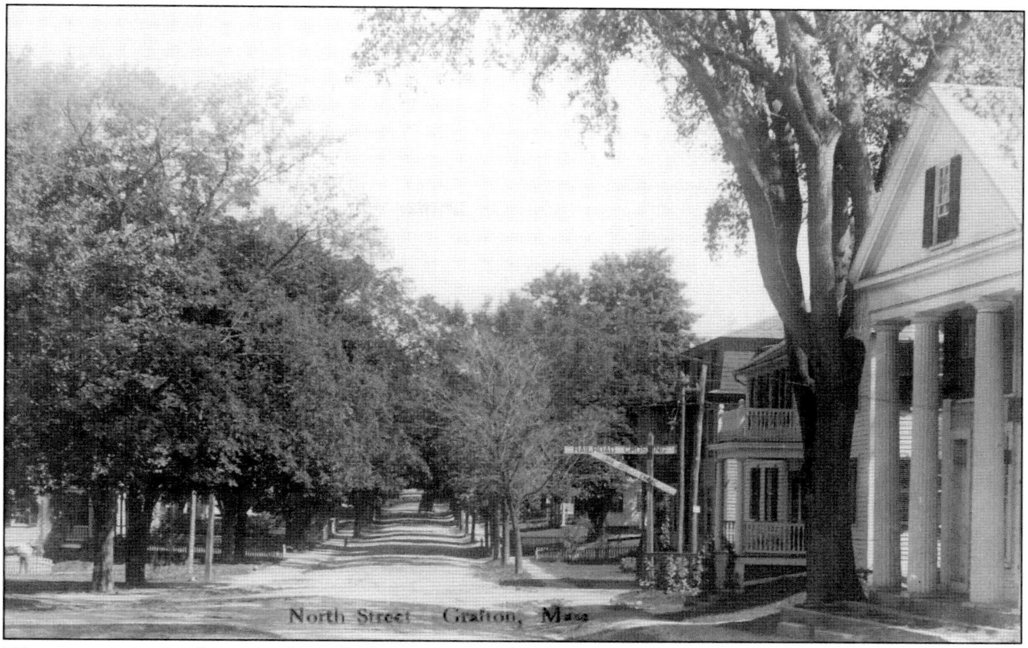

This is a view looking up North Street around 1920. On the far right is the Grafton Savings Bank. Beside it is Georgiana Fiske Keith's private residence, which was removed to make room for a parking lot around 1950.

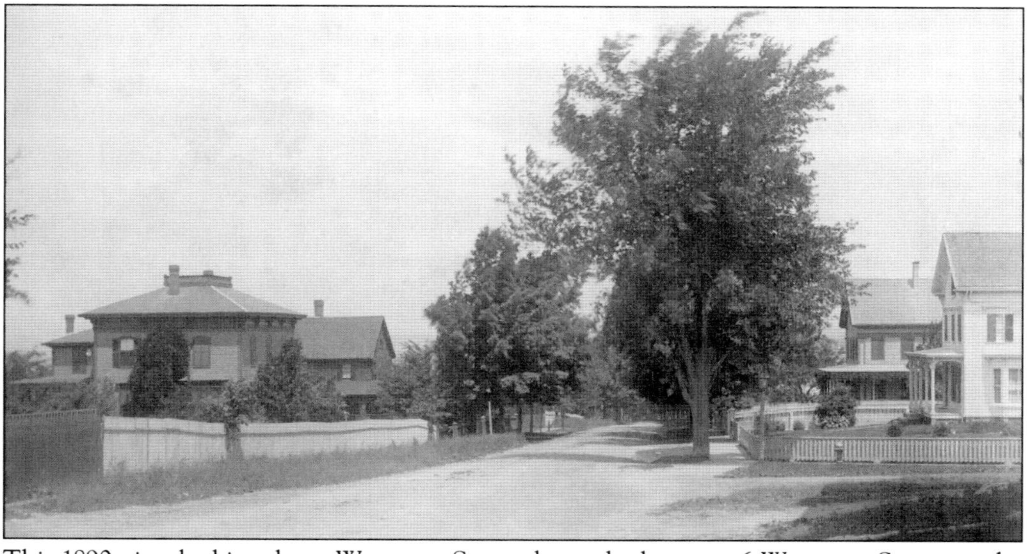

This 1890 view looking down Worcester Street shows the house at 6 Worcester Street on the right. When Worcester Street was created in the early 1850s, this house was moved from the lot now occupied by the Grafton Town House to make room for the new road. The 1720s house now at the corner of Kessell and Worcester Streets was also moved from the same site.

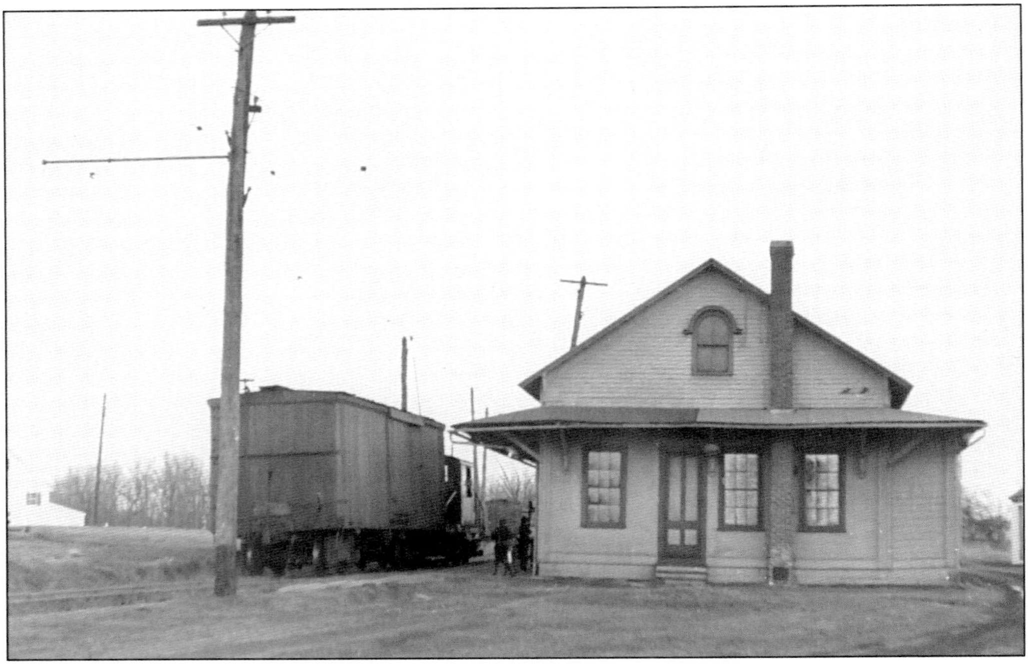

In 1874, the Grafton Center Railroad built a three-mile track connecting Grafton Center to North Grafton. Trains left the center nine times daily to connect with other trains bound for Worcester or Boston. Ridership was about 100 persons per day. The original depot was located behind the Grafton Town House but was moved to Upton Street (above) when the line was expanded into the Grafton & Upton Railroad in 1887. The photograph below shows mail being delivered at the Grafton Center station.

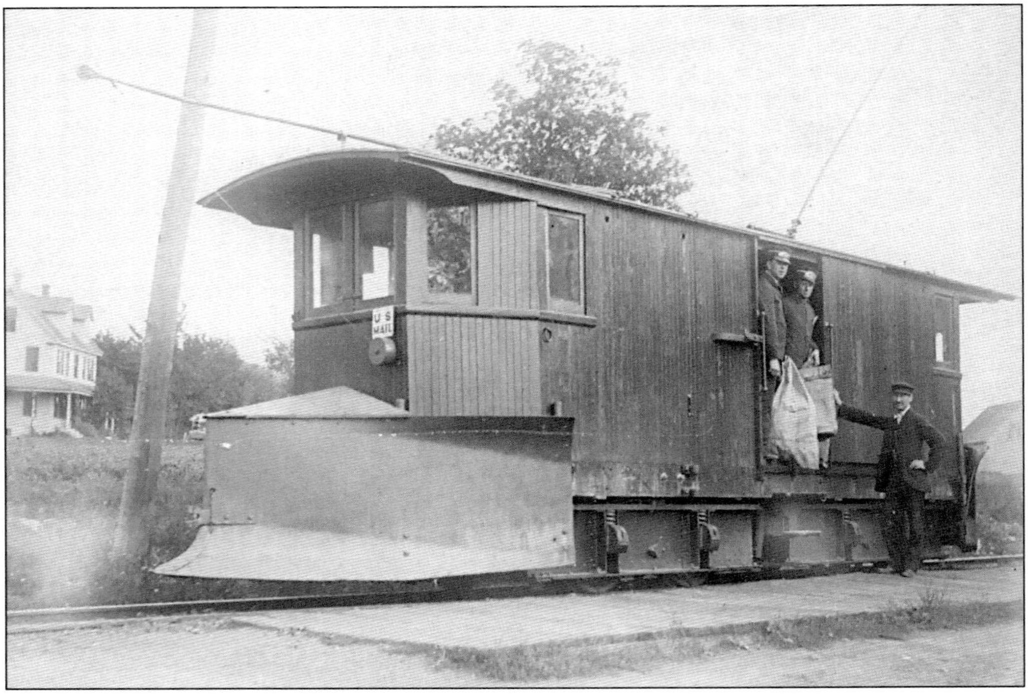

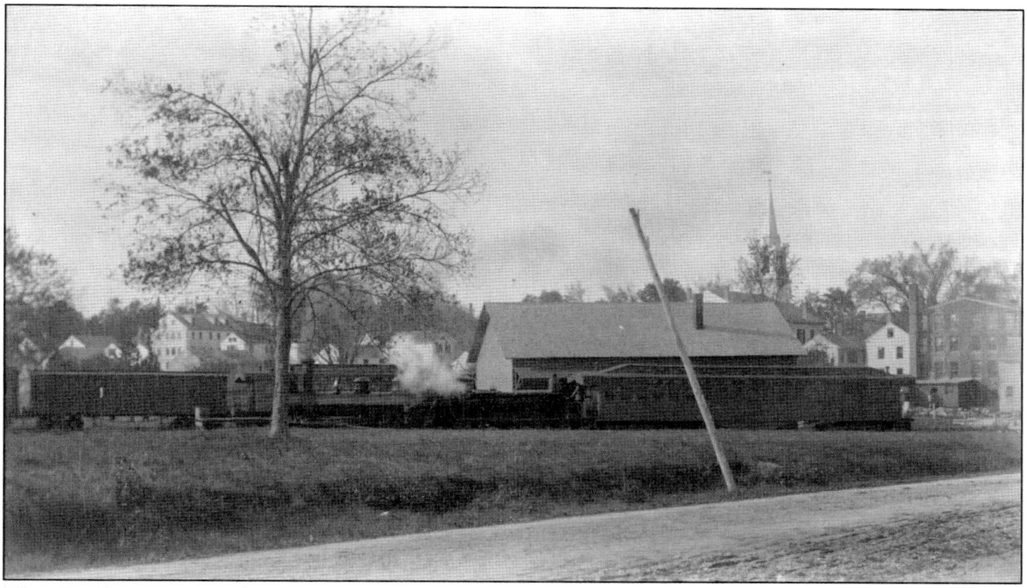

The Grafton Center depot is shown here with South Street in the distance. The Forbush and Brown Shoe Company and the Baptist church can be seen.

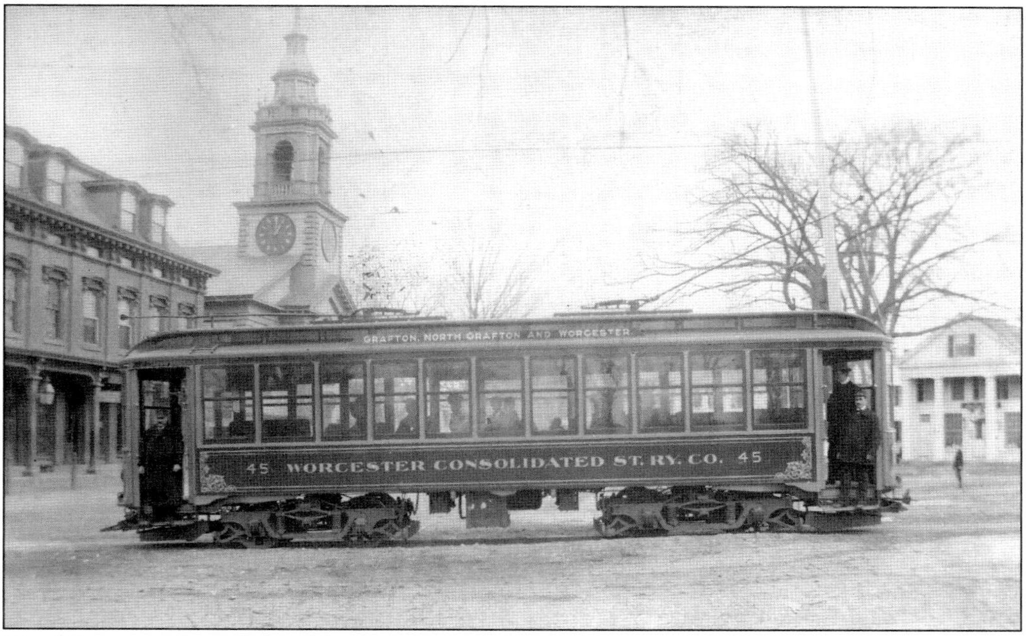

The Worcester Consolidated Railway Company operated this trolley line, connecting Grafton Center with North Grafton. When the road was electrified in 1902, trolleys replaced the passenger service of the Grafton & Upton Railroad. The trolley system operated until 1928 when it gave way to motor buses run by the Johnson Bus Line.

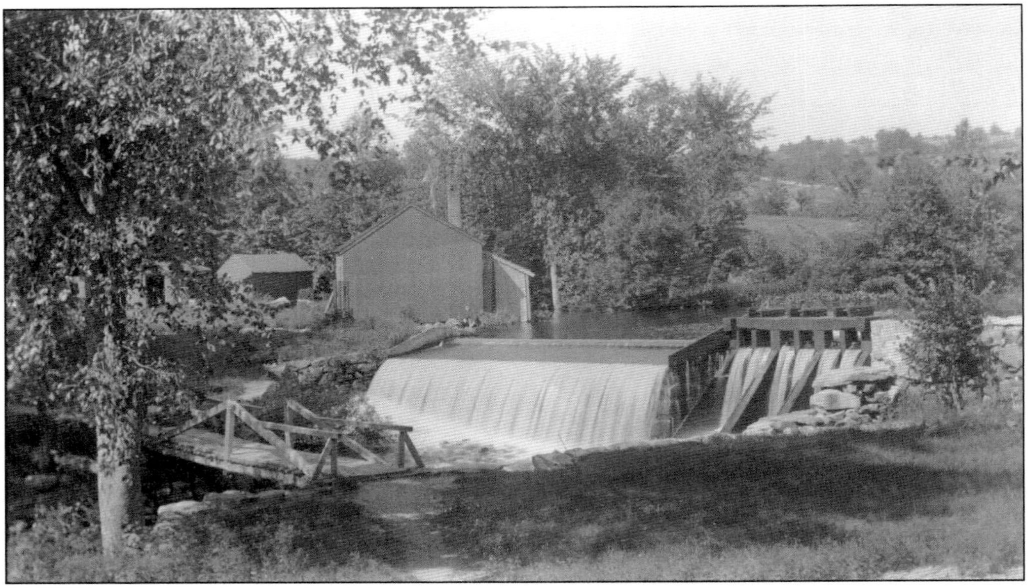

The need for power inspired the town founders to dam the local rivers. The Centerville Dam at the bottom of Brigham Hill was the first to be built. It tapped the Quinsigamond River for power to run a gristmill, a sawmill, and a blacksmith shop. Later, a woolen mill and a cotton mill were built at Centerville as well. A small village with a few shops and residences grew up at this site.

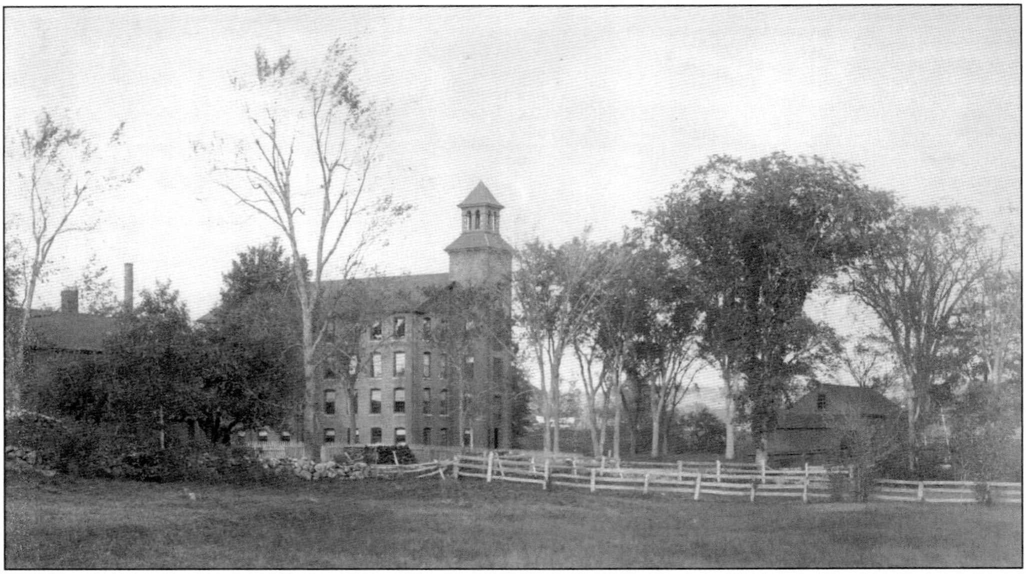

In 1846, Leander Pratt purchased this mill site at Centerville, replaced the old mill with this brick building, and established Pratt's Cotton Mill. In 1872, when the World's Peace Jubilee was held in Boston, 38,000 yards of red, white, and blue sheeting was supplied by the mill to decorate the Coliseum Building. By 1879, the mill was producing 80,000 yards per month of cotton sheeting.

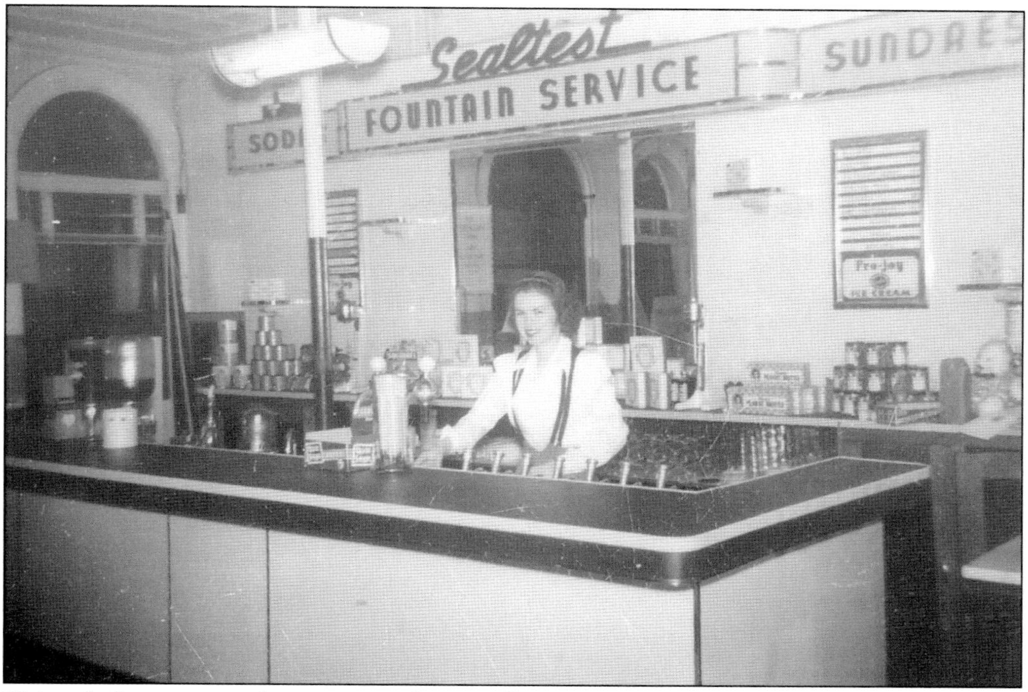

This soda fountain was the prominent feature of Dominic Rossetti's Grafton Pharmacy. Until the 1980s, the pharmacy was a fixture in the old Grafton Town House. Later, the business was moved to 8 Worcester Street, the old Grange Hall building. Here, Ruth Hall is ready to serve.

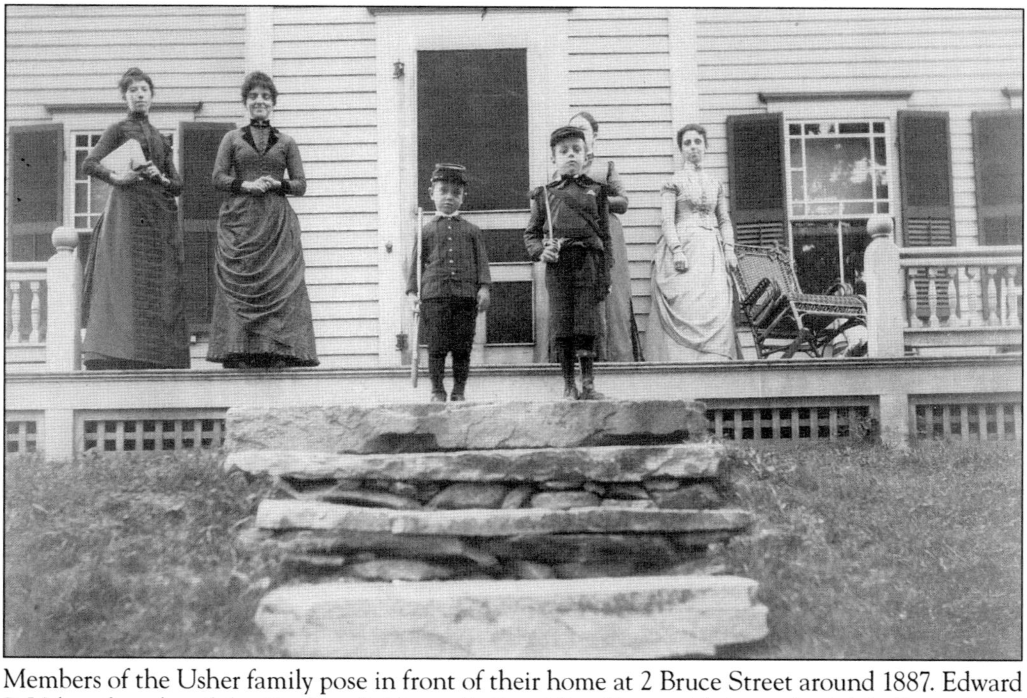

Members of the Usher family pose in front of their home at 2 Bruce Street around 1887. Edward P. Usher, founder of the Grafton & Upton Railroad lived here with his wife, Adela (far right, in a white dress), and their children. Shown on the steps of the porch are their sons Abbott, age four, and Roland, age seven, wearing a leg brace.

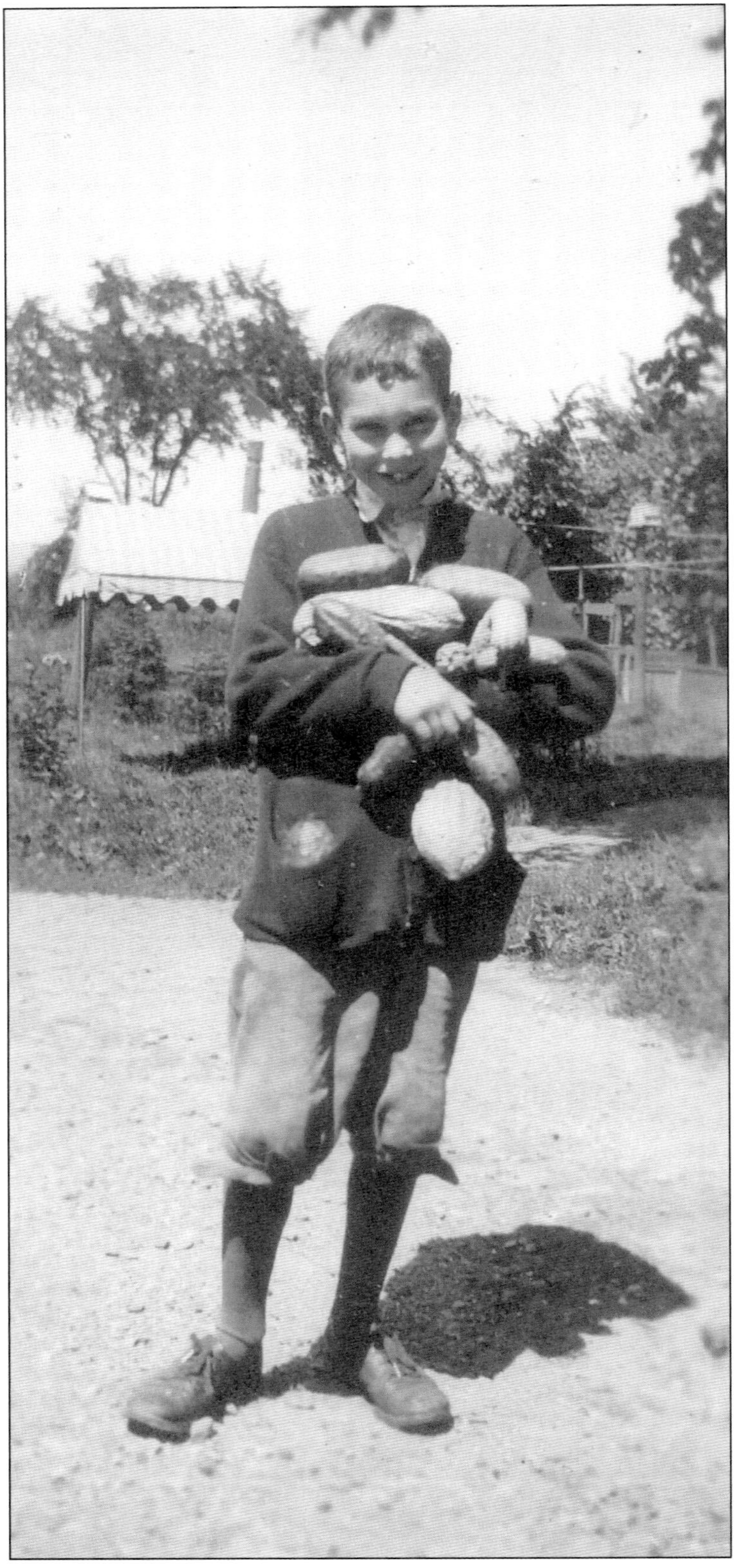

Frederic Anderson (1905–1996) beams with pleasure as he carries an armful of vegetables from the family garden in 1914. Frederic was born in Grafton and earned a degree in agriculture from the University of Massachusetts. He worked as a machinist at Anderson Corporation in Worcester. He was a charter member and director of the Grafton Historical Society and a member of the Grafton Grange.

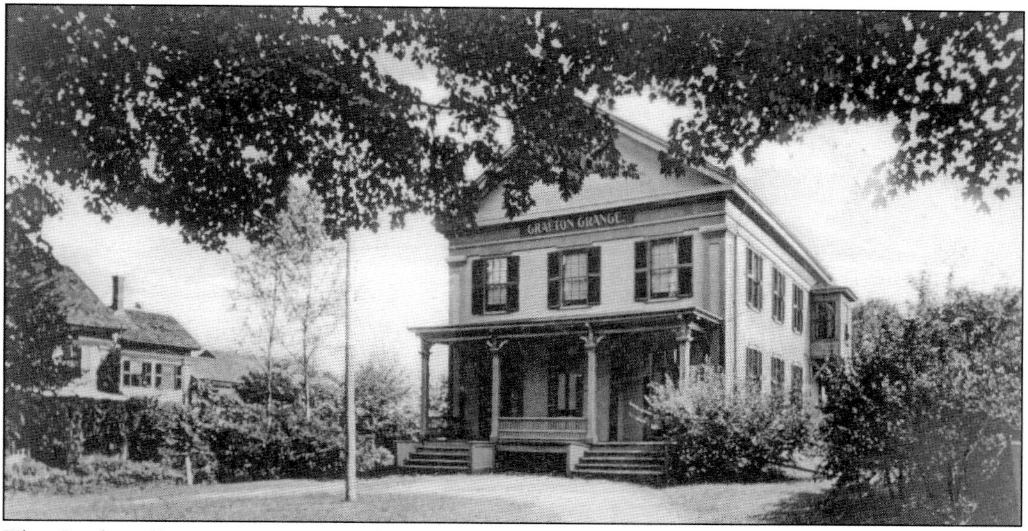

The Grafton Grange was organized in 1875 based on an interest in improving farming methods. In 1901, the organization purchased the old Grafton High School at 8 Worcester Street. That same year, the Grange held a fundraiser called a "plump social." Each gentleman chose a partner who was then weighed. The gentleman paid 5¢ for the first 100 pounds of her weight and 5¢ for each additional 10 pounds.

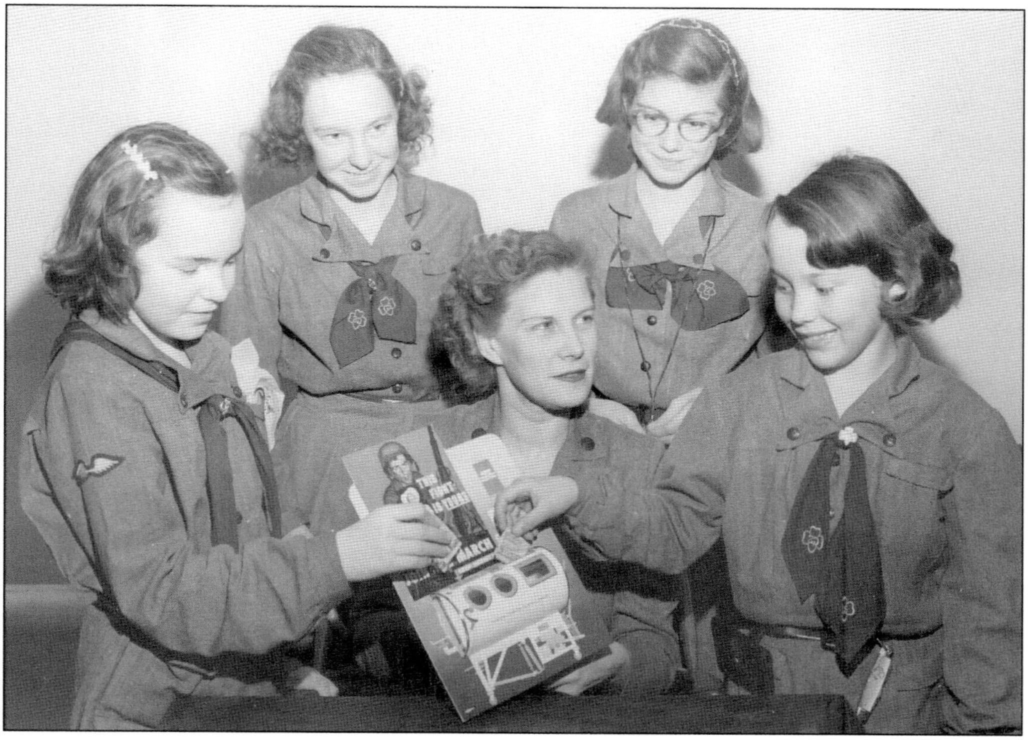
Girl Scouts have been active in Grafton since the late 1920s when the first troop was organized by Mary Riggs. In this 1950s photograph, Margaret Caldwell, leader of Troop 4, looks on as her troop makes a donation to the March of Dimes to purchase iron lungs for polio patients. The Scouts are, from left to right, Carolynne Corey, Joan Gardner, Patricia Clark, and Nancy Troy. (Courtesy Carolynne Grimley.)

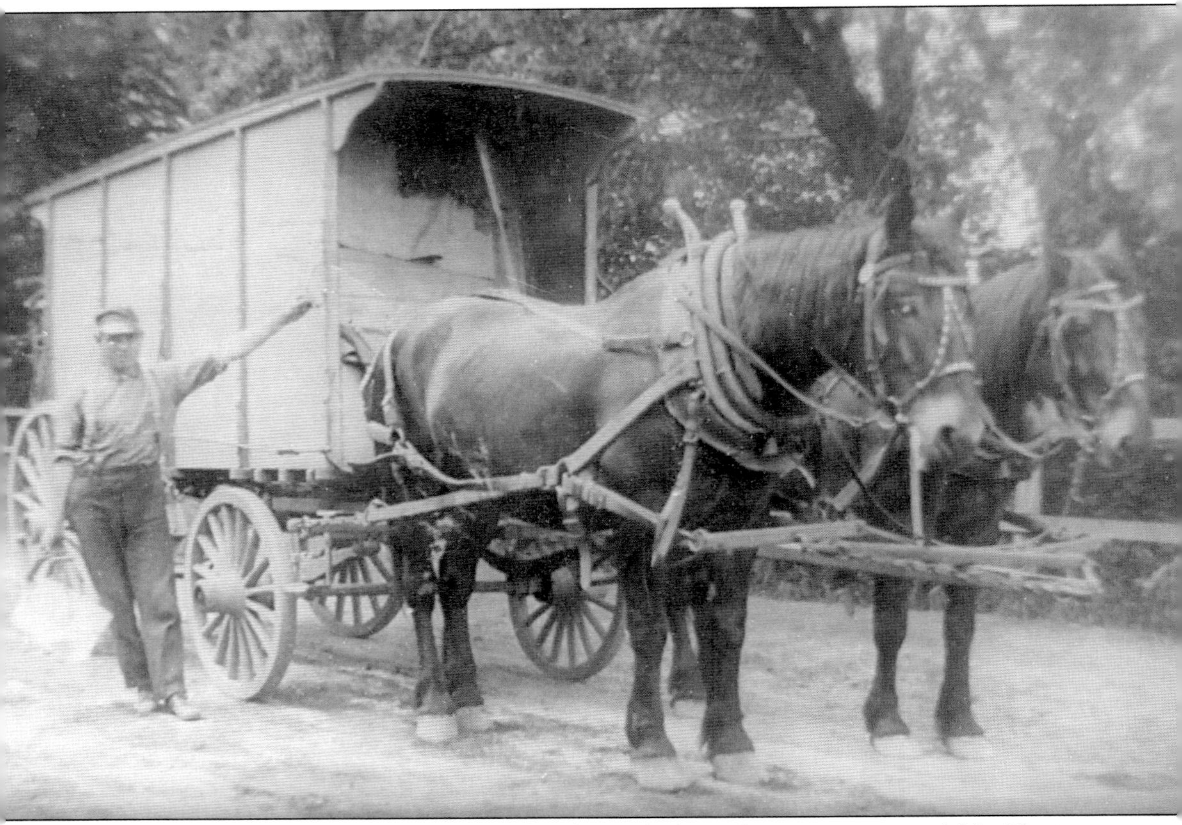

This delivery wagon brought ice to Grafton homes before refrigeration was available. The ice was placed in an icebox and provided cooling until it melted. A special card placed in the window of a house would alert the ice deliveryman to make a delivery. The ice trade was an important New England industry from the early 1800s until World War II. At one time, most Grafton ponds were harvested for ice. The ice would be cut into large blocks, floated to shore, stored in ice houses, and surrounded by sawdust for insulation. Ice stored this way could last for as long as two years. By the 1940s, refrigeration made iceboxes obsolete, and the industry disappeared.

Four

North Grafton

North Grafton was the site of two distinct villages formed early in Grafton history. One was called New England Village and was located on the Quinsigamond River in the north end of town. The other village, known as The Depot, developed after the Boston & Albany Railroad built a depot at the west end of North Main Street.

From the earliest days, sawmills, gristmills, and blacksmith shops were needed to produce equipment for farming and household use. As early as 1760, high-quality scythes were being made near a dam on the Quinsigamond River. In the late 1700s, this was also the site of a shoddy mill, a mill that processed rags. In 1825, another dam was built farther upstream on the Quinsigamond River by William Hovey to supply the Blackstone Canal with water. The following year, all water rights in the area were sold to one company—the New England Manufacturing Company, makers of twines and bags from linen and jute. The village that grew up along this section of the river was called New England Village after the linen mill. The village continued to grow as the company expanded with a new stone factory, tenements for workers, and two churches. Many small businesses were attracted to the area. In 1880, a Scottish firm, Finlayson, Bousfield, and Company, purchased the mill to manufacture linen thread for the shoe, saddler, and bookbinding trades. Additional tenements were constructed for the Scottish and Canadian immigrants who came there to work. The mill also purchased the surrounding farmland for a large dairy farm to help feed the growing population. In 1878, Washington Mills Emery Manufacturing Company set up shop nearby on the site of an old gristmill. They produced natural emery abrasive grain made from ore imported from Turkey. The growing village attracted merchants who established businesses along Main Street.

The Depot area of North Grafton began to develop when the Boston & Albany Railroad built a depot there in 1846. At that time, Jotham Taft was operating a small business on Elm Street, making valentines. In 1848, Joseph Stone, with Jasper Nelson as his manager, began to manufacture shoes. In 1857, Nelson took over the growing business and became wealthy. After his death, his son built up an 18-acre estate in the neighborhood and erected many structures in the surrounding area for his workers. Soon, other businesses were opened nearby, creating a village separate from New England Village.

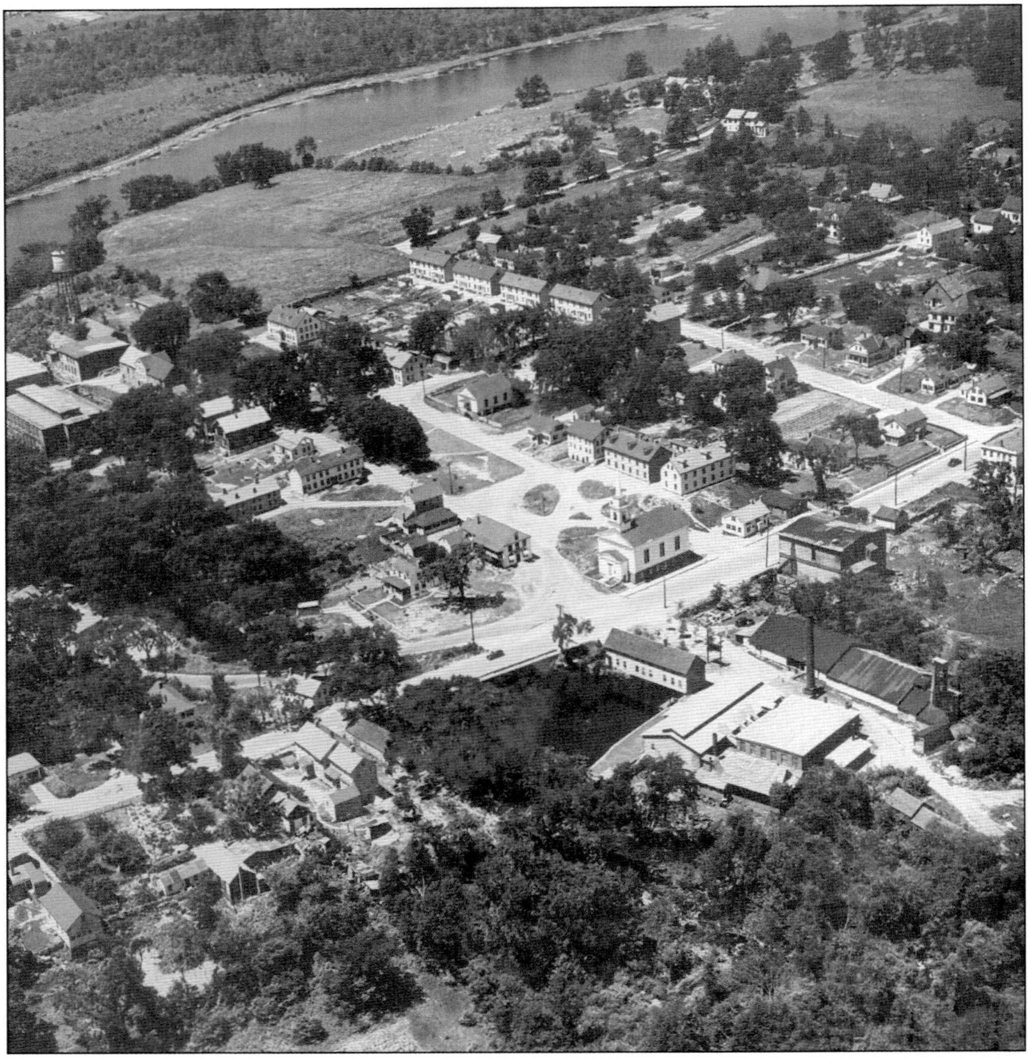

New England Village was one of the small villages that formed around the mills in North Grafton during the late 18th and early 19th centuries. In this aerial view of the village, the Quinsigamond River can be seen across the top of the photograph. The Second Baptist Church is in the center with rows of tenements nearby. Washington Mills Emery Manufacturing Company is at lower right, and the linen mill is at the upper left. (Photograph by Robert Wilson.)

This view of the millpond beside Washington Mills Emery Manufacturing Company in New England Village shows the bridge, the falls, and the Second Baptist Church. Tenements and a store can be seen on the slope behind the church.

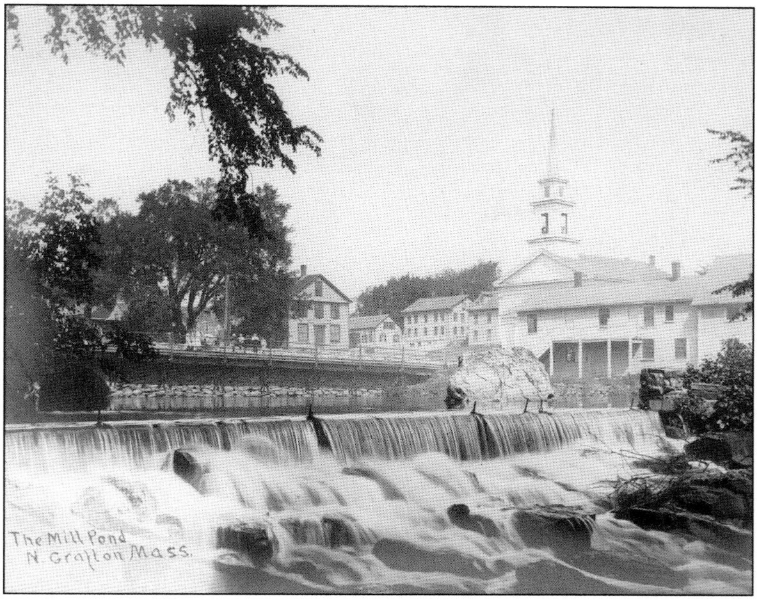

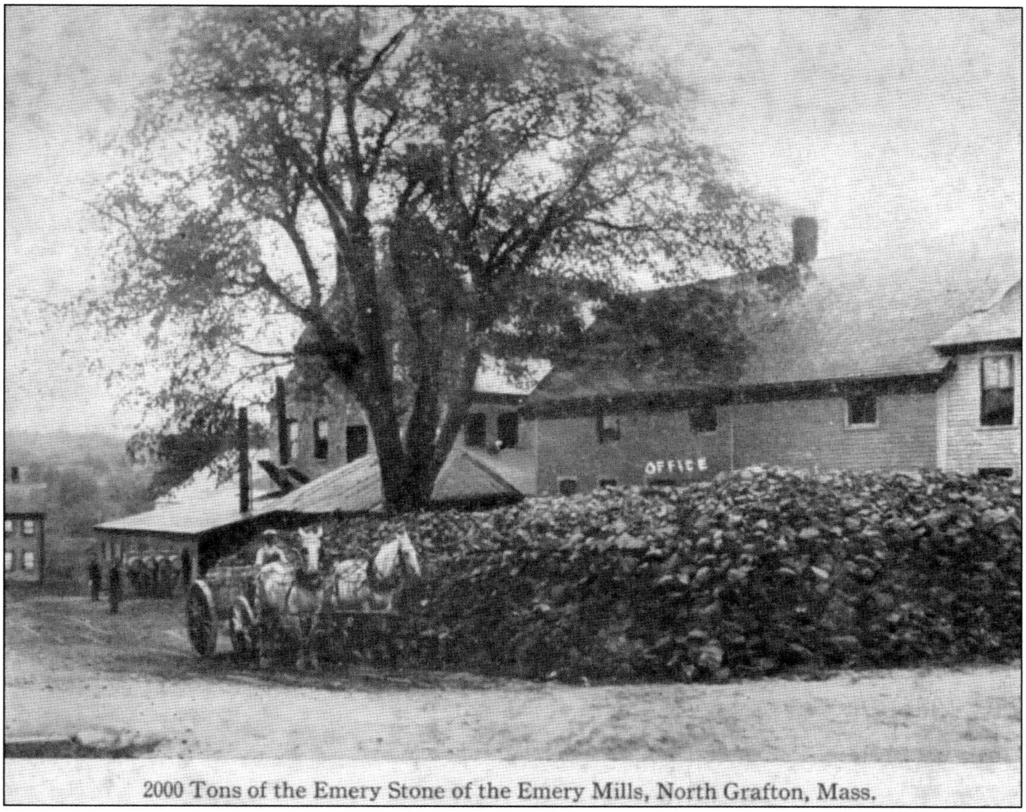

A horse-drawn wagon is parked beside a large pile of emery stones in front of the Washington Mills Emery Manufacturing Company office. The company came to New England Village in 1878 and engaged in the production of abrasive grain made from Turkish emery. The emery stone was imported from mines on the Gallipoli Peninsula and carried to port by camels. (Courtesy of Donald Clark.)

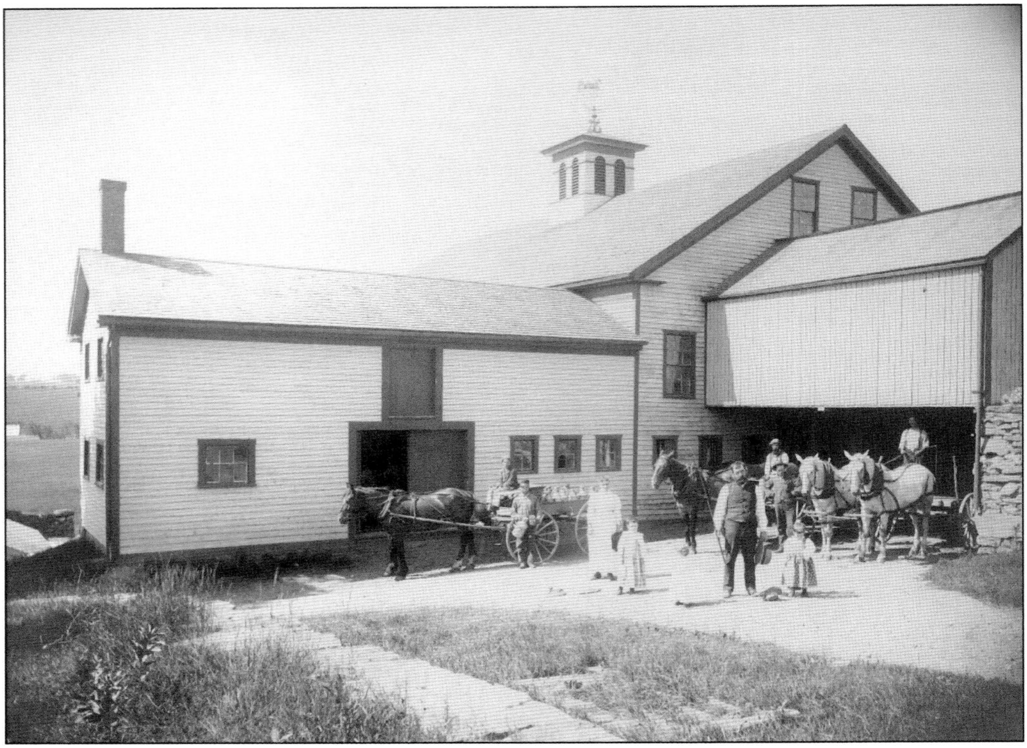

Blackberry Hill Farm was established to provide for the workers who came to North Grafton to work in the linen thread mill. In 1920, J. Frank Johnson (front and center), former farm manager for the mill, bought the farm. Johnson is seen here with farmhands and family, including his son Raymond (the toddler to the left of his father), who took over the farm after his death. The barn was destroyed in the hurricane of 1938. (Courtesy of the Johnson family.)

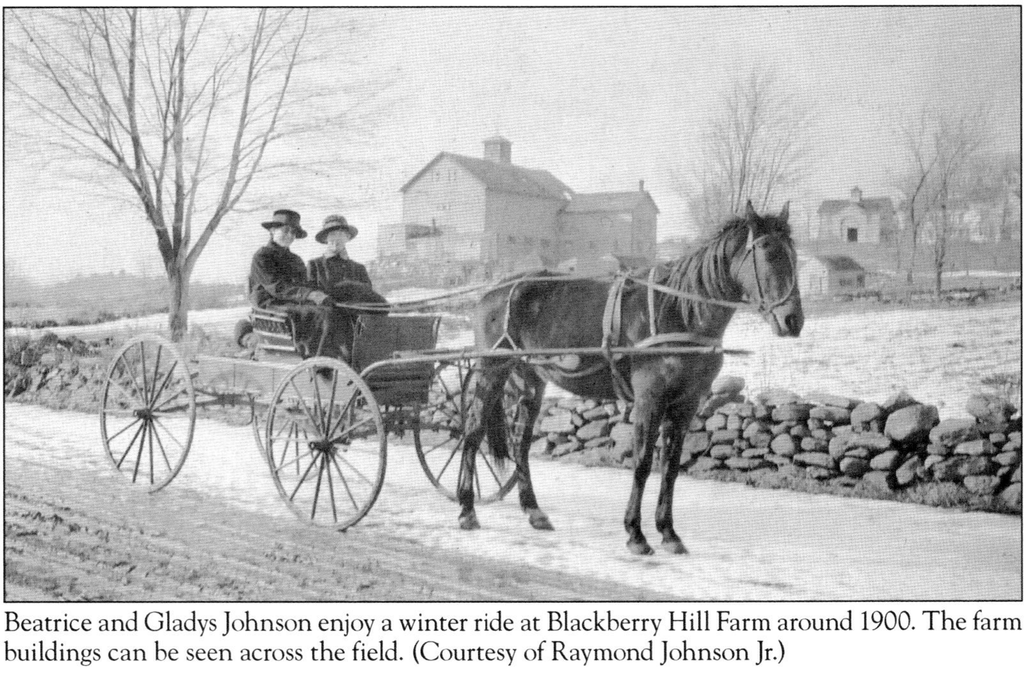

Beatrice and Gladys Johnson enjoy a winter ride at Blackberry Hill Farm around 1900. The farm buildings can be seen across the field. (Courtesy of Raymond Johnson Jr.)

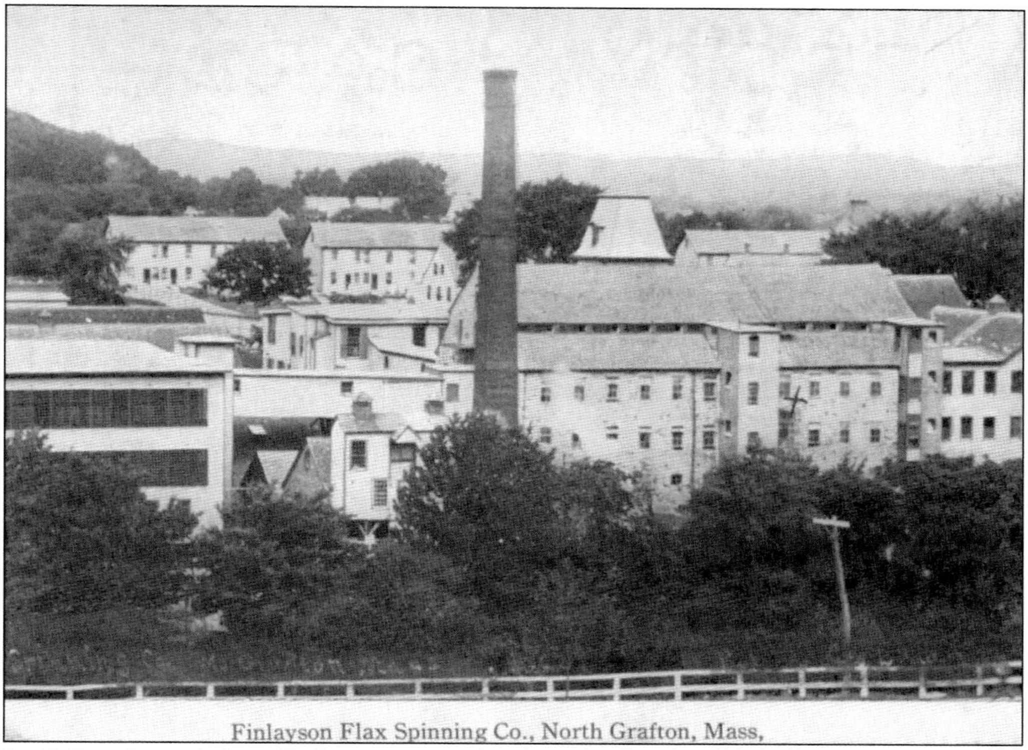

In 1880, a Scottish firm, Finlayson, Bousfield & Company, purchased the upper mill in New England Village and manufactured linen thread for the shoe, saddler, and bookbinding industries. The mill established a dairy farm nearby on Blackberry Hill to provide milk for its workers and to care for the horses used to transport mill products. The factory was closed in 1931, and the property sold off in 1937.

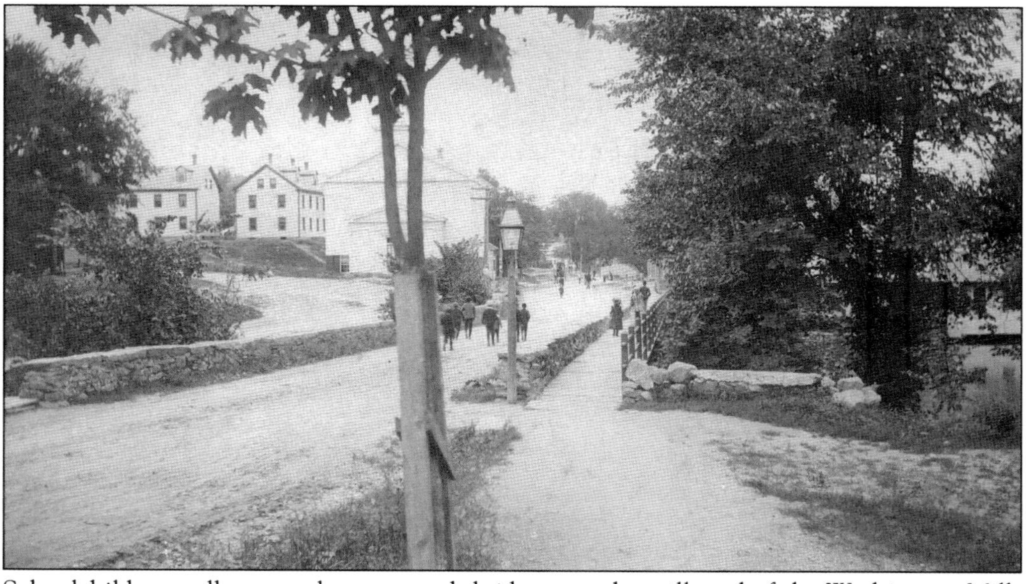

Schoolchildren walk across the stone arch bridge near the millpond of the Washington Mills Emery Manufacturing Company around 1910. The Second Baptist Church is straight ahead. New England Village tenements can be seen behind the church.

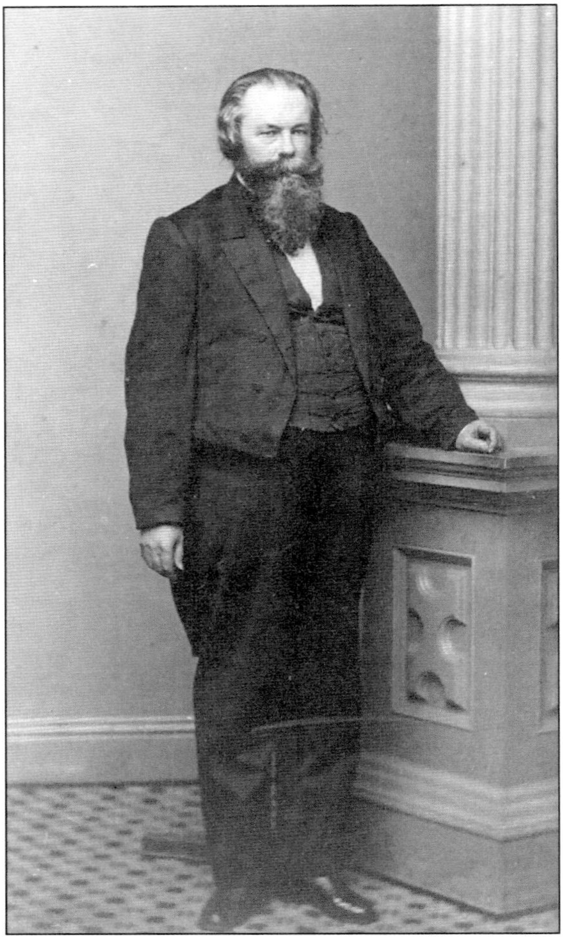

Ethan Allen, an inventor and manufacturer of firearms, came to North Grafton in 1832 to set up a business making cutlery. He built a dam at Waterville Street to harness the waterpower needed to run his machines. His most famous invention was the pepperbox pistol, a self-cocking revolver that was the only multi-shot weapon available on the civilian market at that time.

Three boys proudly drive the delivery wagon for Pratt Brothers, a feed store that supplied hay, grain, and coal, as well as poultry and dairy feeds. It was located at the dam on Waterville Street.

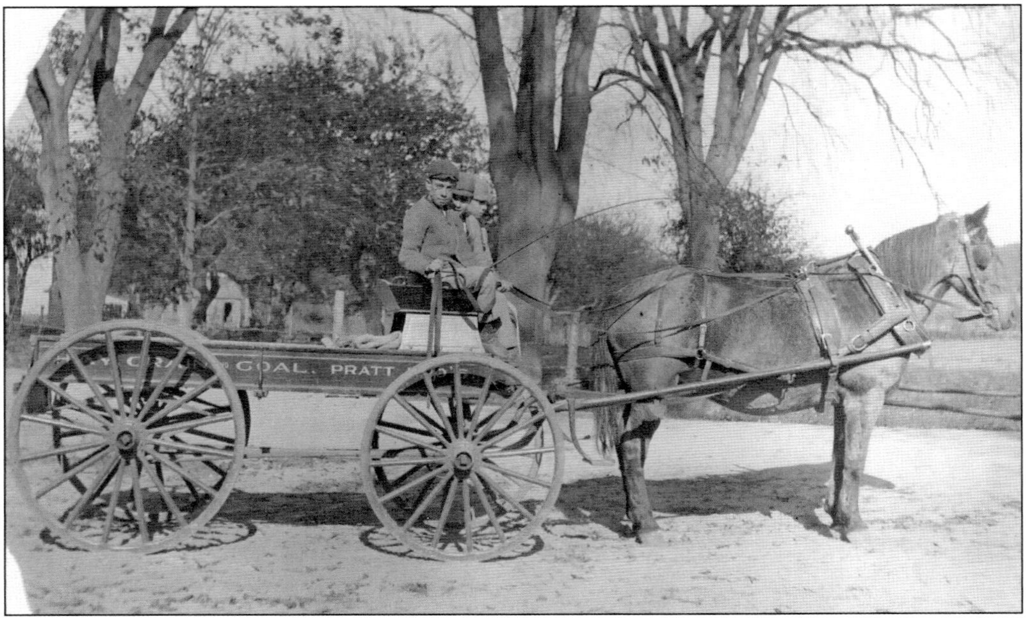

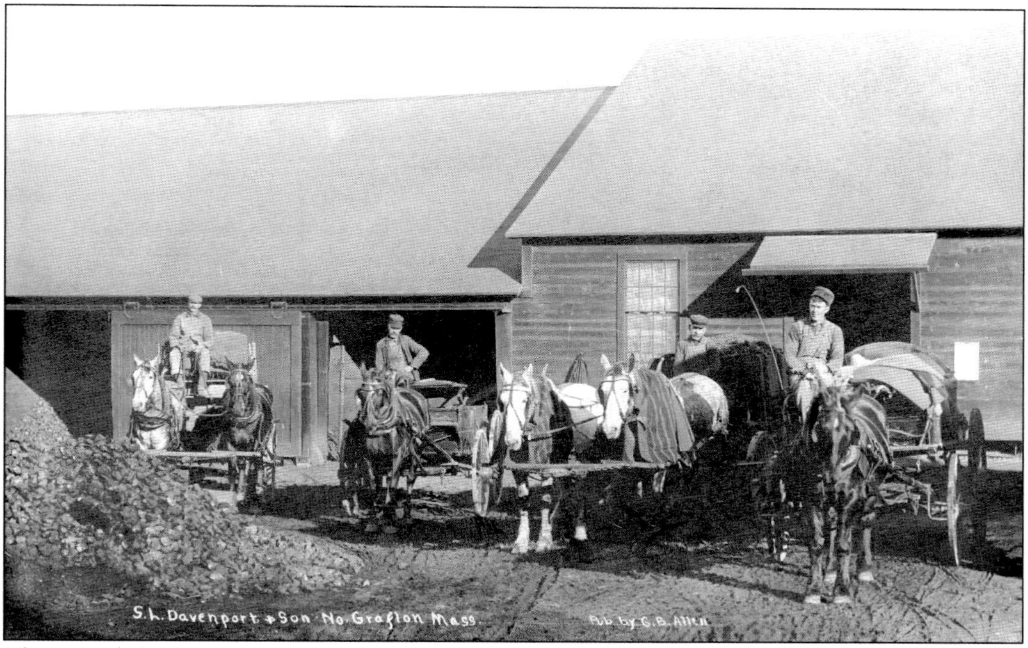

These coal sheds, pictured with horse-drawn delivery wagons, were located at 58 North Main Street in North Grafton. The company was run by Stearns Longley Davenport, father to S.L. Davenport, owner of Creeper Hill Orchards. (Courtesy of Amy Callihan.)

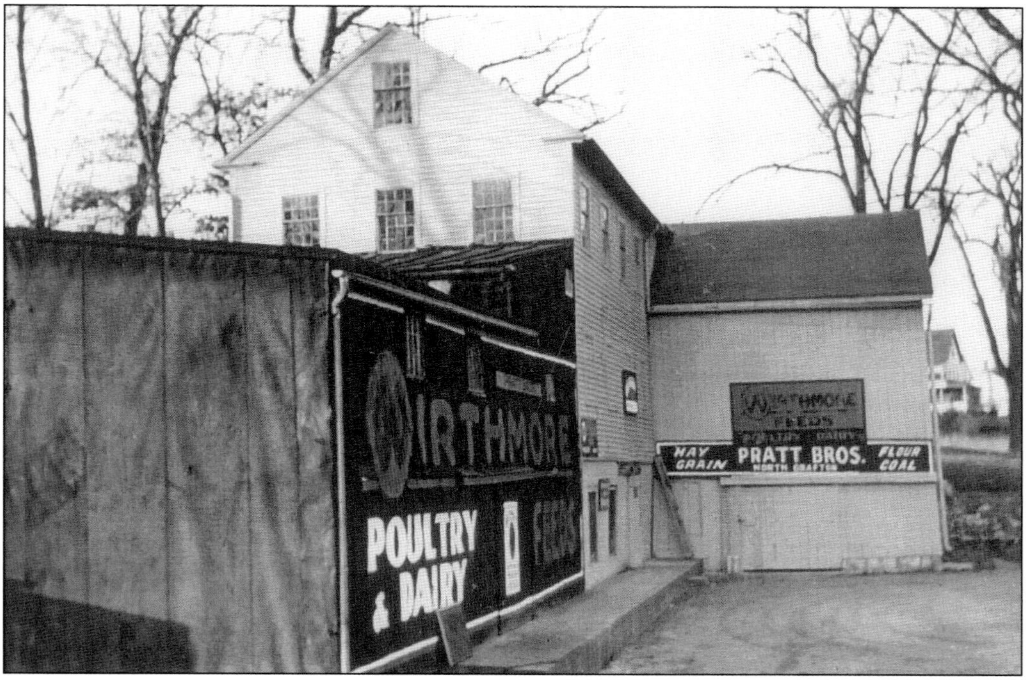

Pratt's feed store is shown at the Waterville Street dam, originally created by Ethan Allen to provide power for his gun-making business. In later years, the waterpower was used for a machine shop, a jewelry shop, a gristmill, and a cider mill. Beginning in 1909, brothers Burt and Clarence Pratt conducted a business in coal and grain here. The pond nearby is named after them.

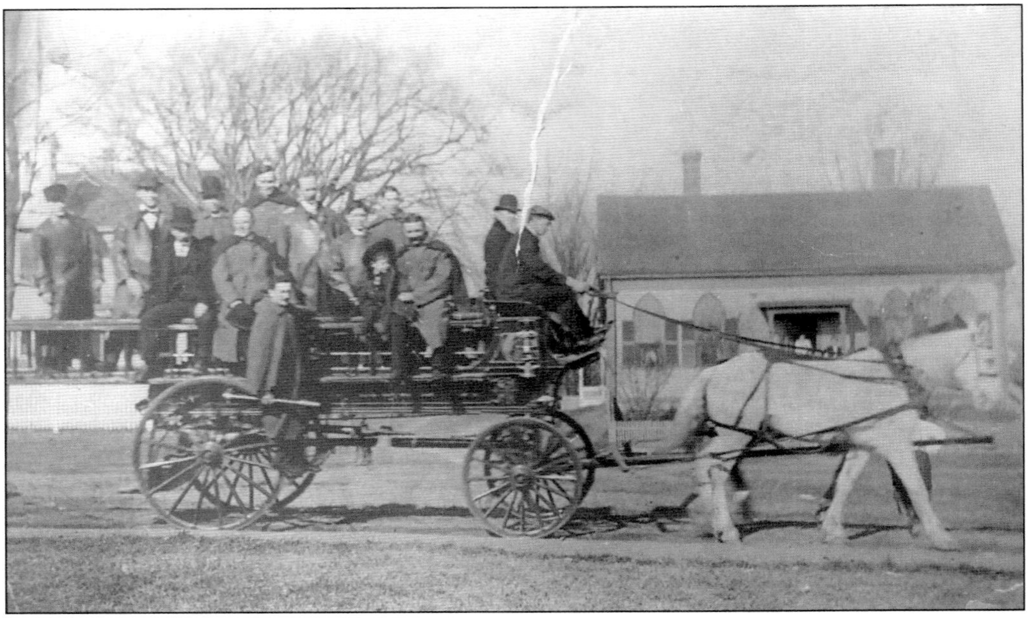

The Henry Crippen Hose Company was the fire brigade serving New England Village. Founded in 1852, it was originally called the Emperor Fire Company. In 1889, Henry Crippen was made captain of the brigade. His son had great financial success in the West and, upon his return to New England Village, purchased new equipment for the fire company. The hose company was then renamed to honor his father. (Courtesy Grafton Fire Department.)

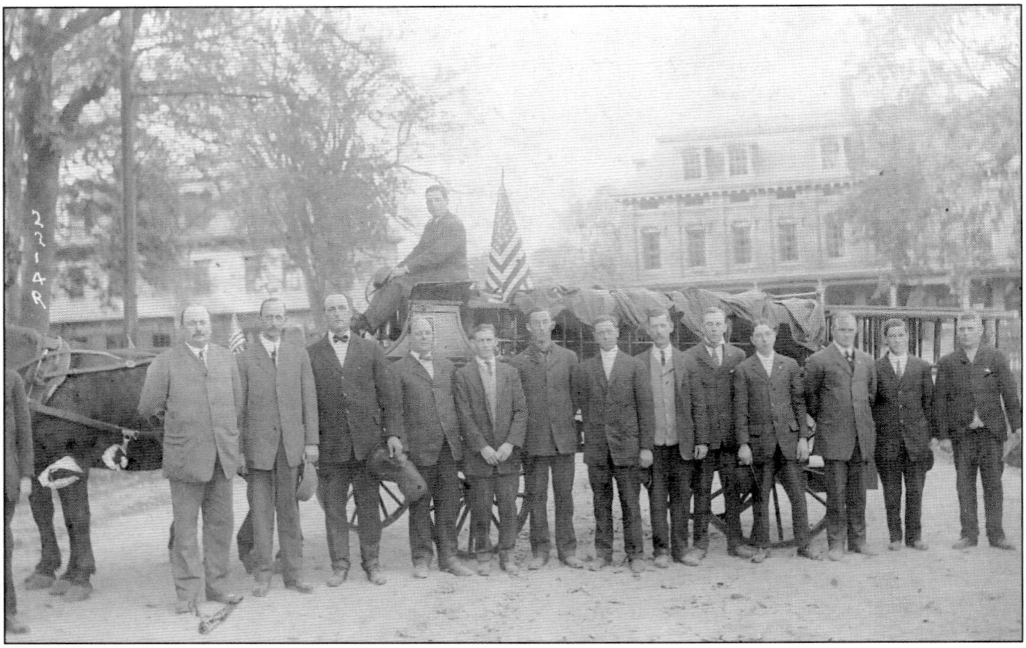

The Henry Crippen Hose Company of North Grafton poses in victory at a fireman's muster in 1910 in Grafton's Central Square. This fire company competed with the two other Grafton fire companies, as well as those from surrounding towns, to see which was the fastest at various fire-suppression techniques. The driver shown is Ralph Johnson; the man standing seventh from left is Leroy Knowlton. (Courtesy of Patricia Knowlton.)

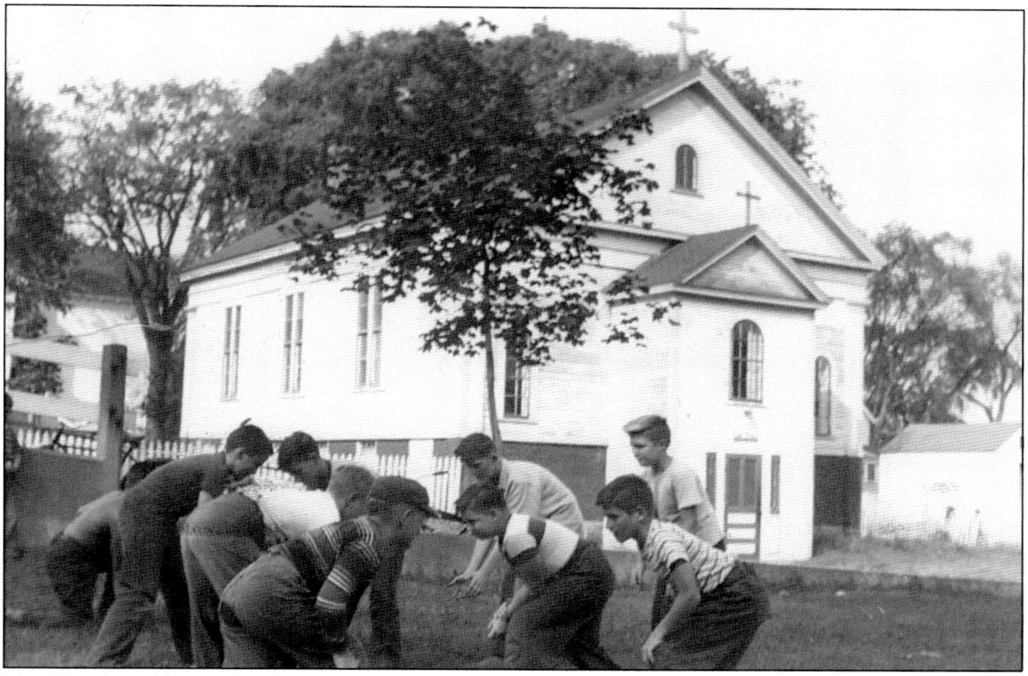

Neighborhood boys play football at Whitney Park in front of the Methodist church in the 1950s. A congregation was organized between 1842 and 1843 to serve a growing number of Methodists who worked at the nearby mill in New England Village. Before the church was constructed, services were held in the office of the stone mill building. The mill donated the land, and the church was built in 1847.

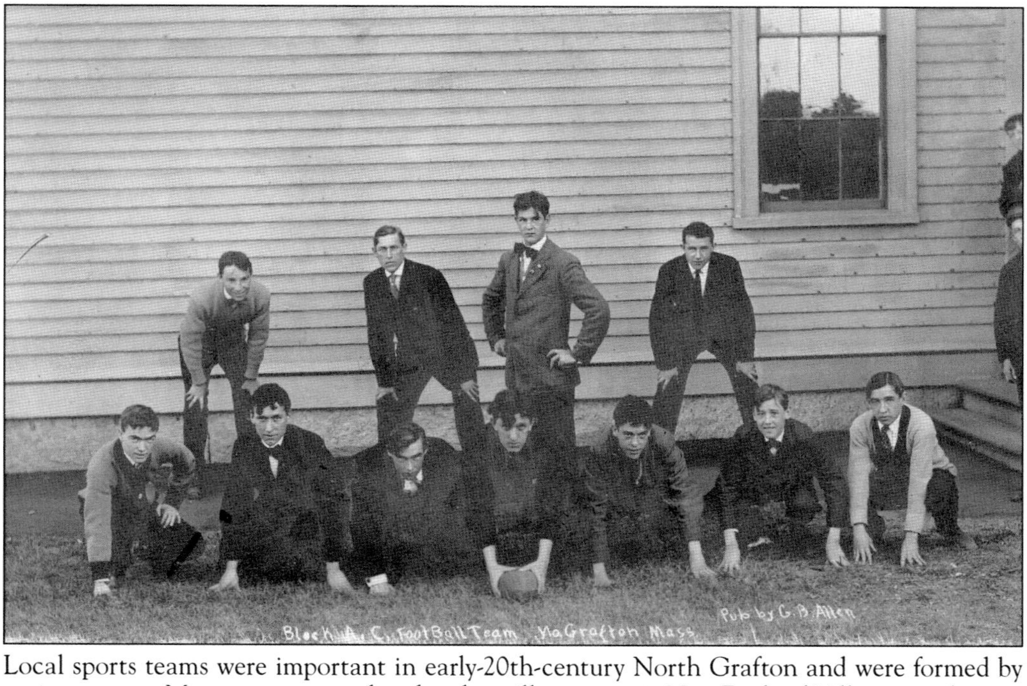

Local sports teams were important in early-20th-century North Grafton and were formed by various groups. Many games were played at the mill common in New England Village, now known as Whitney Park. These boys represented tenement blocks A and C in football.

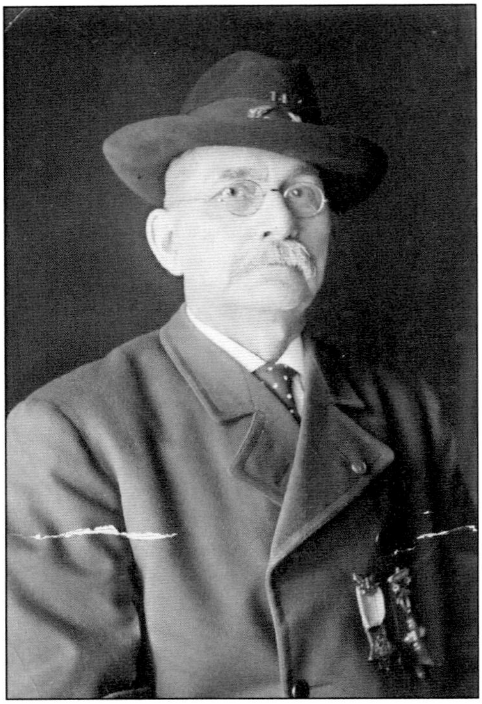

Sidney Whitney was born on Waterville Street in North Grafton in 1847 and served in the Union army during the Civil War. He married Estelle Putnam and lived in North Grafton after the war. In the early 1930s, he purchased the New England Village common from the mill, and the area was renamed Whitney Park. Whitney Park was the site of concerts, church picnics, and other community celebrations for the village. (Courtesy of Amy Callihan.)

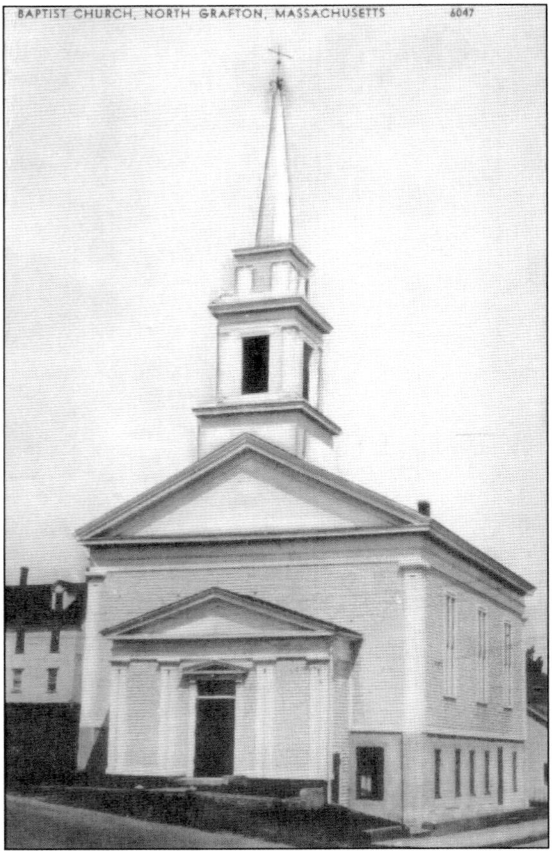

The Second Baptist Church was founded in 1836 by 43 brethren from Shrewsbury, Boylston, and New England Village. After meeting in private homes and then at the schoolhouse, the group was offered meeting space at the nearby mill. In 1838, the mill donated a piece of land where a new church was built. In 1844, this congregation allowed women to vote on church matters for the first time.

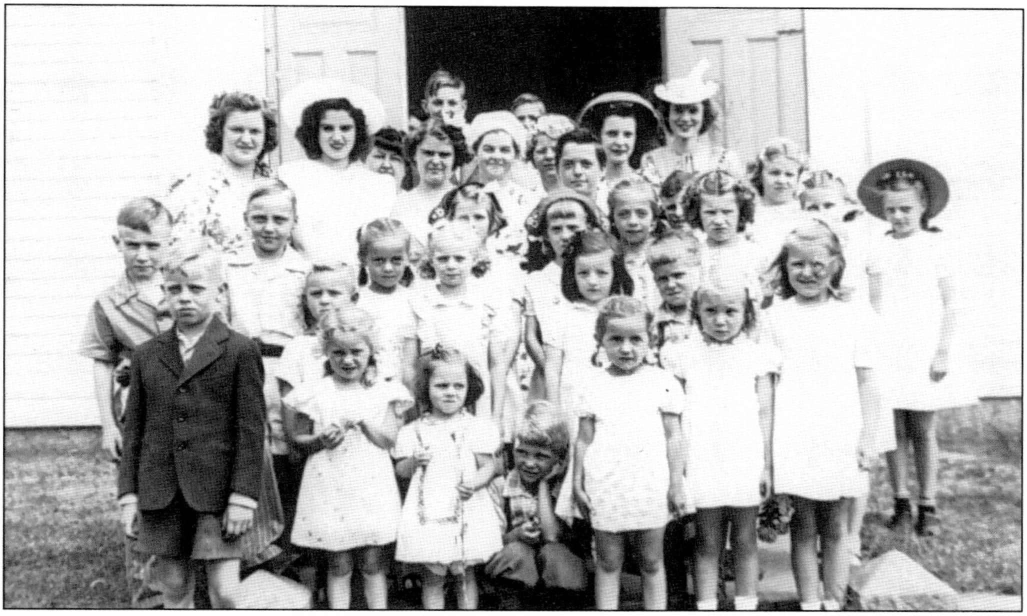

Sunday school children pose on the steps of the Second Baptist Church on Children's Sunday, June 18, 1944. Included in the group are William Budge, Don Giles, Howard Richardson, Lois Ohman, Priscilla Aronberg, Jane and Nancy Kelly, and Betty Ohman. (Courtesy of Viola Johnson.)

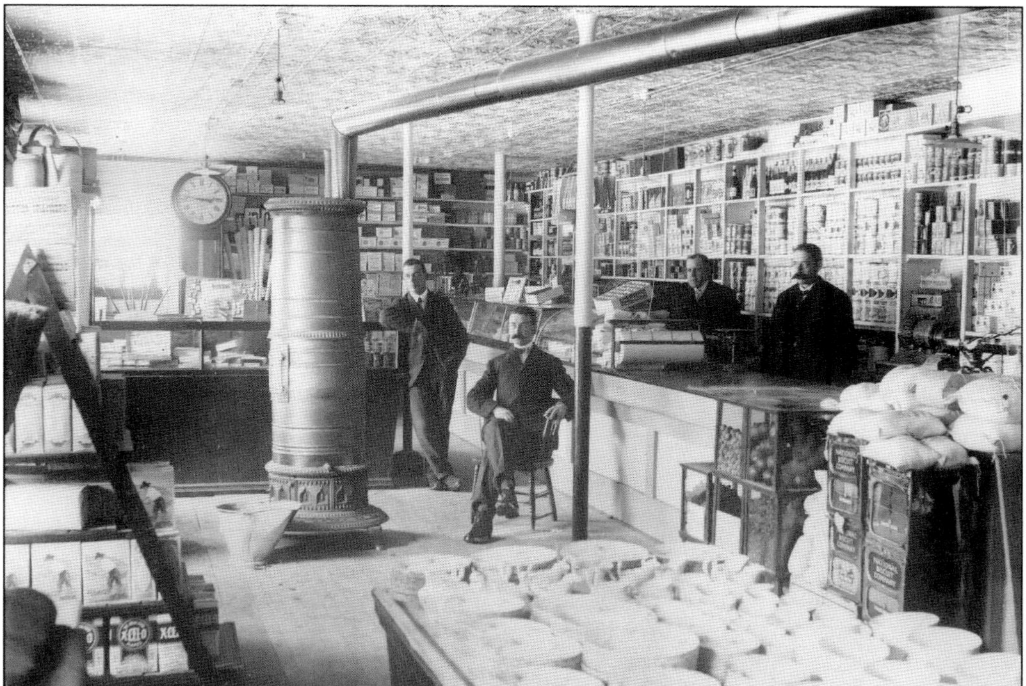

When the Second Baptist Church was built in 1838, funds were inadequate, so half the basement was deeded to a storekeeper who operated a general store there. No liquor was allowed to be sold on the premises. The church lot grew smaller as parcels of land were taken by the railroad for tracks, by the water company for pipelines, and by the town for road widening. The church was demolished in 2010.

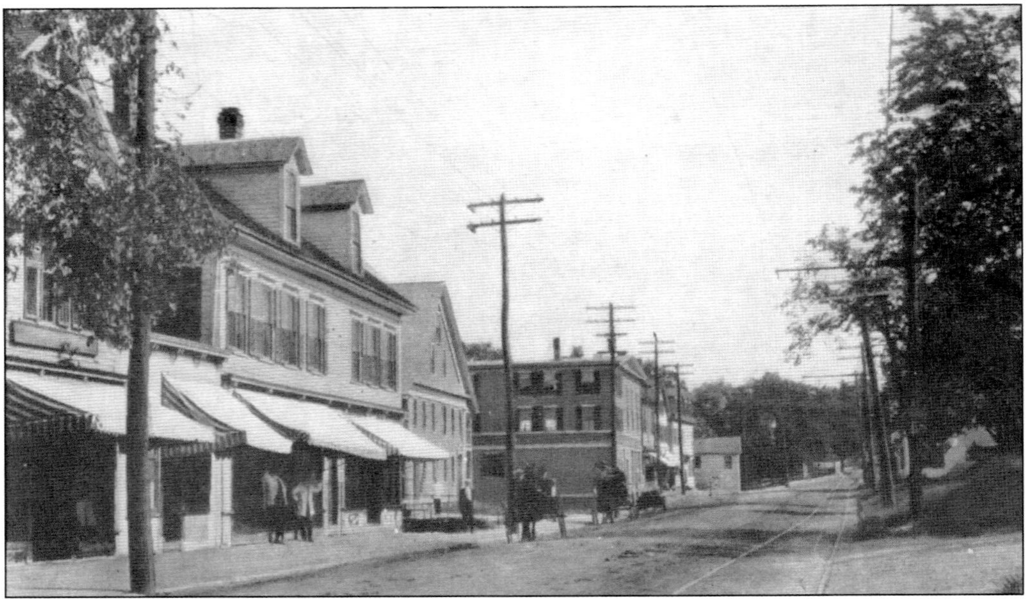

The New England Village commercial buildings and Barker's Hall can be seen in this view looking south on North Main Street. Barker's Hall was built by William T. Barker to house his general store. The hall over the store was used for entertainment. Trolley tracks are evident on the right. The adjacent block housed a variety of businesses over the years. Among them are Ludy's Newsroom, Hatch's Bakery, Prue's Cobbler Shop, and First National Store.

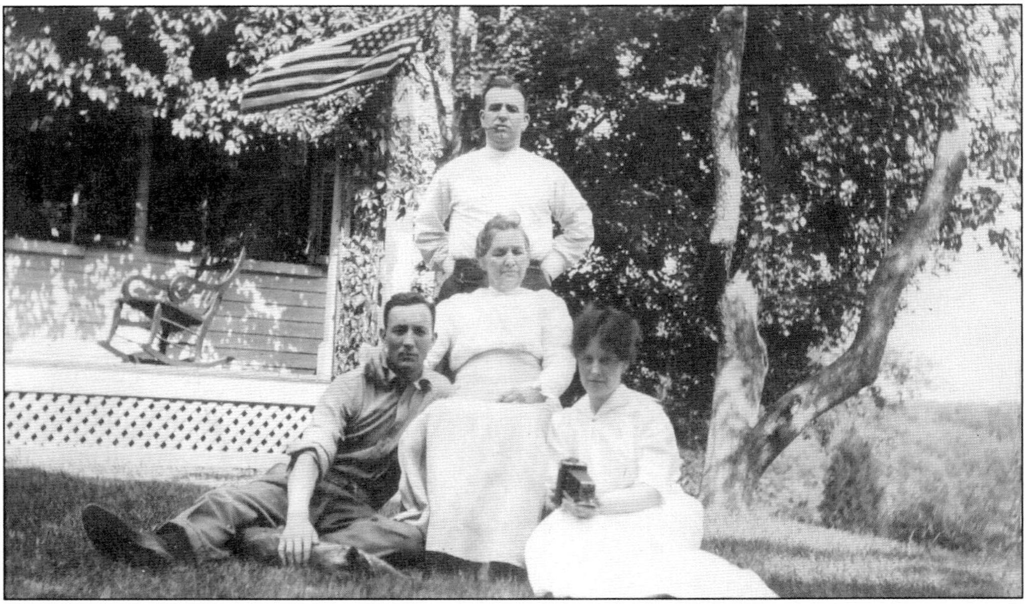

The Dickson family, ready for a Fourth of July celebration, pose on their lawn on Worcester Street. The family emigrated from Scotland on July 3, 1892, to work in North Grafton. Every year they enthusiastically celebrated both the Fourth of July and the anniversary of their arrival. (Courtesy of Elizabeth Stinson.)

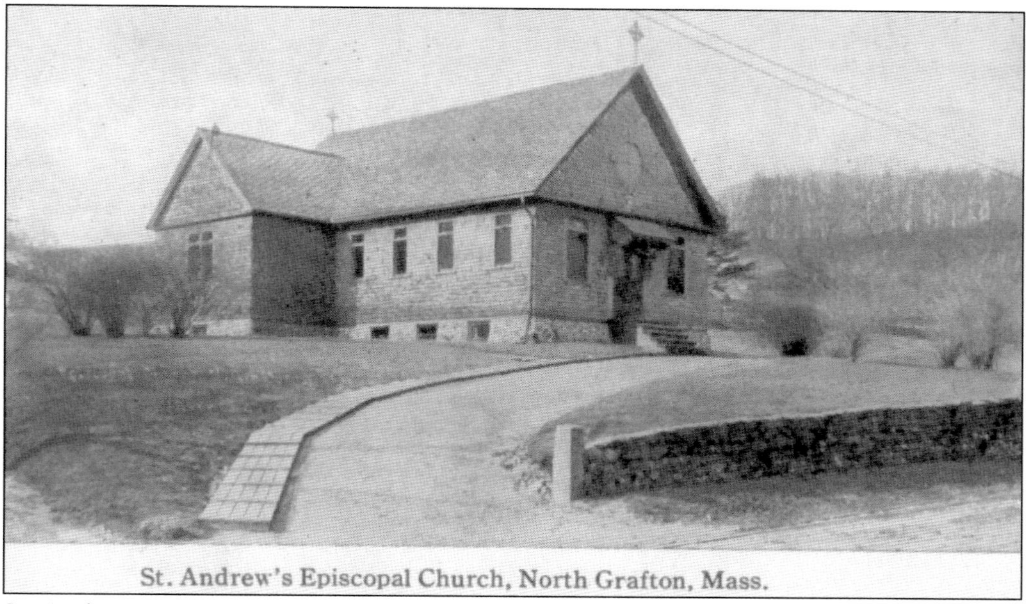

St. Andrew's congregation, established in 1893, met in Barker's Hall while funds were being raised for a church building. The land for the church was donated by owners of the linen thread mill. After World War II, with the congregation expanding, a new church was built on the old location. The steeple was the first in the United States to be made of fiberglass. (Courtesy of Donald Clark.)

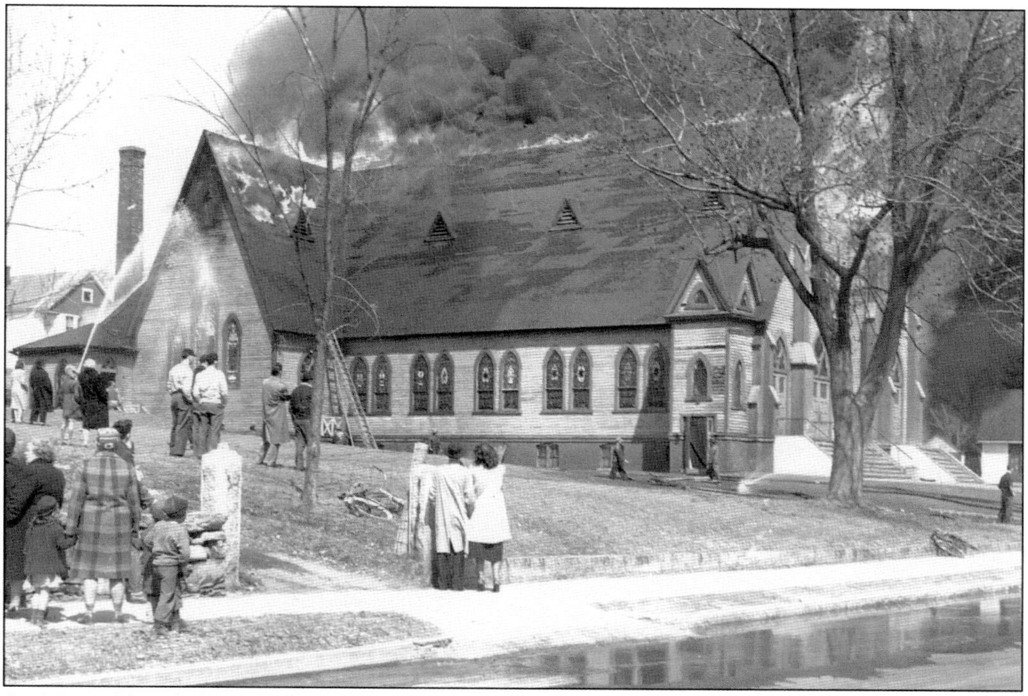

St. Mary Church began offering services to Catholics in North Grafton as a mission in 1882. Initially, the people of North Grafton worshiped in a roofed-over basement. In 1887, new plans were drawn up for a Romanesque building, and by 1896, it was completed. On March 30, 1948, disaster struck the church when a fire of unknown origin broke out, and it burned to the ground.

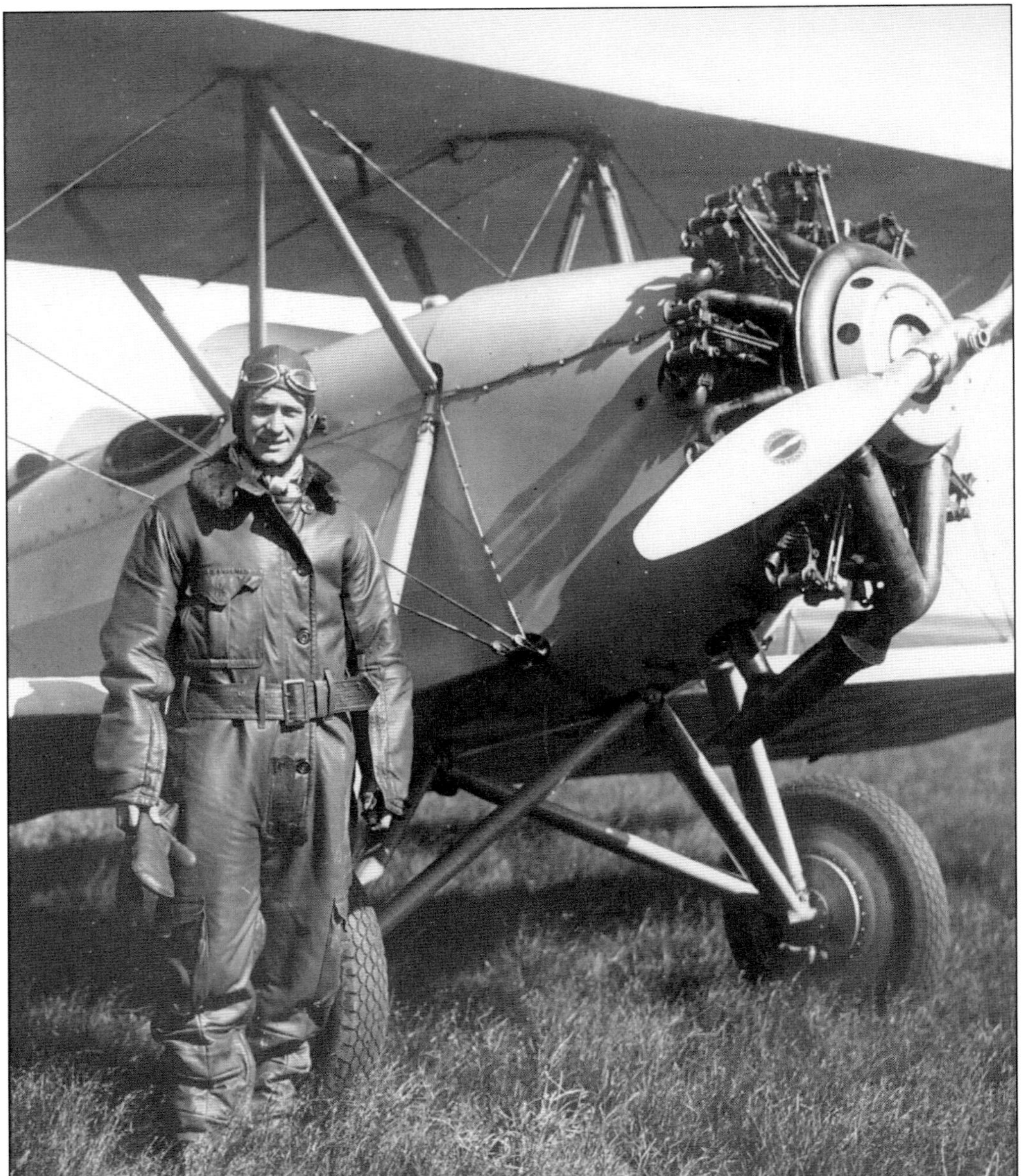

James Whittall stands beside his Driggs Dart II at Grafton Airport in 1927. The airport was opened in 1925 as a private flying field by Whittall and his brother Whitin. In 1927, the field was chosen as the best site for Worcester Airport, and it operated under that name. Eventually airplanes became too large for the short runways in the Grafton field, and the airport closed in 1951.

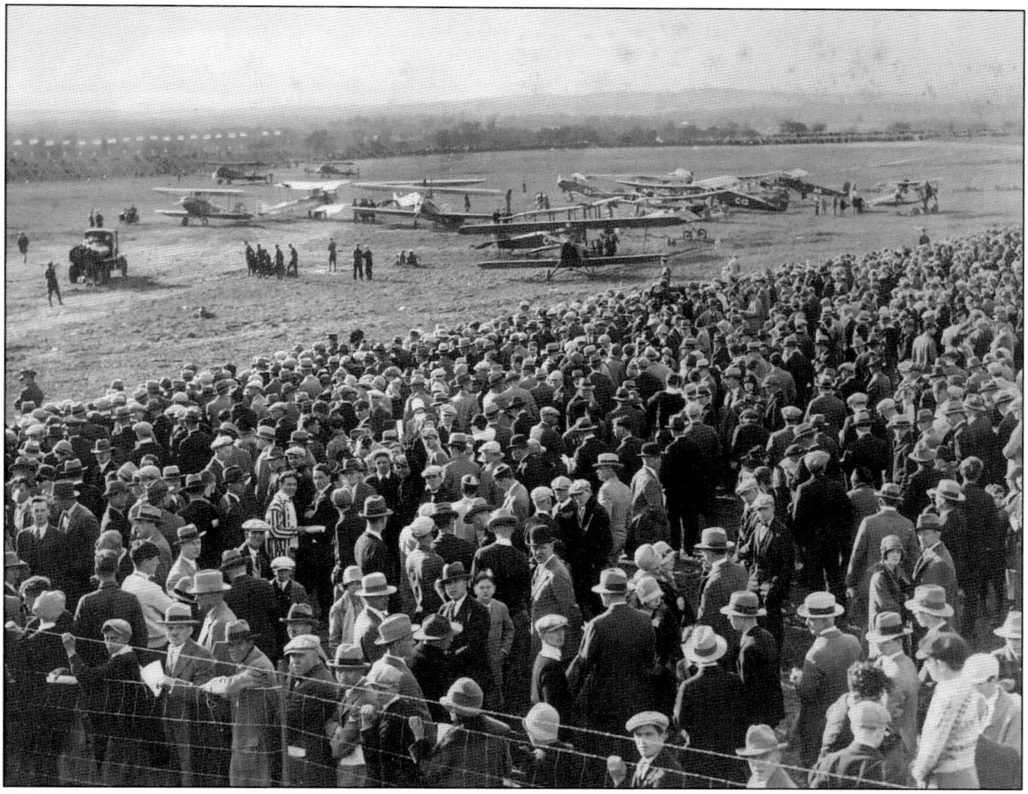

The grand opening of Grafton Airport in 1927 featured air races, acrobatics, parachute jumps, and flying exhibitions. Famous aviators from around the world came to perform, and throngs of people clogged the highways to get to North Grafton.

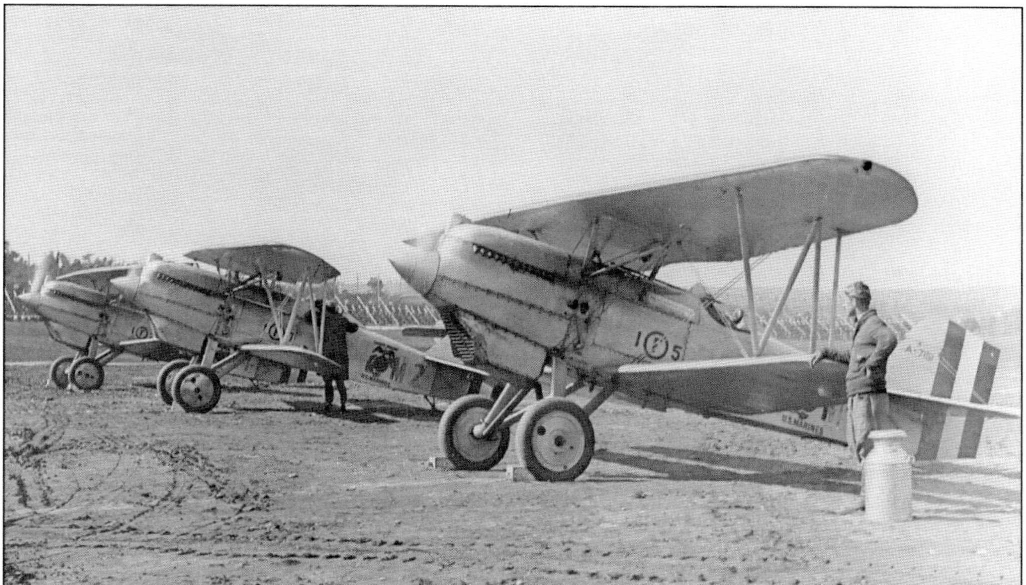

These Marine pursuit planes participated in the grand opening of the airport. The airport hosted several flight schools in the 1930s and 1940s.

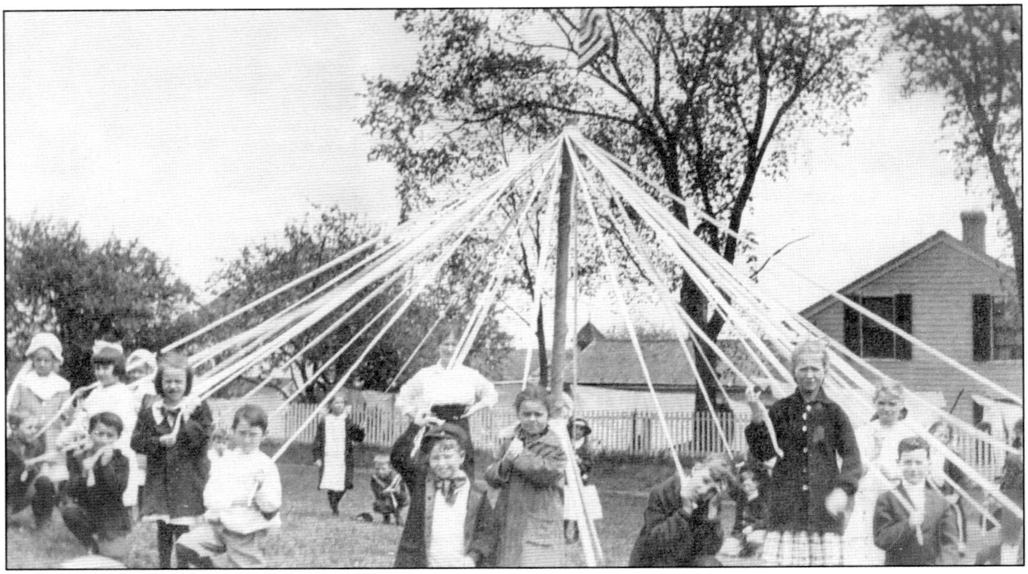

Young North Grafton girls celebrate May Day with a maypole dance near the Perry Hill School. Holding a ribbon and singing, each girl dances around the pole until the ribbons are wound tight. They then dance in the opposite direction until the ribbons are unwound. (Courtesy of Elizabeth Stinson.)

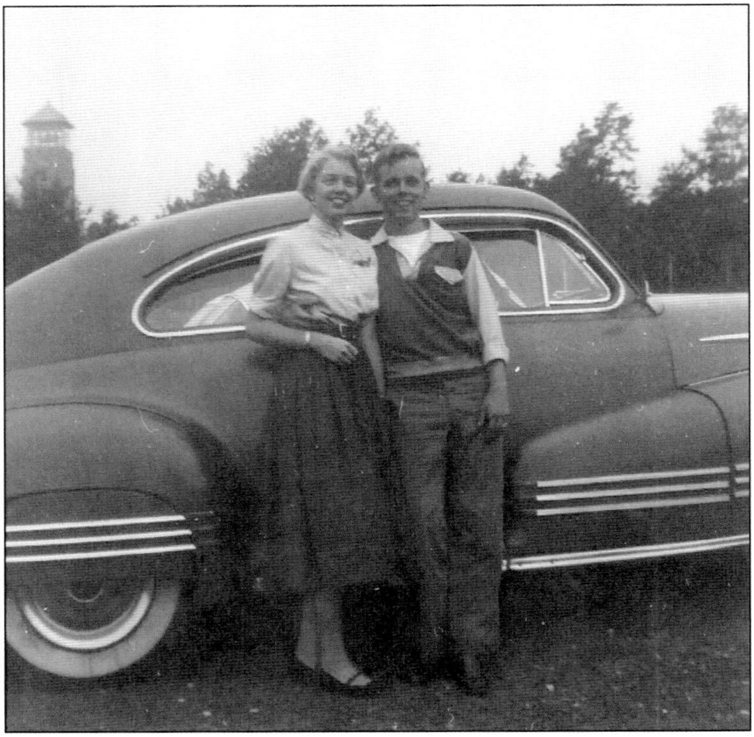

Marlene Temple and William Budge are shown beside Budge's 1947 Pontiac in which they enjoyed many hours of sightseeing around the region. Cars and leisure time were great pleasures for young people in the years following World War II. (Courtesy of Marlene Budge.)

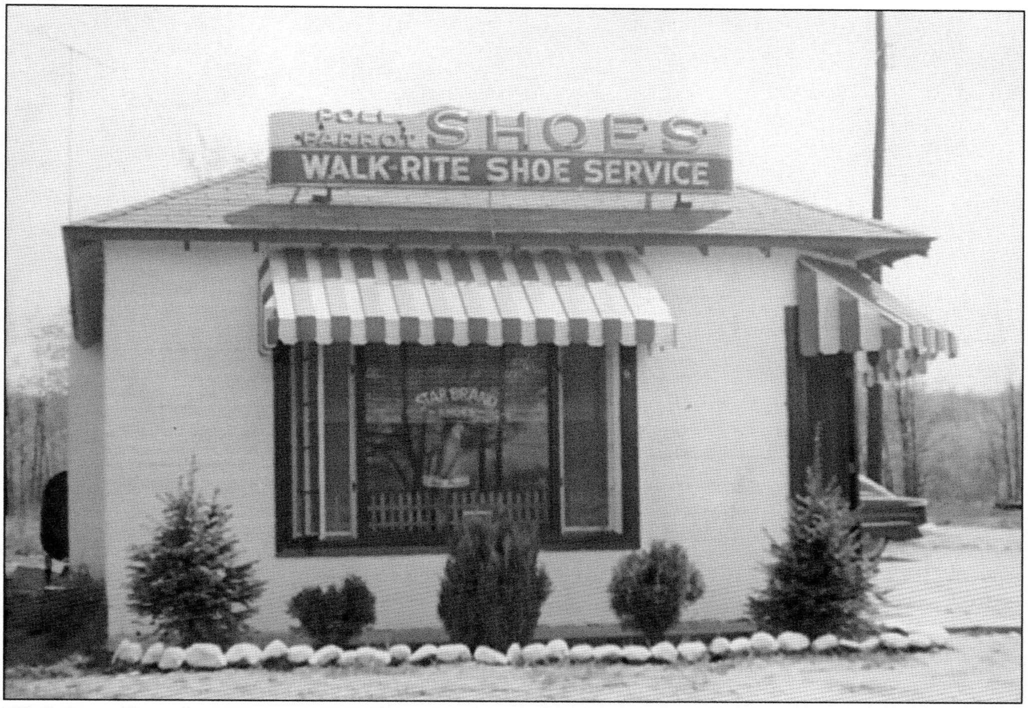

Walk-Rite Shoe Service was opened in North Grafton by Charles N. Bolack in 1955. Previously, he had sold shoes door-to-door in the area. In the late 1950s, he opened Taylor Rental, built the North Grafton Shopping Center, and founded the *Grafton News*. In 1959, the shoe store was sold to his brother Francis Bolack. (Courtesy of Marianne Rososky.)

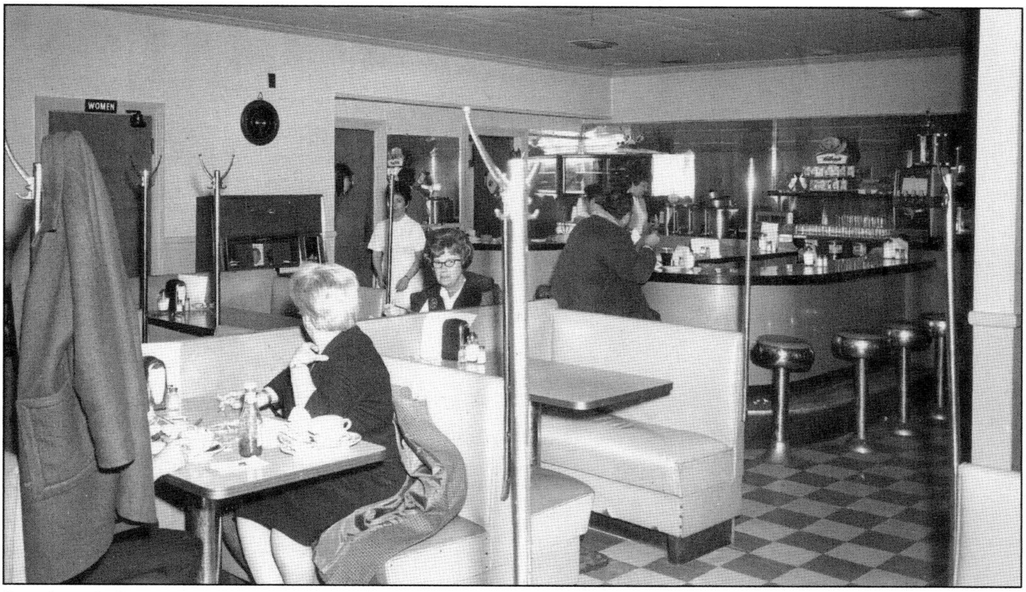

Leofanti's Restaurant was opened in the 1940s by Aldo and Leo Leofanti. An establishment called the Pig and Whistle had once operated at this location. This interior view of Leofanti's Restaurant was typical of the 1950s. Adults enjoyed breakfast and lunch here. Other folks would line up for homemade ice cream, and teenagers would go there after dances to play the jukebox. (Courtesy of Caroline Prout.)

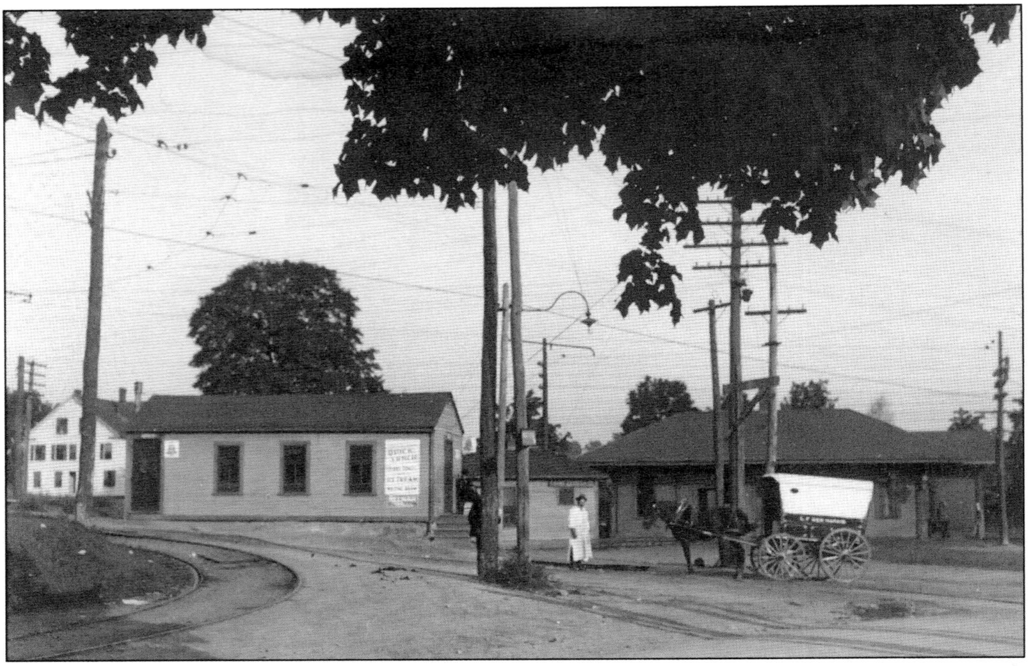

L.F. Desmarais, a local butcher, stands in front of his delivery wagon at Depot Square in North Grafton. The depot was located at the west end of North Main Street. In 1887, a connector track was built to tie North Grafton to the Boston-Albany line. A turnstile and a spur were built at the North Grafton site. The depot building was torn down in 1961 after all passenger rail service had ended.

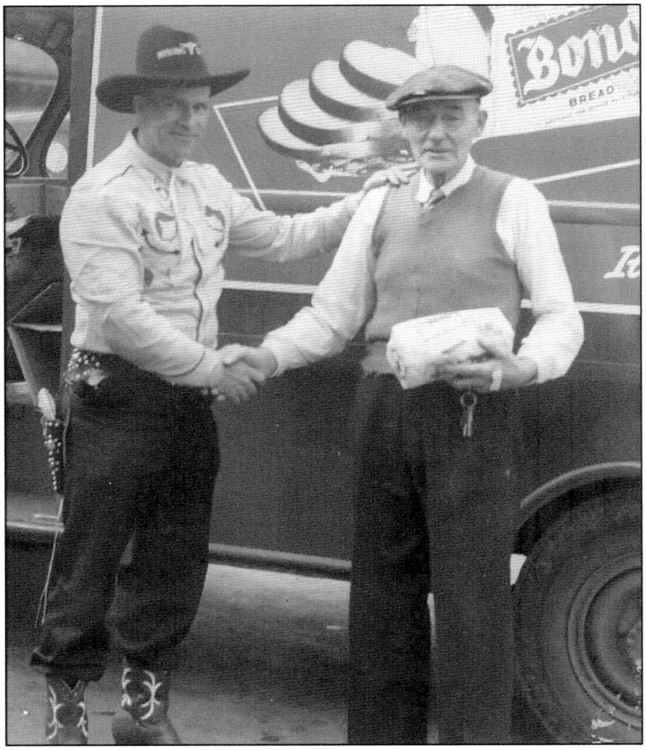

Pictured around 1950, North Grafton grocer Joe Wilson greets a cowboy advertising Bond Bread. Competition for bread customers was fierce in the 1950s, and bakeries tried many advertising tactics. This visit to North Grafton was part of a successful sales campaign by the Bond Bread Company.

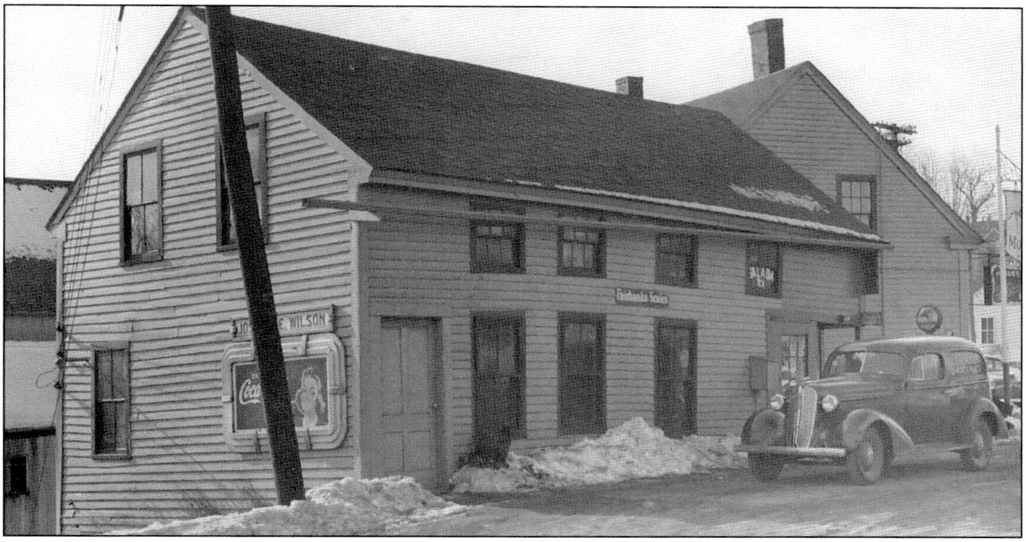

For over 30 years, Joe Wilson operated his general store across from the railroad depot in North Grafton. Wilson's store served as the social center for The Depot neighborhood. At one time, Wilson drove the mail truck between Grafton and North Grafton. He served on the board of selectmen and for 10 years was a police officer.

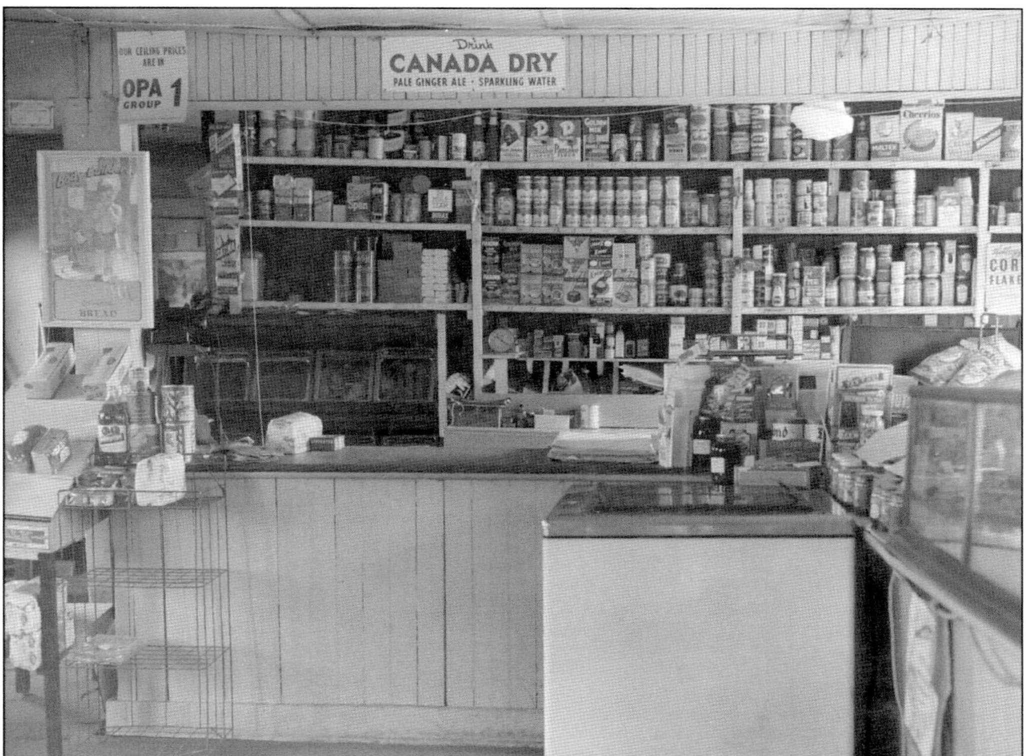

The shelves of Joe Wilson's store were always full. One could get almost anything there: penny candy, news, gossip, or a helping hand. One fixture of the store was the roll of brown paper and the spool of string used to wrap parcels before paper bags became available. Marion Bodge served as the store clerk for over 28 years.

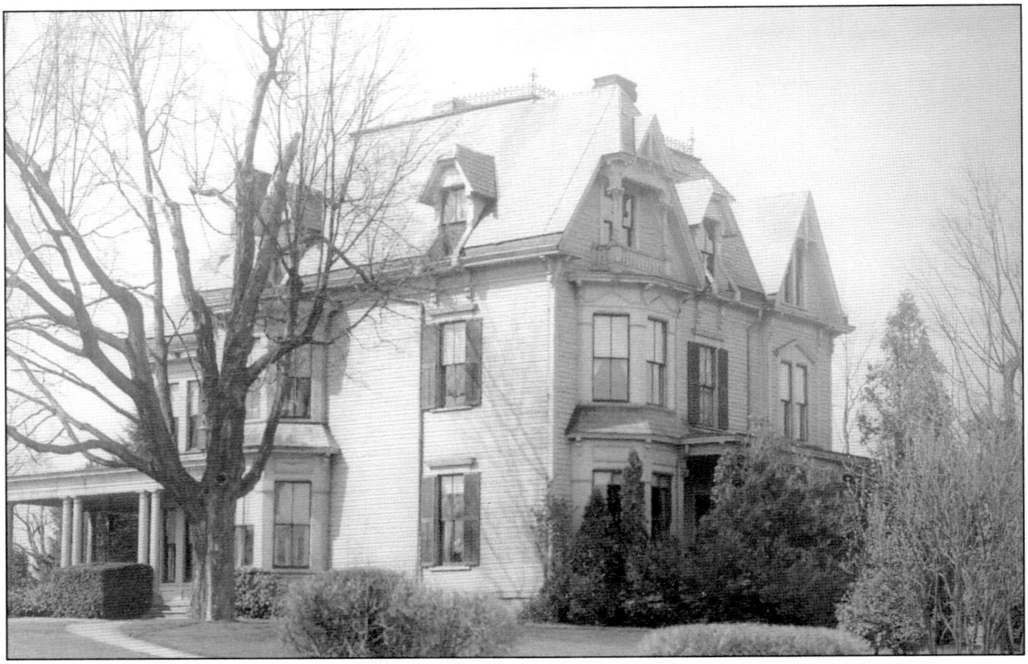

The Nelson Mansion was built in 1878 by Jasper Nelson, founder of the Nelson Shoe Company. The mansion was located on his 18-acre estate near the Shrewsbury border. The estate was bequeathed to the Town of Grafton by Nelson's son Charles for use as a park and library. In 1935, the mansion became the Nelson Memorial Library but was destroyed by fire in 1974.

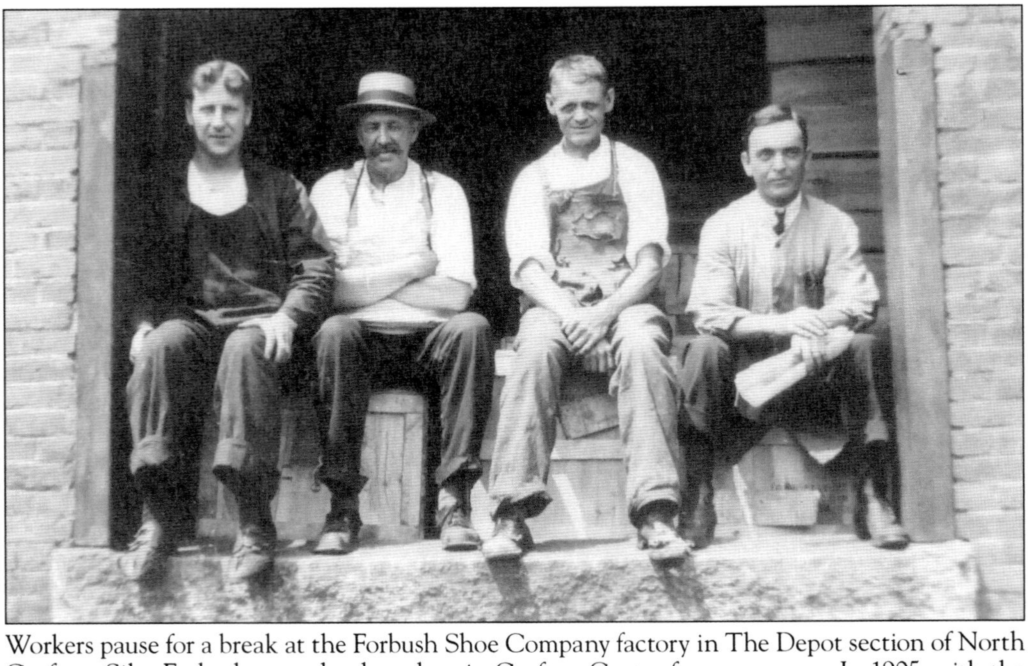

Workers pause for a break at the Forbush Shoe Company factory in The Depot section of North Grafton. Silas Forbush owned a shoe shop in Grafton Center for many years. In 1905, with the shoe industry fading in Grafton Center, he bought the Nelson Shoe Company near the North Grafton depot. The factory specialized in the production of dress shoes for men. It was sold in 1932 and became a yeast factory.

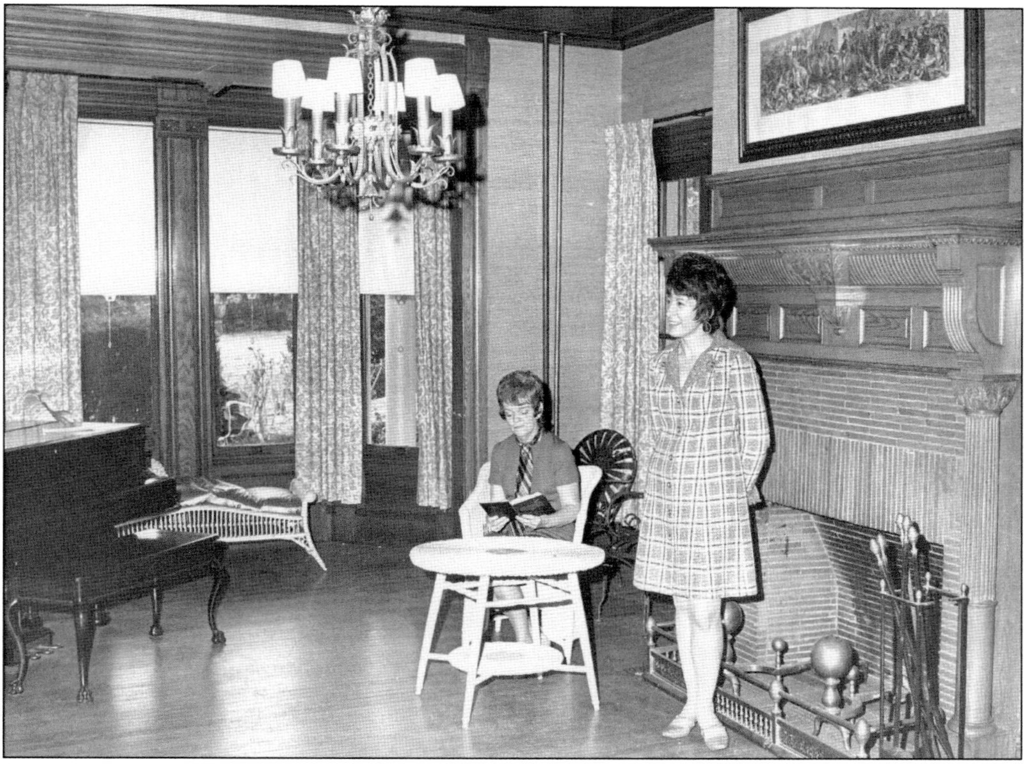

June Lufkin (right) and Elinor Bonin (left), librarians, enjoy the music room at the Nelson Mansion after it had been transformed into the Nelson Memorial Library. During the early 1900s, skilled artisans were hired from Europe to decorate the mansion with carved woodwork, frescoed ceilings, gold leaf stenciled walls, and marble fireplaces. (Courtesy of the *Worcester Telegram.*)

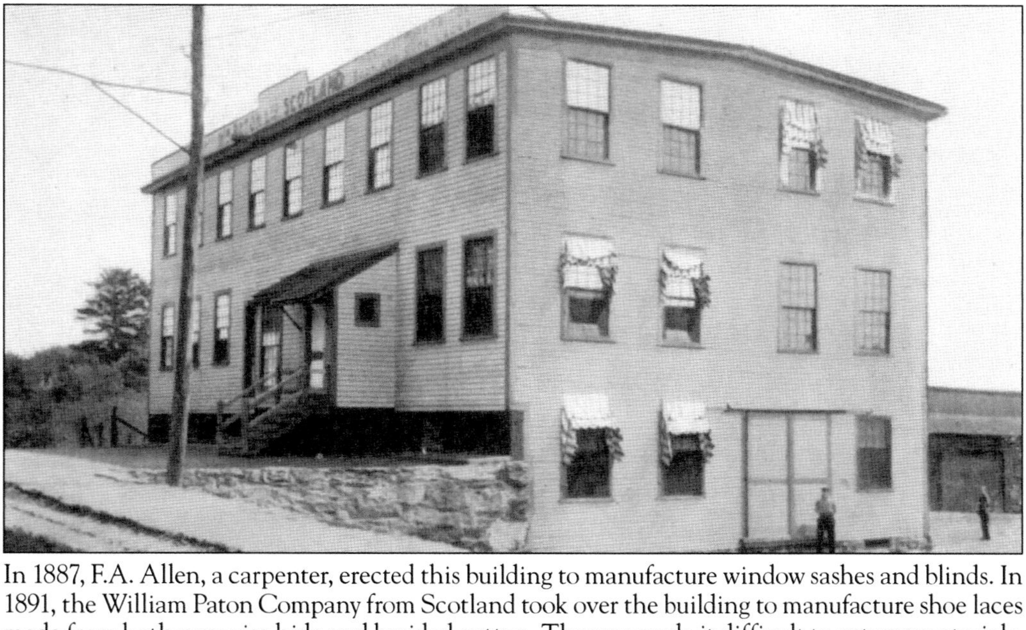

In 1887, F.A. Allen, a carpenter, erected this building to manufacture window sashes and blinds. In 1891, the William Paton Company from Scotland took over the building to manufacture shoe laces made from both porpoise hide and braided cotton. The war made it difficult to get raw materials, and the factory closed in 1916. The building burned in 1918. (Courtesy of Ann Morgan.)

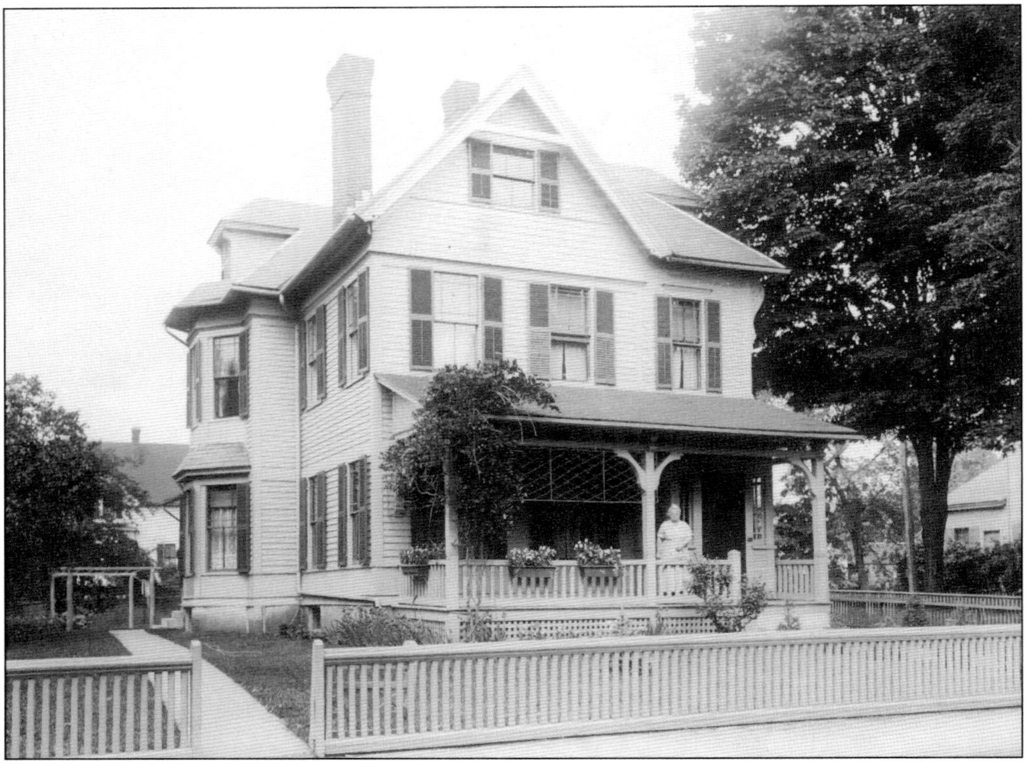

Amy Putnam Wing stands on the front porch of her home on Nelson Street. Her husband, Oliver M. Wing (1859–1924), was employed by the Nelson Shoe Company, eventually becoming secretary of the firm. He also served as treasurer of the Grafton Savings and Cooperative Bank and owned the Wing Insurance Agency in Grafton Center. (Courtesy of Amy Callihan.)

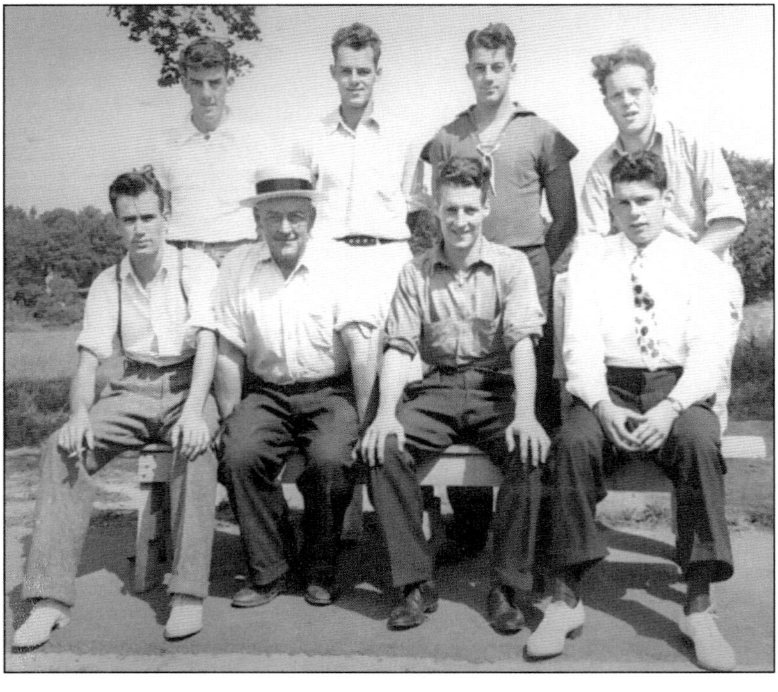

The North Grafton Horseshoe Team of 1938 is shown here. From left to right are (first row) Arthur Marr, "Cap" Simmons, Kitson Belanger, and Bernard Fleming; (second row) Charles Wade, Floyd Holland, Clayton Holland, and Arthur Bradish.

Elizabeth Ryerson joins other neighborhood children for an afternoon of ice skating at Windle Pond near Nelson Street. While the younger children skated, the older children played ice hockey. The entire neighborhood enjoyed the bonfires lit to keep everyone warm. (Courtesy of Elizabeth Stinson.)

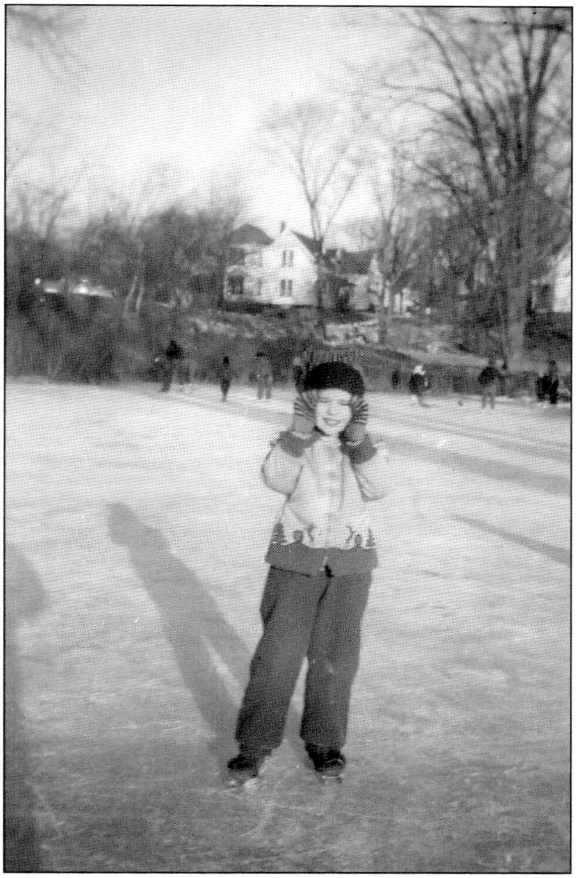

In the 1940s and 1950s, the Grafton Riding and Driving Club sponsored many horse shows at Nelson Park, attracting folks from all over the region. Today, the park boasts playing fields for softball, baseball, and soccer.

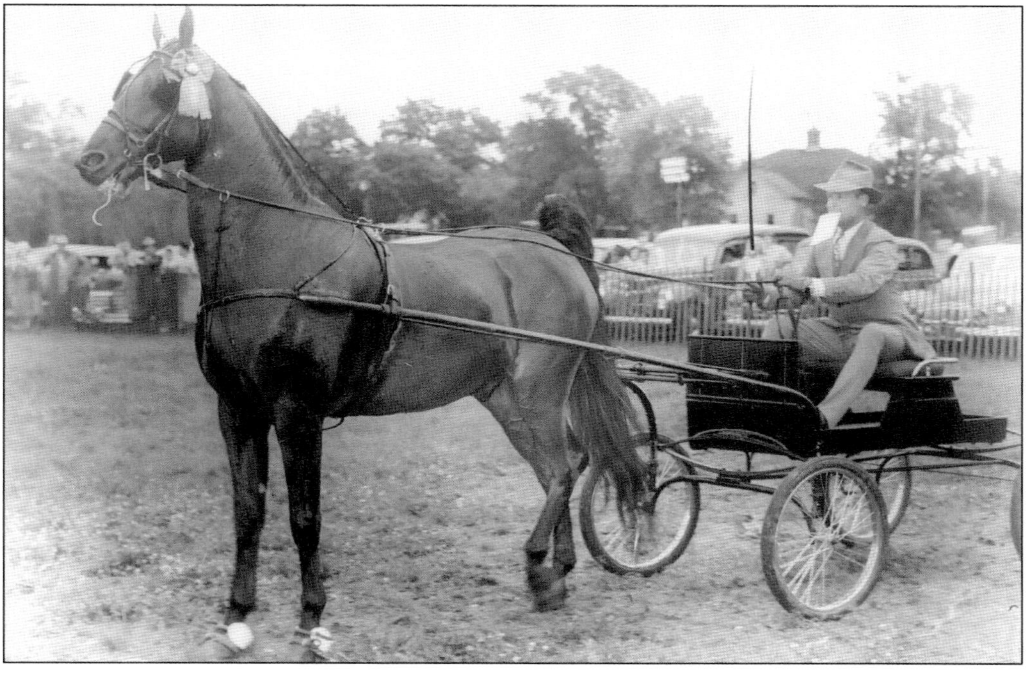

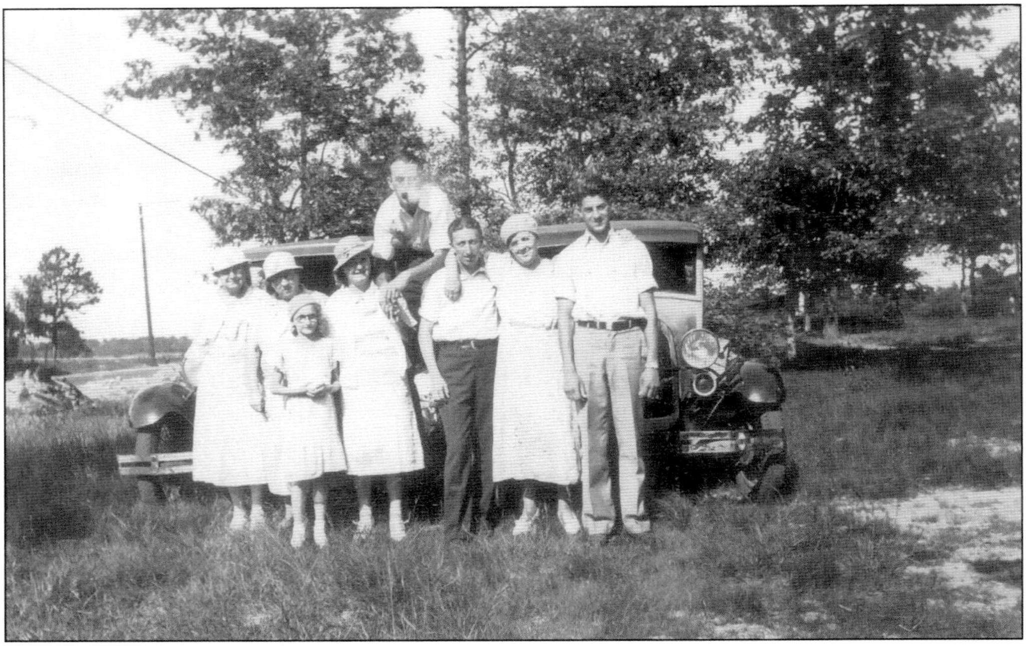

The residents of The Depot neighborhood formed a strong social group, enjoying many activities together. Preparing for a summer drive in the late 1930s are, from left to right, Emma Bull, Harriet Rice, Beatrice Rice, Doris Bull, Aubrey Bull, two unidentified, and Clayton Holland. (Courtesy of Jacqueline Davison.)

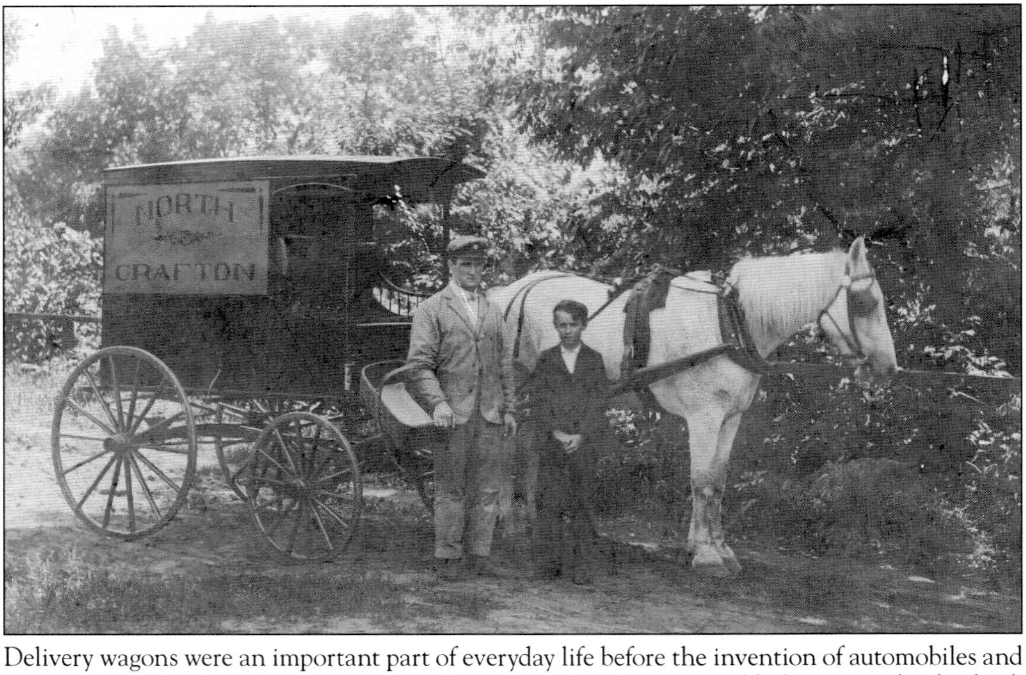

Delivery wagons were an important part of everyday life before the invention of automobiles and refrigeration. Food needed to be replenished every day. Patrons would place an order for food, and the grocer would have it delivered to their door. Here, a North Grafton deliveryman stands beside his horse with basket ready. He delivered bread for the store operating in the basement of the Second Baptist Church.

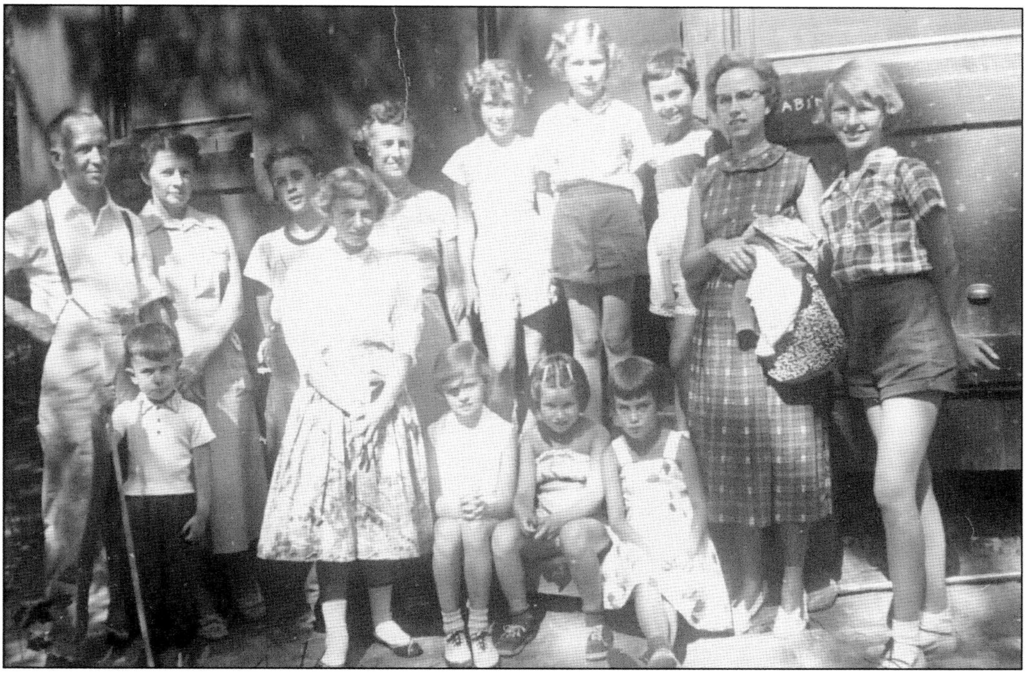

Families from The Depot area gather for a photograph at Camp Green Erie for Girl Scouts. This group of girls belonged to the neighborhood North Grafton Girl Scout Troop 222 in the 1950s. The Nason, Perkins, Kelly, and Fowler families are represented. (Courtesy of Jacqueline Davison.)

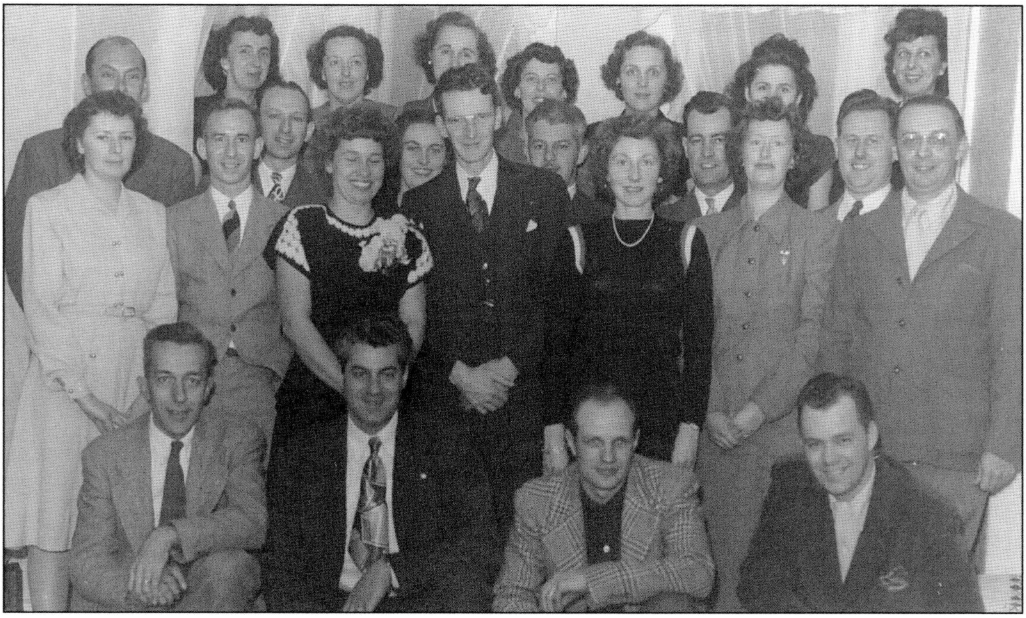

The North Grafton Couple's Club is shown in 1948. From left to right are (first row) Philip Brook, Clayton Holland, Ludger Witherell, and Bradley Pratt; (second row) Jean Nason, William Nason, Ethel Firth, Jack Firth, Evelyn Brook, Shirley Witherell, and Walter Matson; (third row) Robert Bull, James Allen, Betty Wallace, Russell Holland, Albert Hamilton, and Charles Wallace; (fourth row) Marion Matson, Jane Wilson, Jeanette Holland, Ruth Bull, Madeline Holland, Jean Hamilton, and Patricia Pratt.

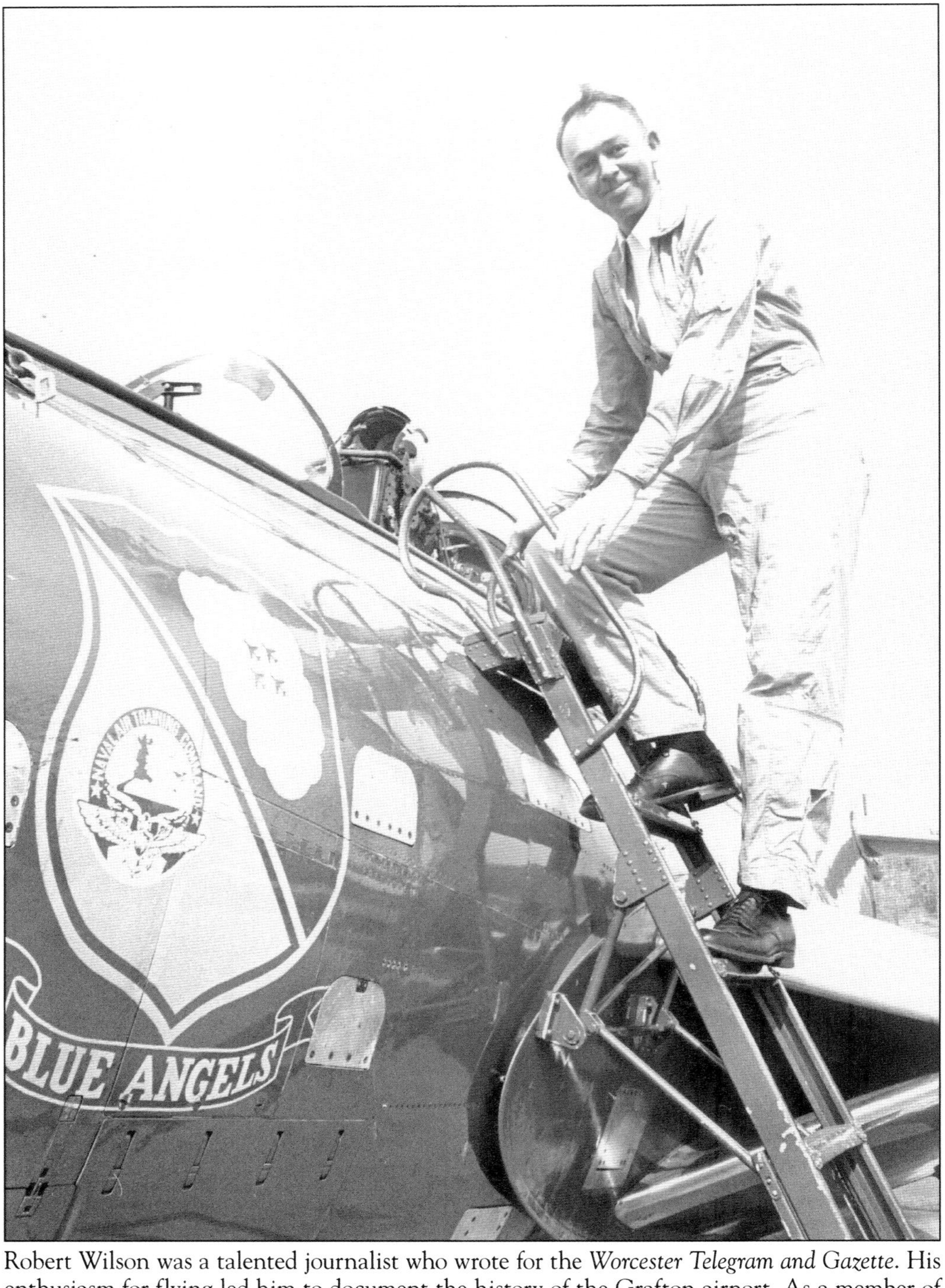

Robert Wilson was a talented journalist who wrote for the *Worcester Telegram and Gazette*. His enthusiasm for flying led him to document the history of the Grafton airport. As a member of the Grafton Historical Society, he collected and preserved many photographs and documents pertaining to Grafton history and the airport. In 1985, he coauthored a publication, *Grafton at 250*, a brief history of Grafton in the 20th century.

Five

South Grafton

The Blackstone River played a central role in the evolution of the textile industry in South Grafton. Three villages grew up along the Blackstone River: Farnumsville, Saundersville, and Fisherville, each located around a textile mill using waterpower from the river. Area businesses benefited from the opening of the Blackstone Canal in 1828; it provided a cheaper water route for the transport of goods to the coast.

Farnumsville grew up around Peter Farnum's woolen mill, built on Depot Street in 1812. Multifamily housing for workers appeared on Harding Street and along Providence Road. There was a boardinghouse for men; women boarded with families. A community house was built on Depot Street across from the mill. In its years as a textile mill, the mill burned down twice, was rebuilt, closed due to financial problems several times, and operated under many different business names. Its various names included Blackstone Woolen Company, Wright and Morse, A. Morse and Son, Farnumsville Cotton Mills, Excelsior Mills, and Wuskanut Mills. In the 1950s, J.J. O'Donnell Woolens revived the mill and operated it successfully for 10 years, closing in the late 1960s.

Saundersville was created in 1829 when David Wilkinson built a mill along the Blackstone River near the Sutton border. In 1835, he sold out to the Saunders brothers, Israel, Benjamin, and Esek, who built a new three-story granite mill and called the business Saunders Cotton Mill Company. Tenements were built nearby to house the Canadian, Irish, Polish, and Greek immigrants who made up the workforce. In 1880, Esek Saunders, who had taken over the business, sold out to the Whitin brothers of Whitinsville. In 1929, the Vanadium Wire Company converted the property for the production of steel wire but went out of business during the Depression. In the 1950s, the building housed chickens for Saunders Poultry Farm, owned by Chester Hospod. The mill was finally demolished in the 1970s.

The mill at Fisherville was built in 1831, also by Peter Farnum. At the time, the area was called Upper Farnumsville, but the name was officially changed to Fisherville in 1882. The mill operated under many different names: Canal Cotton Company, E.F. Fisher and Sons, and Fisher Manufacturing Company. For 80 of those years, it was owned by a member of the Fisher family and produced cotton cloth and toweling. The Fisher family supported the construction of tenements and two churches.

The three villages of Farnumsville, Saundersville and Fisherville make up South Grafton. The mill owners helped to finance schools, churches, and community centers. Each village attracted its own grocers, bakers, tailors, barbers, and merchants of every sort. Residents were loyal to the village in which they lived.

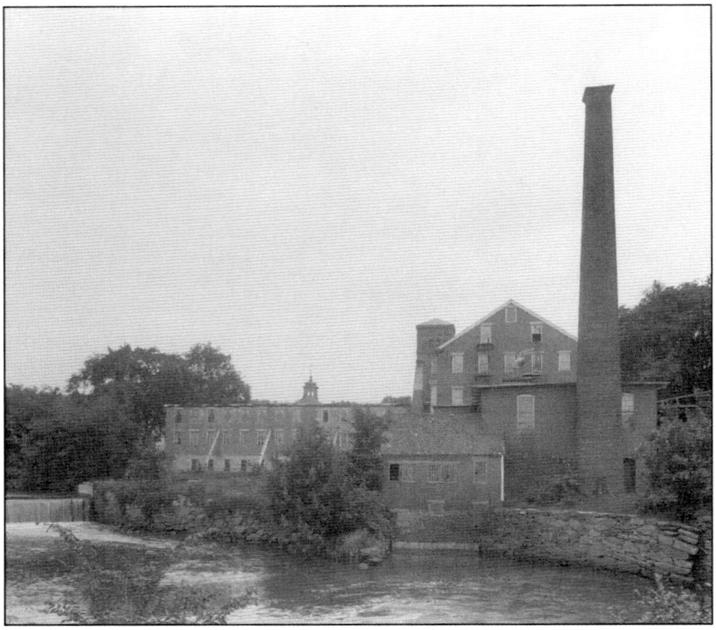

Wuskanut Mill is viewed from the Blackstone River with Depot Street on the right. The dam providing power to the mill can be seen on the left. Peter Farnum built his first Grafton woolen mill at this site in 1812. Over the years, the mill burned down twice, was rebuilt, closed several times, and operated under many different names.

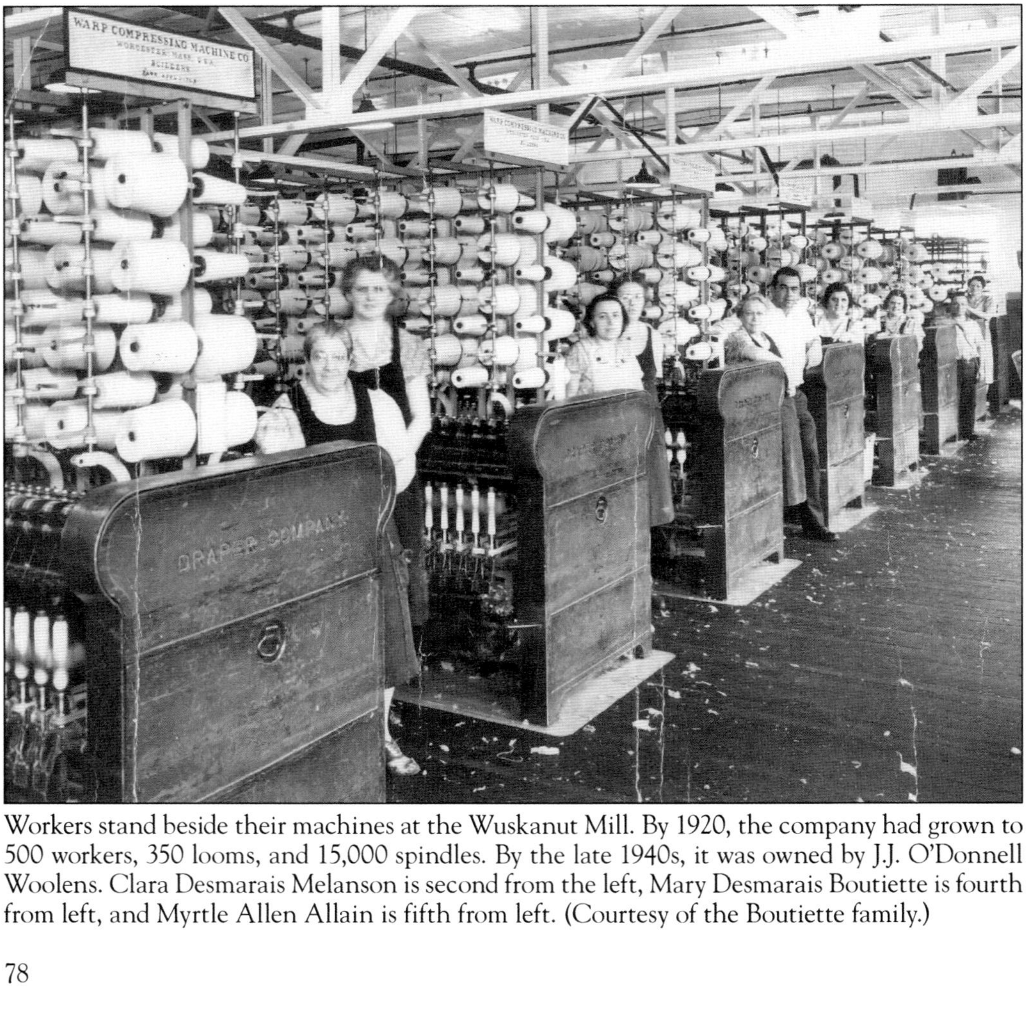

Workers stand beside their machines at the Wuskanut Mill. By 1920, the company had grown to 500 workers, 350 looms, and 15,000 spindles. By the late 1940s, it was owned by J.J. O'Donnell Woolens. Clara Desmarais Melanson is second from the left, Mary Desmarais Boutiette is fourth from left, and Myrtle Allen Allain is fifth from left. (Courtesy of the Boutiette family.)

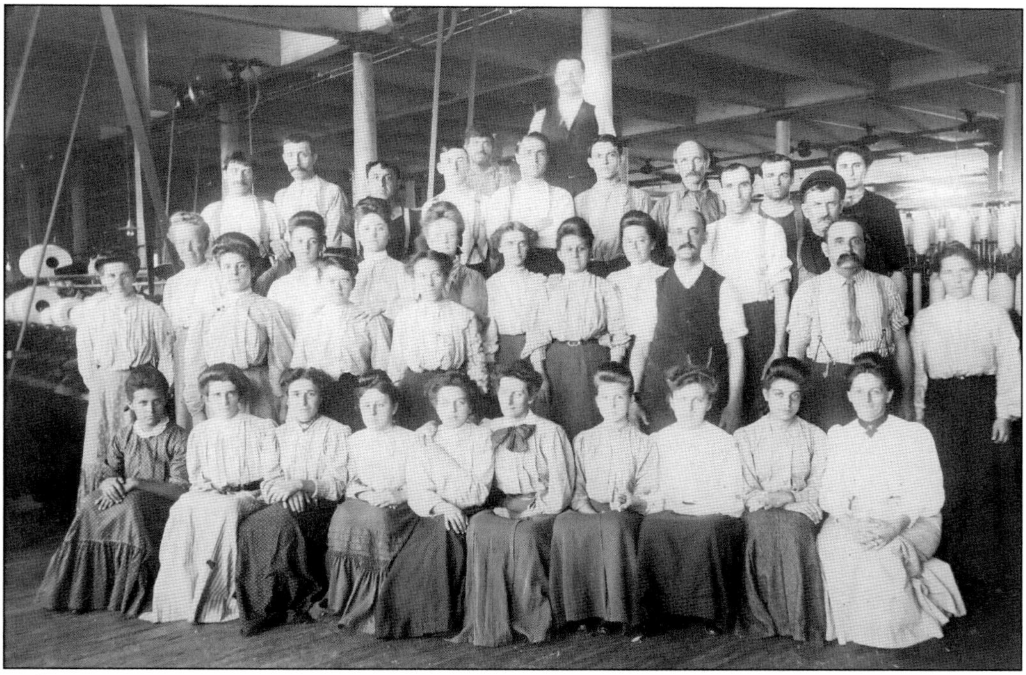

Mill workers at Wuskanut Mill pose for a formal photograph around 1910. The early textile mills along the Blackstone River originally hired children to work the mills because they were the cheapest labor. When school attendance requirements and child labor laws put an end to the practice, women workers became the preferred labor for the same reason. Men were usually hired as mill supervisors or to perform jobs requiring technical ability or strength.

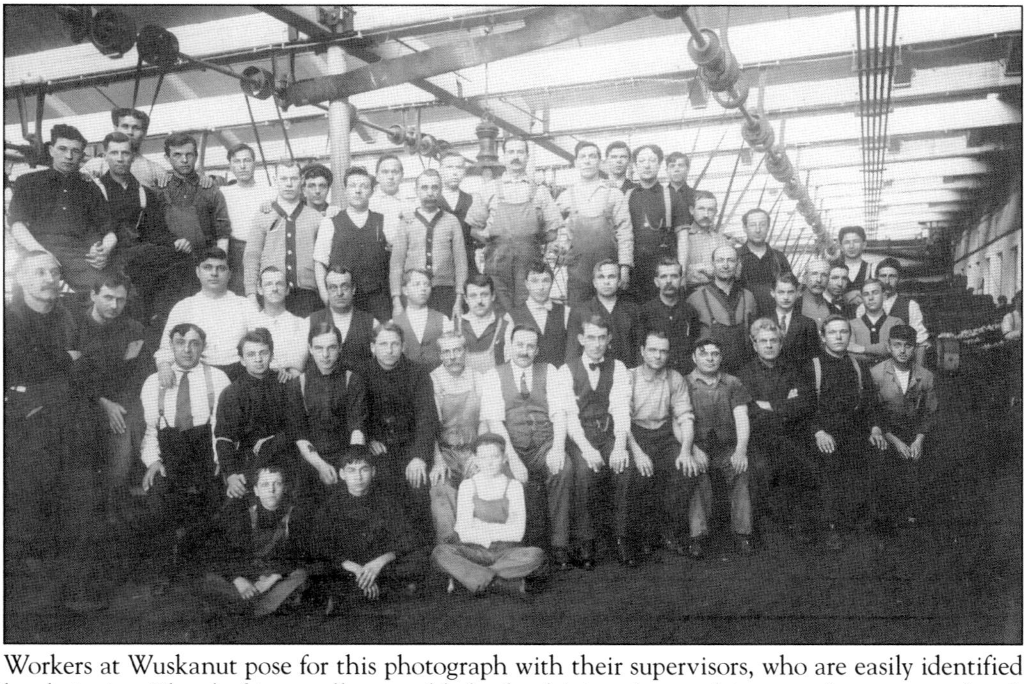

Workers at Wuskanut pose for this photograph with their supervisors, who are easily identified by their ties. The shafting, pulleys, and belts for driving the machines can be seen overhead. (Courtesy of Boutiette family.)

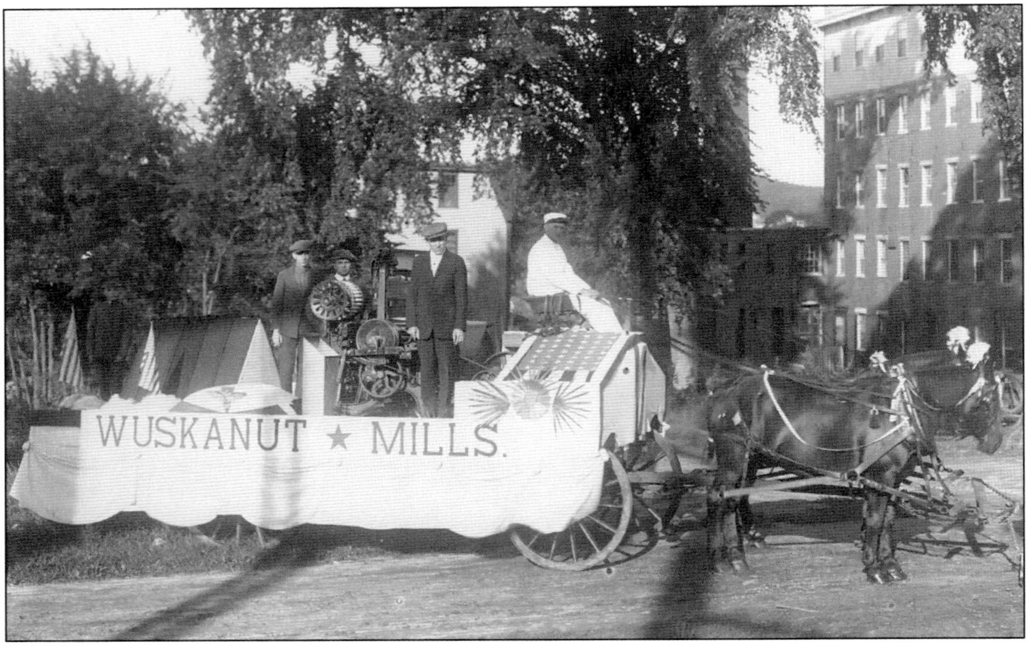

This horse-drawn float sponsored by the Wuskanut Mill was part of the parade in 1918 celebrating the end of World War I. The float featured a piece of machinery newly purchased by the mill. The parade traveled down Providence Road and onto Main Street. (Courtesy of Joseph Boutiette.)

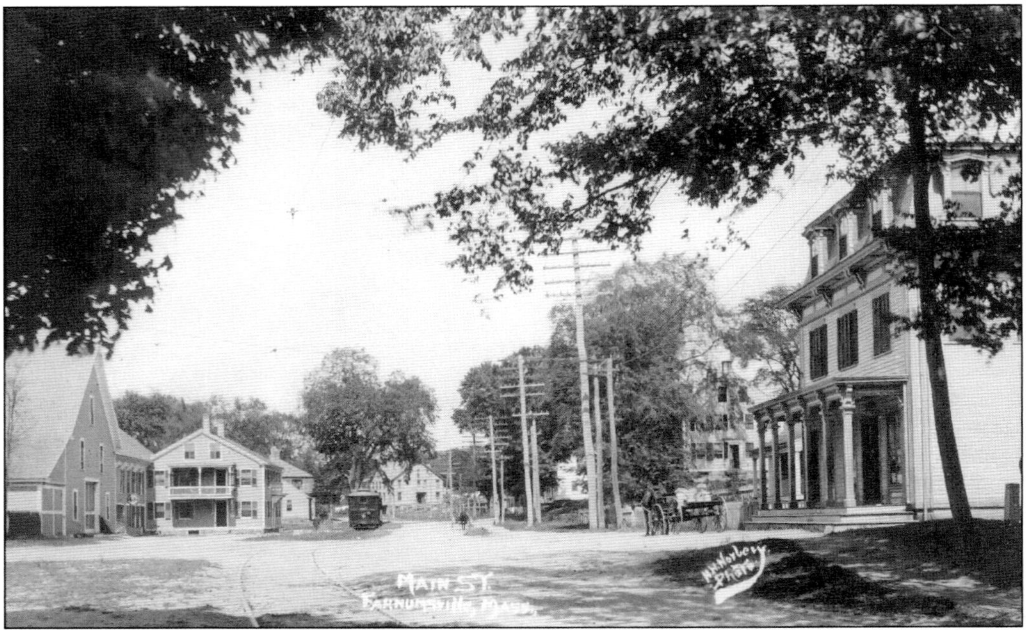

This view of Providence Road looking north shows a pharmacy building on the far right. This building, erected in 1872, has had various names, including the Wuskanut Pharmacy, Lynch's Pharmacy, and Finn's Pharmacy. Trolley tracks are evident in the foreground. (Courtesy of Eileen Tomkiewicz Flynn.)

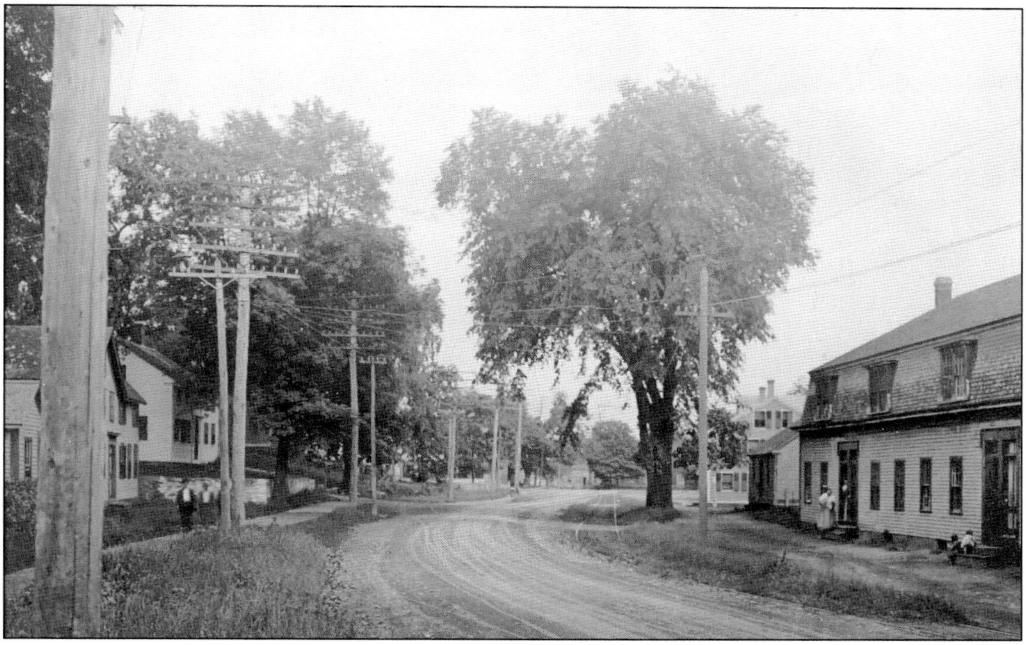

Looking south, this view of Providence Road shows the housing for mill workers at far right. Single-family houses in this scene were probably built for management workers. Trolley tracks can be seen along the roadway.

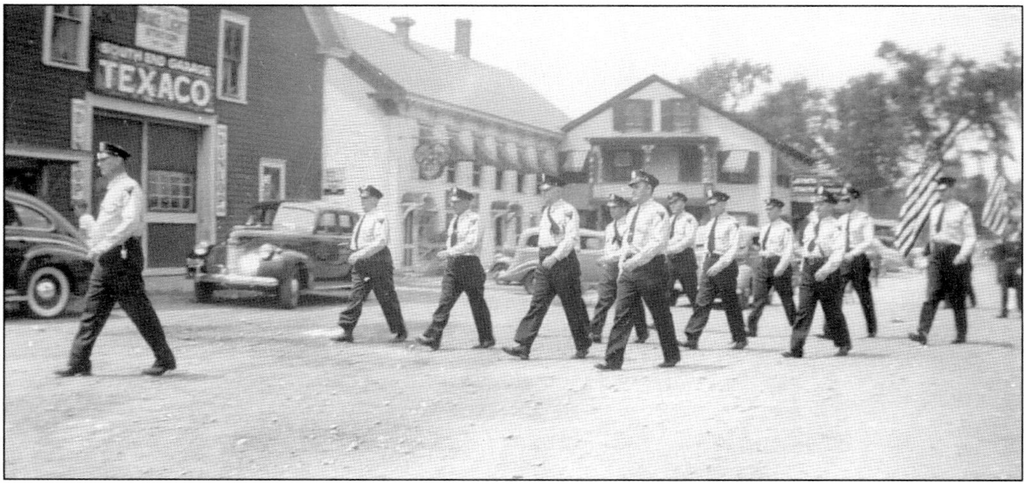

Men in uniform march past Jim's Inn on Providence Road in a 1941 parade. Jim's Inn was a popular Farnumsville bar. In 1980, operating as Lord Zachary's Inn, it was destroyed by fire.

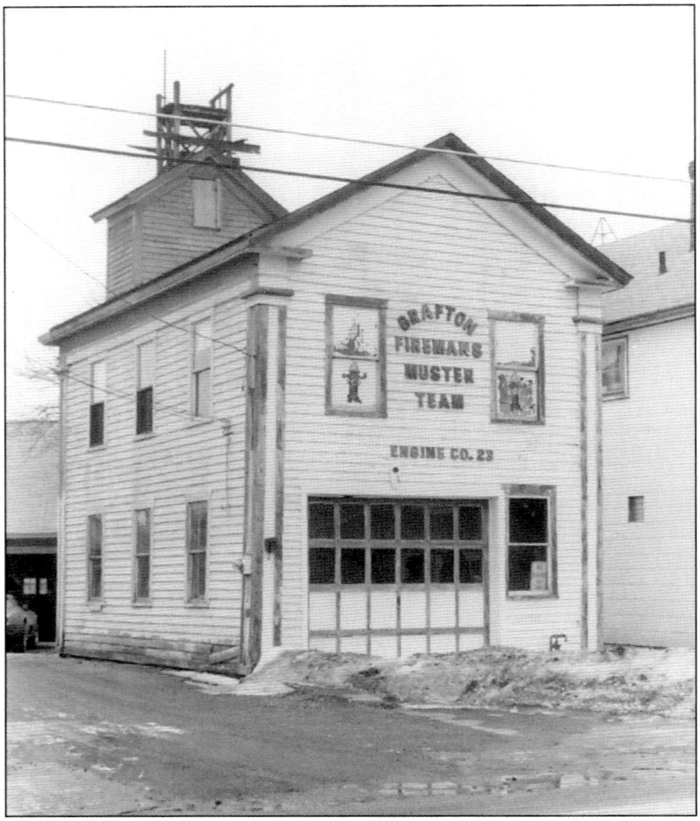

The Farnumsville Fire House, built in 1853, was equipped with a Howard & Davis hand tub fire engine and was known as the Blackstone Engine Company No. 3. The company operated with a crew of 40 men. Restoration of the firehouse began in 1996, led by Ralph Michniewicz and supported by Philip Gauthier and Daniel and Maryann Finn.

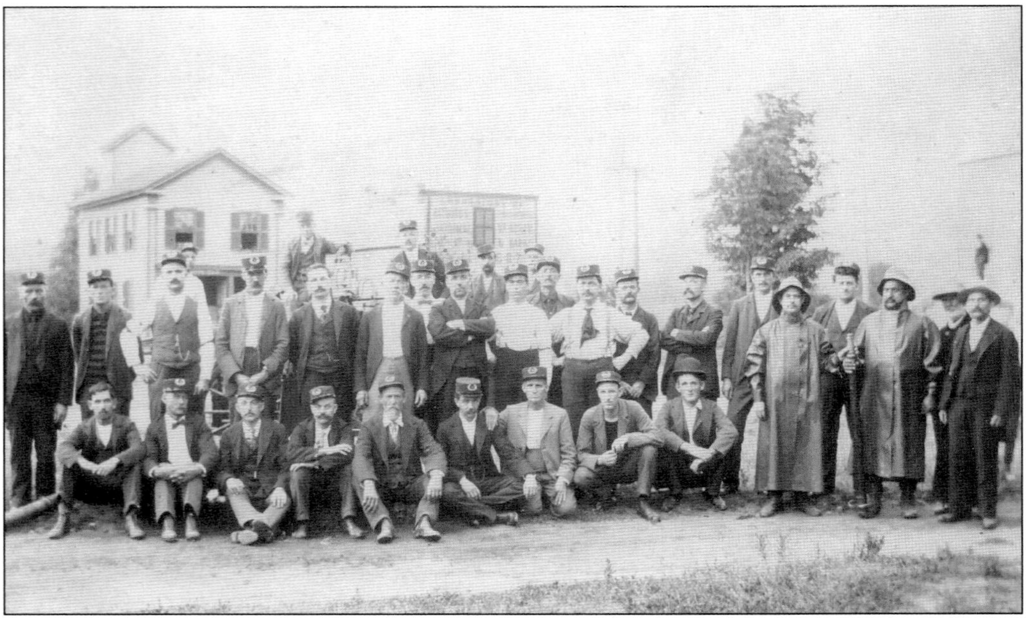

The Blackstone Engine Company No. 3 is shown here posed in front of the Bitgood's store in Farnumsville. Bitgood's was a laboratory that made herbal medicines from roots and barks and sold them to the public. The Farnumsville firehouse can be seen in the background. (Courtesy of Grafton Fire Department.)

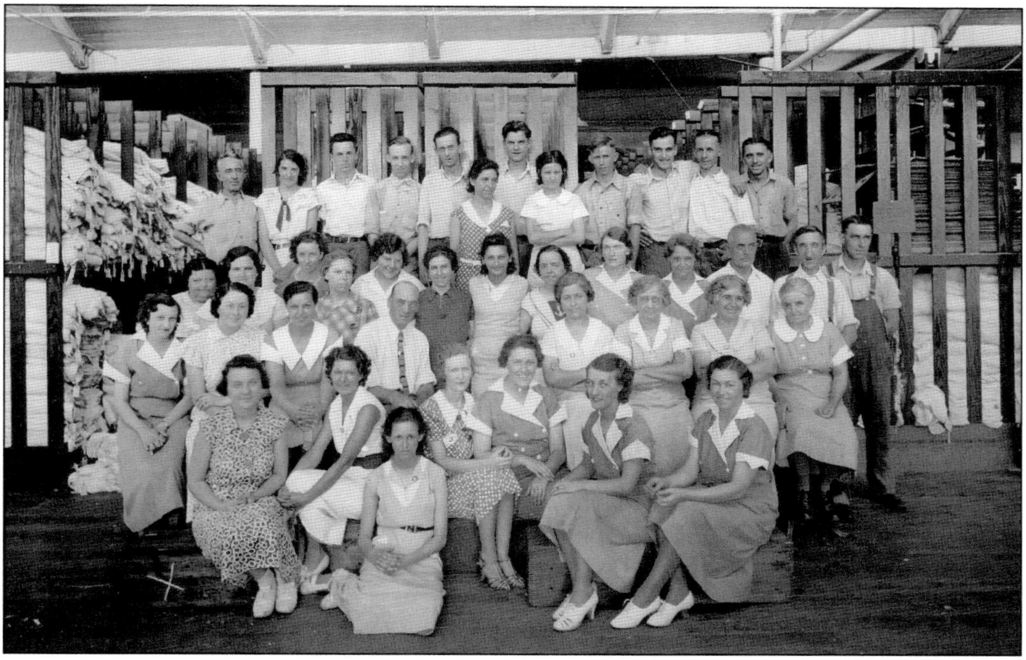

Women workers at Wuskanut Mill pose for a photograph in 1936. Stacks of fabric can be seen on nearby racks. Helen Lemoine is the woman at far right in the first row. (Courtesy of Nancy Lemoine.)

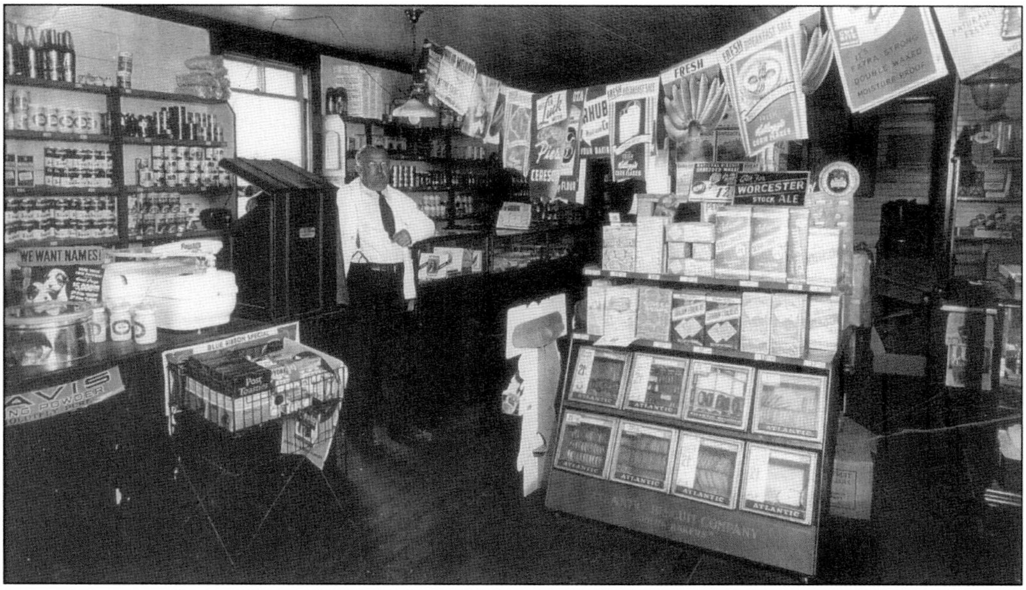

Klocek's General Store on Cross Street provided the Farnumsville village with groceries, beer, wine, tobacco, and other household products. Owner Frank Klocek is seen here amid displays of Campbell's soup, Kellogg's Corn Flakes, Atlantic Biscuits, Worcester Stock Ale, an assortment of penny candy, and cigars. The store was a favorite spot for Farnumsville residents in the 1940s and 1950s. (Courtesy of Ronald Klocek.)

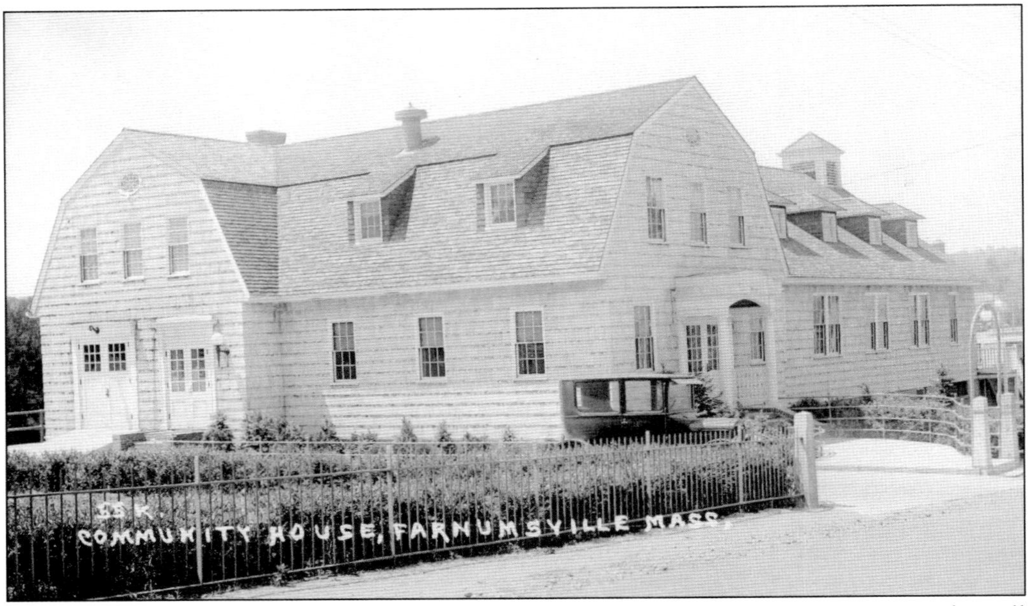

A community house on Depot Street was built by the mill to provide a recreation spot for mill workers. It included a recreation hall where the South Grafton Girl's Club, led by Mary Maguire Morin, met in the 1940s. A bowling alley downstairs was owned and operated by Henry and Lucien "Kite" Morin.

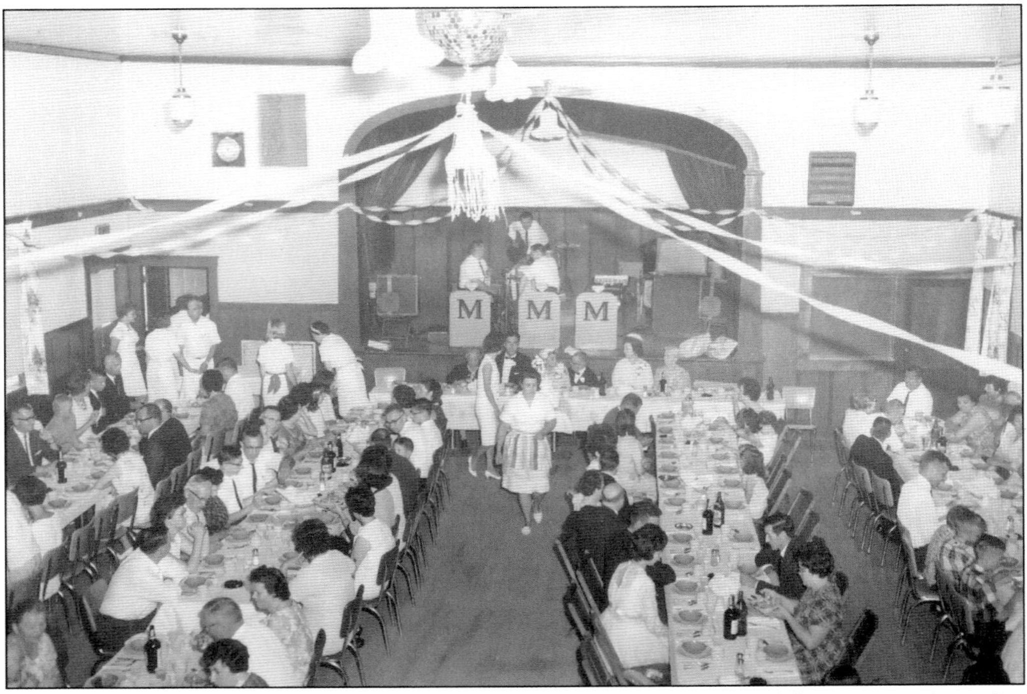

The Polish National Home was a popular site for many community celebrations, such as this wedding reception for Blanche and Frank Obara. Many Polish immigrants came to the South Grafton area around 1900. After years of fundraising and construction, the home opened its doors in 1935. It has provided a haven for the Polish community ever since. (Courtesy of the Rawinski family.)

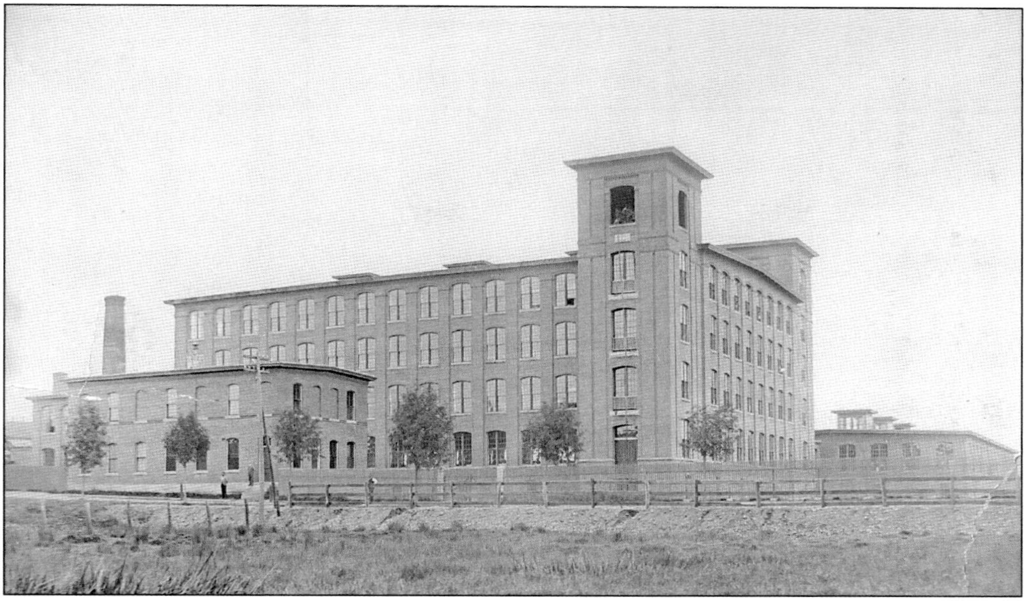

In 1830, Timothy McNamara bought land along the Blackstone River and worked jointly with the Blackstone Canal Company to build a dam near Cross Street. The first textile mill at this site was in operation by 1832. For most of its history, members of the Fisher family were owners. In 1868, George and Albert, sons of Erastus Fisher, were made partners and the company became E. Fisher and Sons. Later, when it was called Fisher Manufacturing Company, George became the agent and Albert became a supervisor. The mill was expanded several times to become one of the largest cotton mills in the Blackstone Valley. In 1879, it produced 1.5 million yards of cloth, continuing to manufacture textiles until 1949. The above photograph shows the mill before 1890; below, the expanded mill is surrounded by floodwaters in the 1930s.

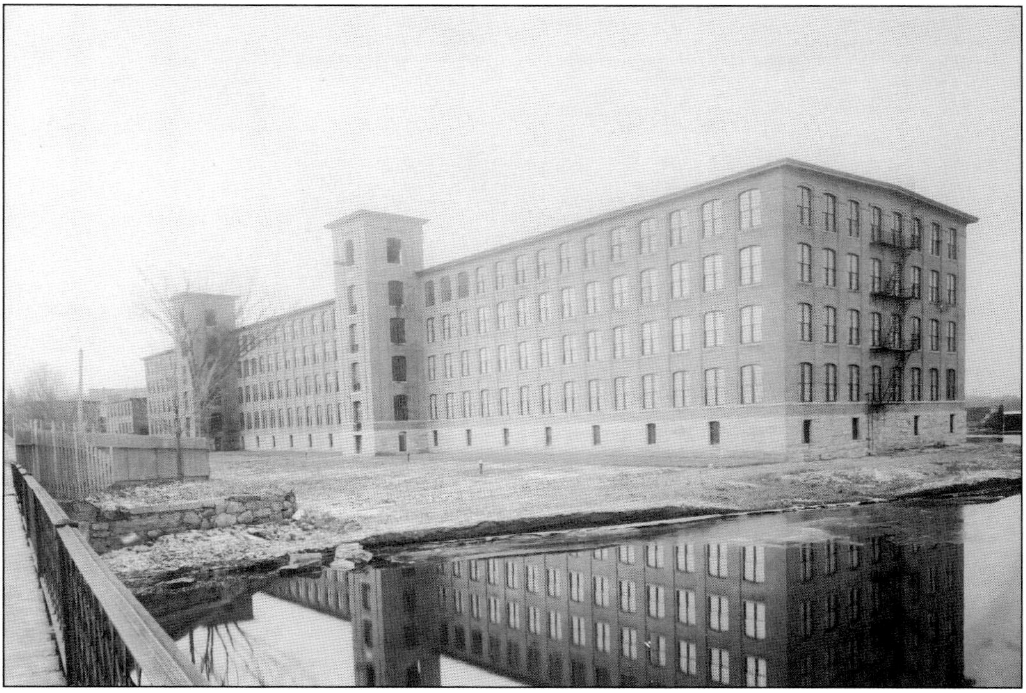

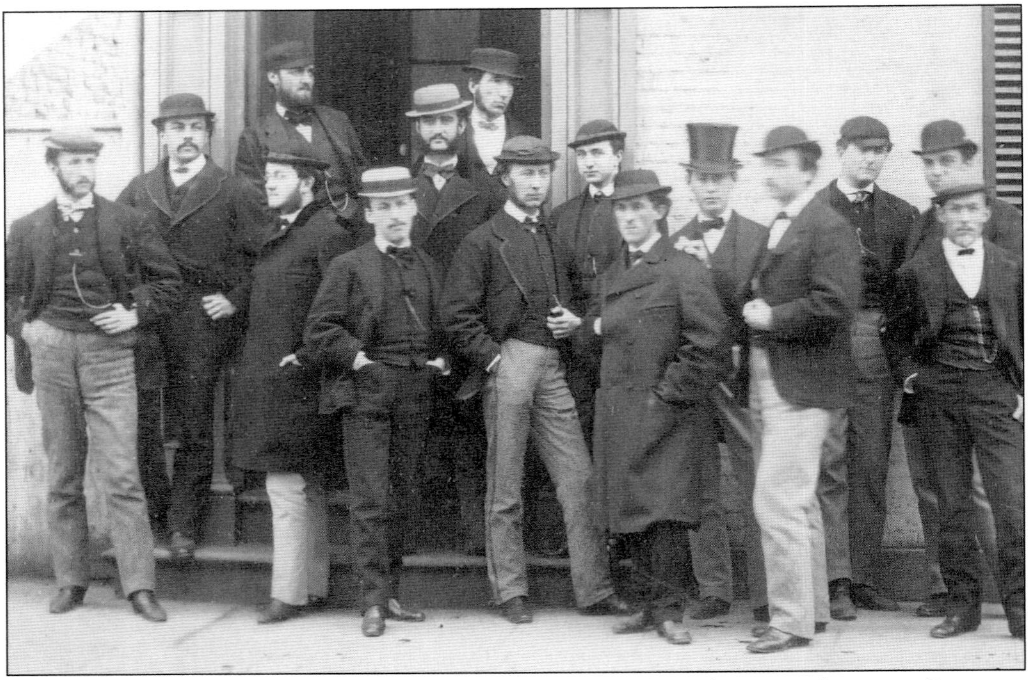

George Fisher, the man in the tall silk hat, stands outside the Fisher Manufacturing Company with some of his employees. In 1868, he joined his father as a partner in the mill. He built a large mansion in Grafton Center, and when he died, he was one of the richest men in town. He left one-fourth of his fortune to the town for support of the public library.

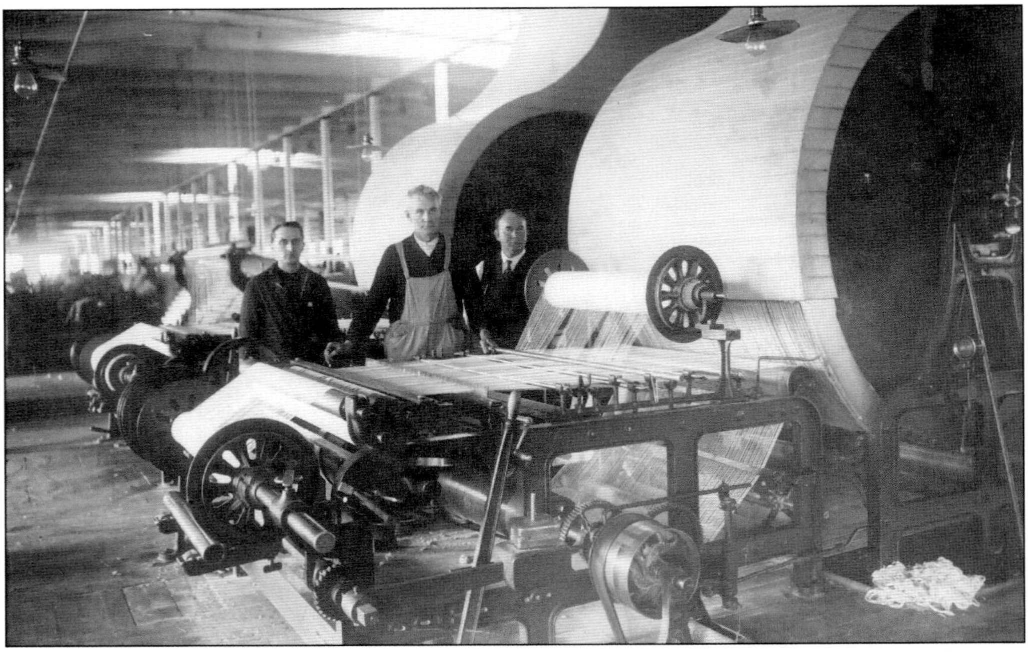

Pictured from left to right, Peter Bonner, James Harding, and a Mr. Relly (the supervisor) are at work at the Fisherville Mill. During the 1940s, the mill produced a loosely woven material that was used as mosquito netting. The noise in the mills frequently caused deafness in workers. The rhythm of the looms could be heard throughout the nearby neighborhoods.

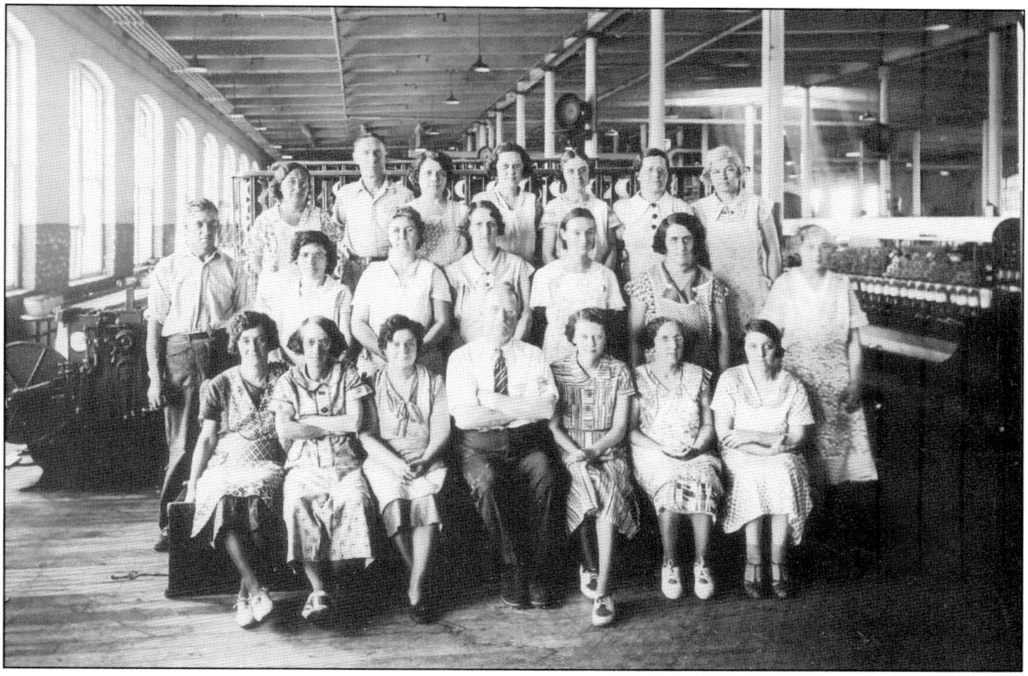

Workers pose in one of the many mill departments around 1936. They are, from left to right, (first row) Stella Pong, Grace Hardback, Laura Fontain, Luke Rooney, Alice Capistrand, Alma White, and Stella Nolan; (second row) Antoine Patnaude, Eva Bilils, a Mrs. Marando, Rosanna Pong, Lillian Healy, Rose Berk, and Mrs. Boucher; (third row) a Mrs. Goodwin, a Mr. Cook, Alice Brook, Eva Ouellette, Cecila White, Mabel Brook, and a Mrs. Gauvin.

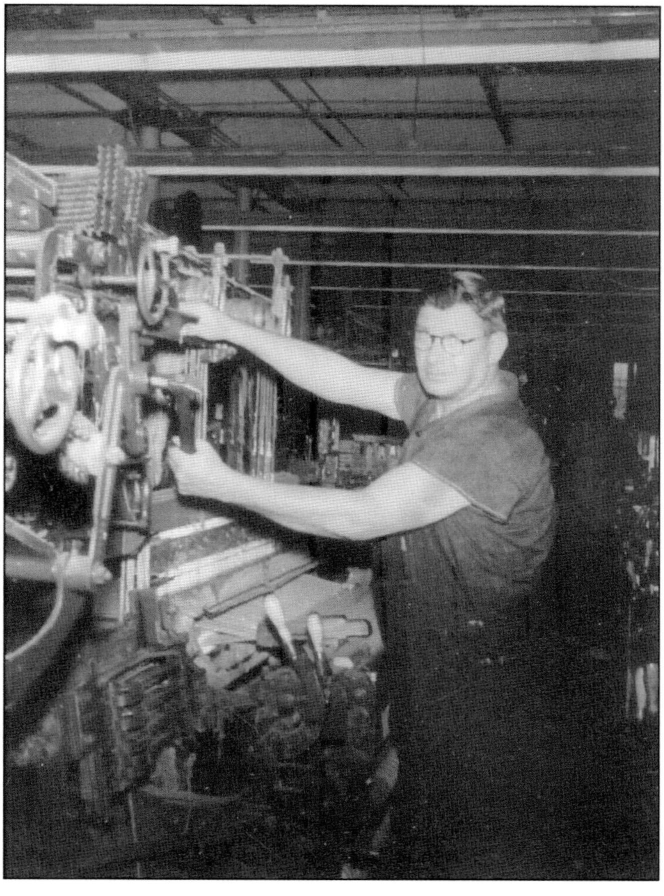

Julian Ribicki, a loom fixer, is shown working at the Fisherville Mill. Loom fixers were required to work quickly and efficiently to fix broken looms. Delay meant a loss of productivity. (Courtesy of the Ribicki family.)

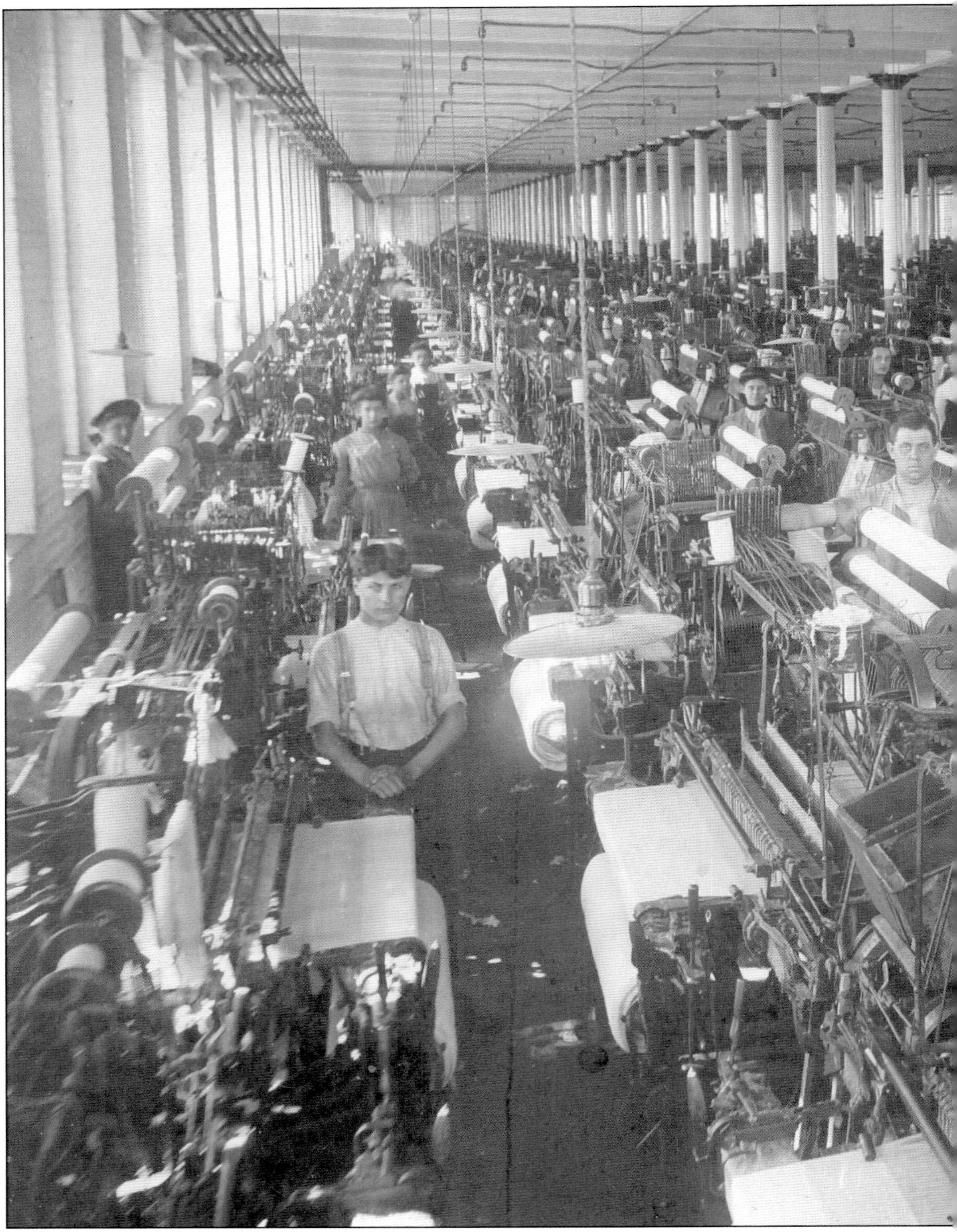

The Fisherville Mill provided employment for hundreds of Polish and French-Canadian immigrants. This c. 1910 view of the interior of the mill shows the size of the workrooms. In the 1920s, the pay for six days' work, 10 hours per day, was $6. Working conditions were poor; air filled with

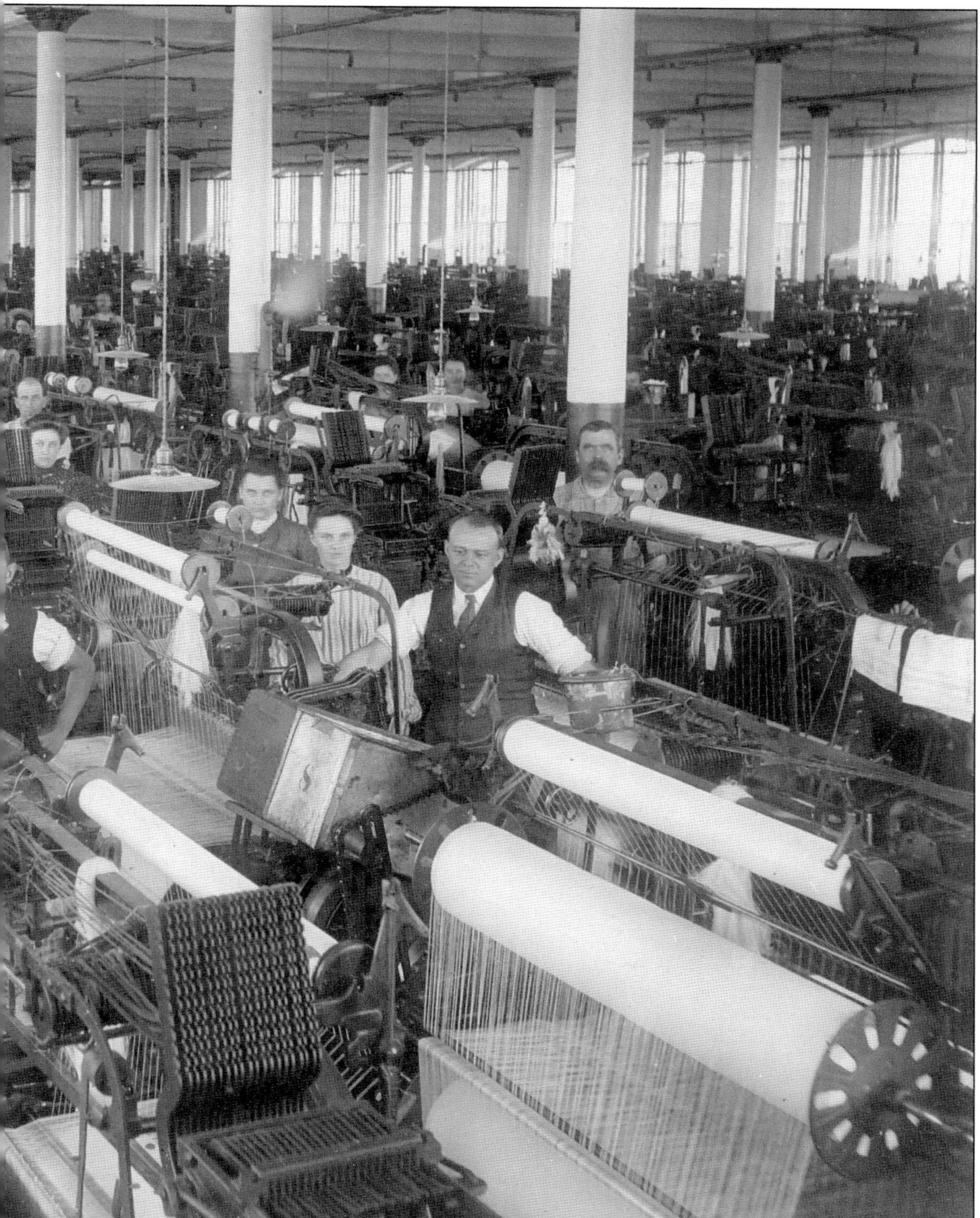

cotton fibers, deafening noise, extreme heat and humidity, and dangerous machines made the work challenging. (Courtesy of St. James Church.)

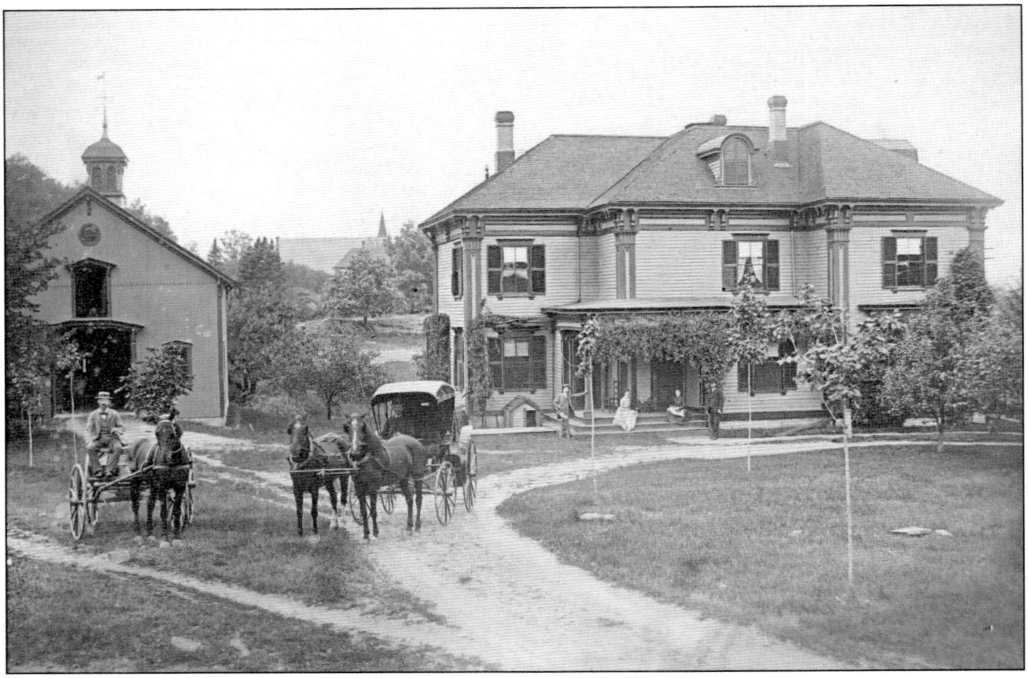

This house at 75 Main Street was the home of Erastus Fisher, who owned Fisher Manufacturing Company, first with his brother Waterman and later with his sons. Upon his death, his youngest son, Albert, took over this house and supervised at the mill. In 1876, Albert also took charge of the company's general store across the street. In 1882, he became postmaster of Fisherville. (Courtesy of Carolynne Grimley.)

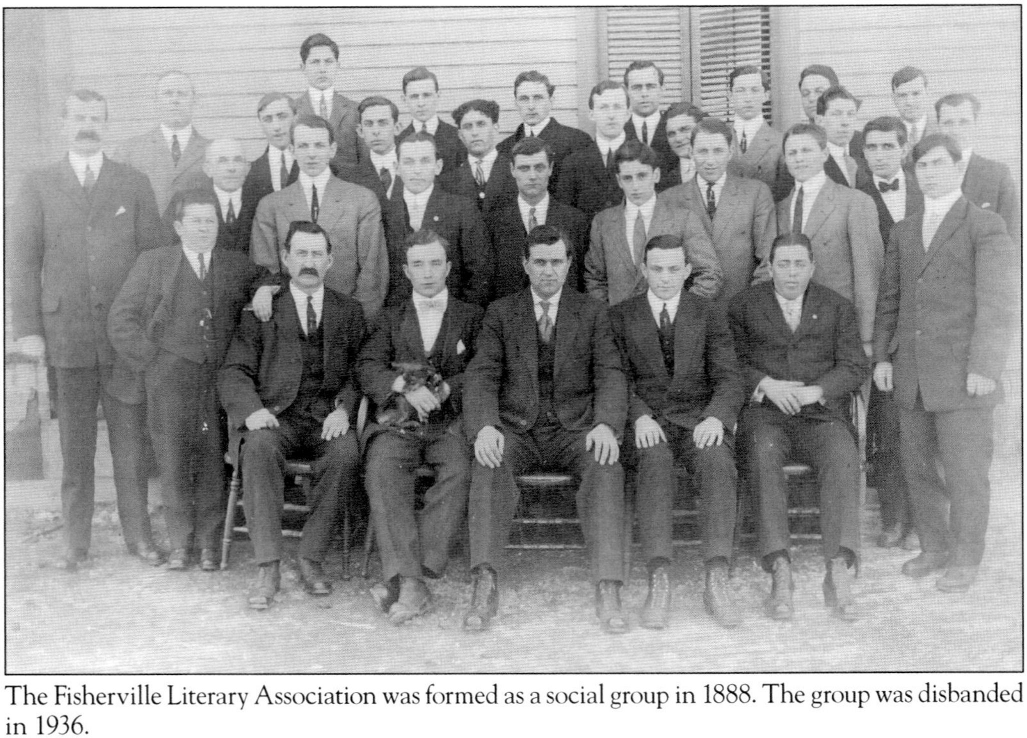

The Fisherville Literary Association was formed as a social group in 1888. The group was disbanded in 1936.

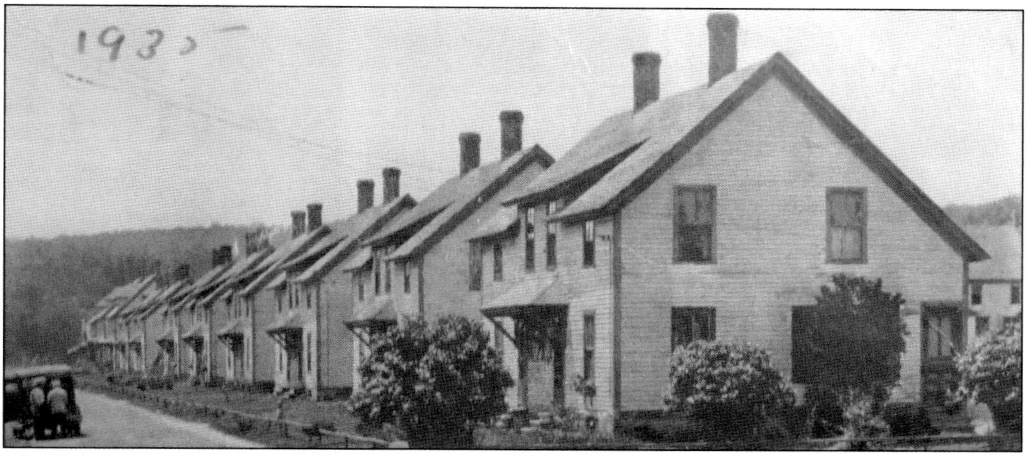

The Fisher Manufacturing Company built these houses for its workers on English Row and Orchard Street. Known as New Village, this area included a large boardinghouse for single employees and rows of two- or four-family homes. The area of tenements located on Railroad Court behind the Fisher store came to be called Old Village.

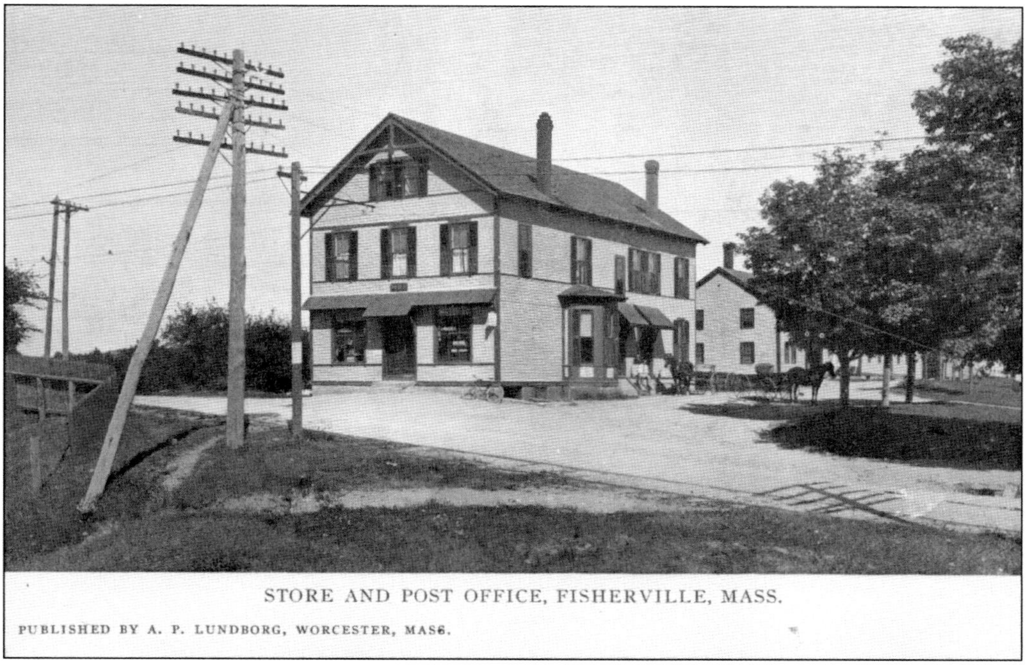

The A.L. Fisher store and post office were located on Main Street near Old Village. The houses there had been built for earlier generations of mill workers and were less desirable. Because the lots had no room for children to play or space for a garden, families were motivated to work hard and save money to buy their own homes. Later, this store became Sareault's Market.

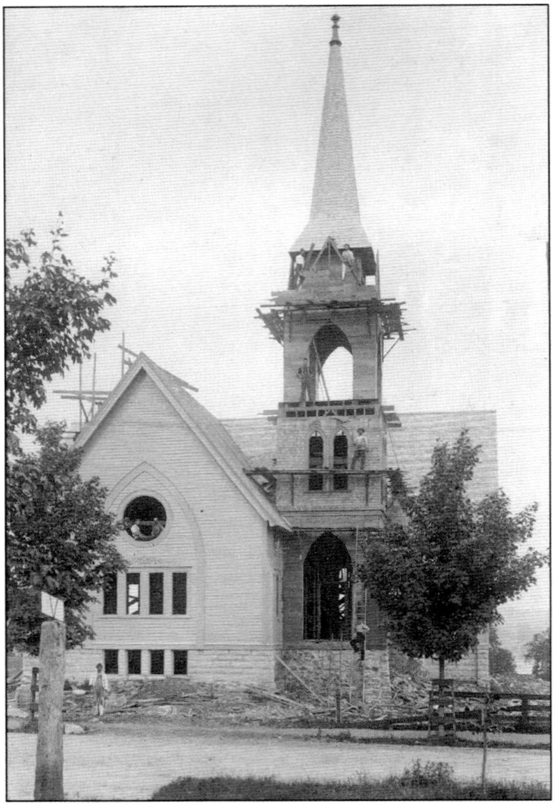

The Union Congregational Church, seen here under construction, was originally organized in 1860 as the Saundersville Congregational Church. For many years, the congregation met on the second floor of the post office building at the corner of Main and Elmwood Streets. In 1895, the church reorganized to serve all the mill villages and the name was changed. This structure was then built on land donated by the Fisher Manufacturing Company.

The South Grafton Library was built in 1938 as a branch of the Grafton Public Library. The land was donated by the Fisherville Mill, and funds for the building were supplied by David E. Merriam. Minnie Briand, Olive Morin, and Ethel Ernshaw were librarians there.

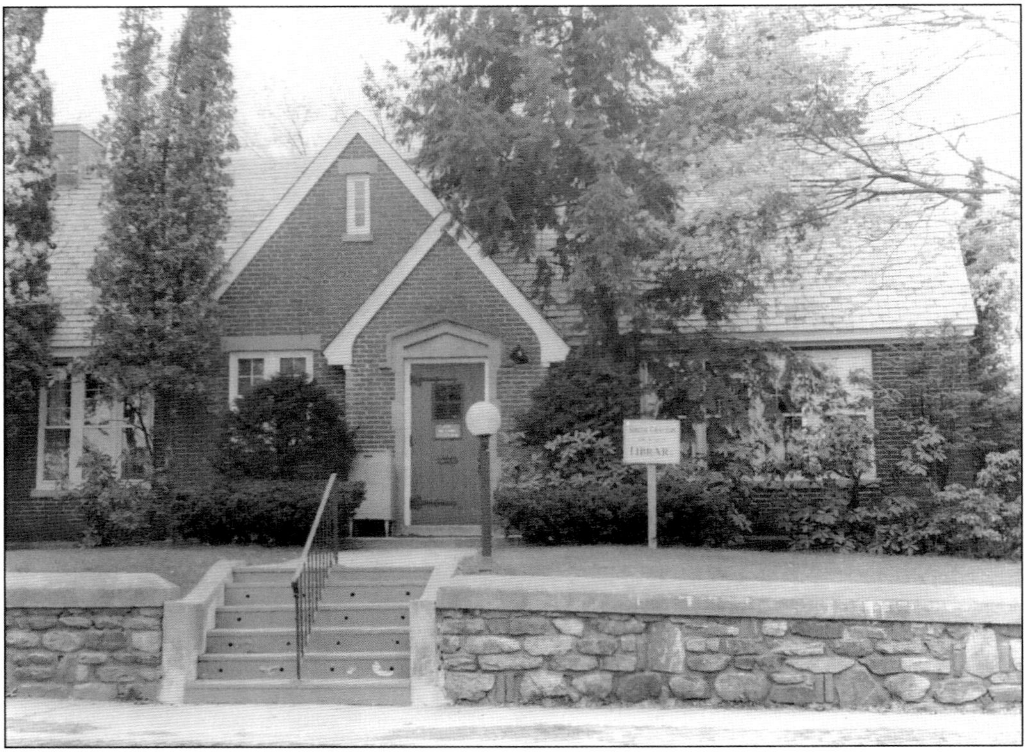

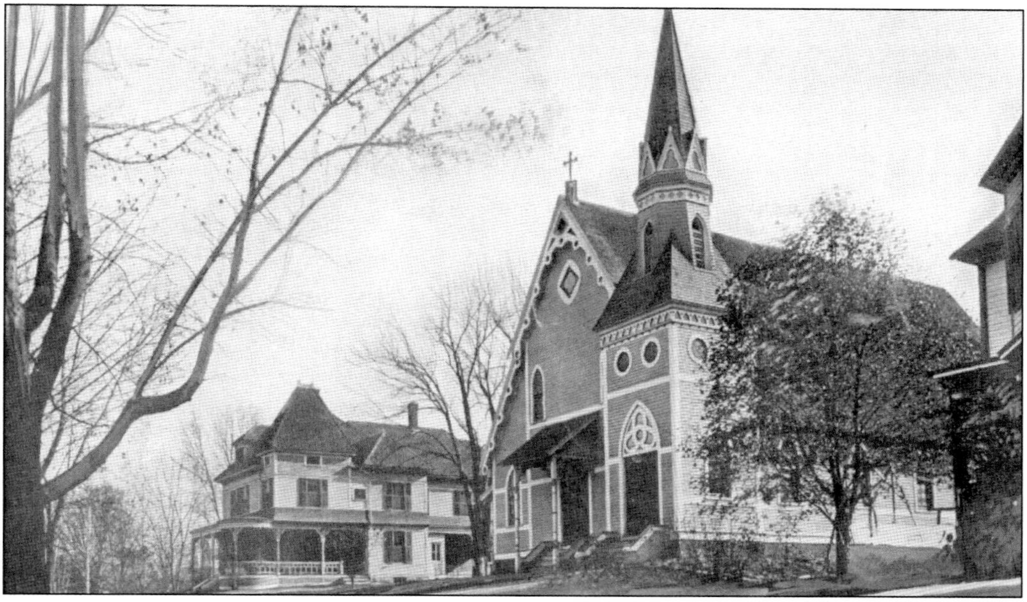

In 1883, Fr. James Boyle oversaw the building of St. James Church on land donated by the Fisher Manufacturing Company. The rectory was completed in 1887. In 1945, when fire destroyed the church, parishioners attended Mass at the Wuskanut Hall until the church was rebuilt.

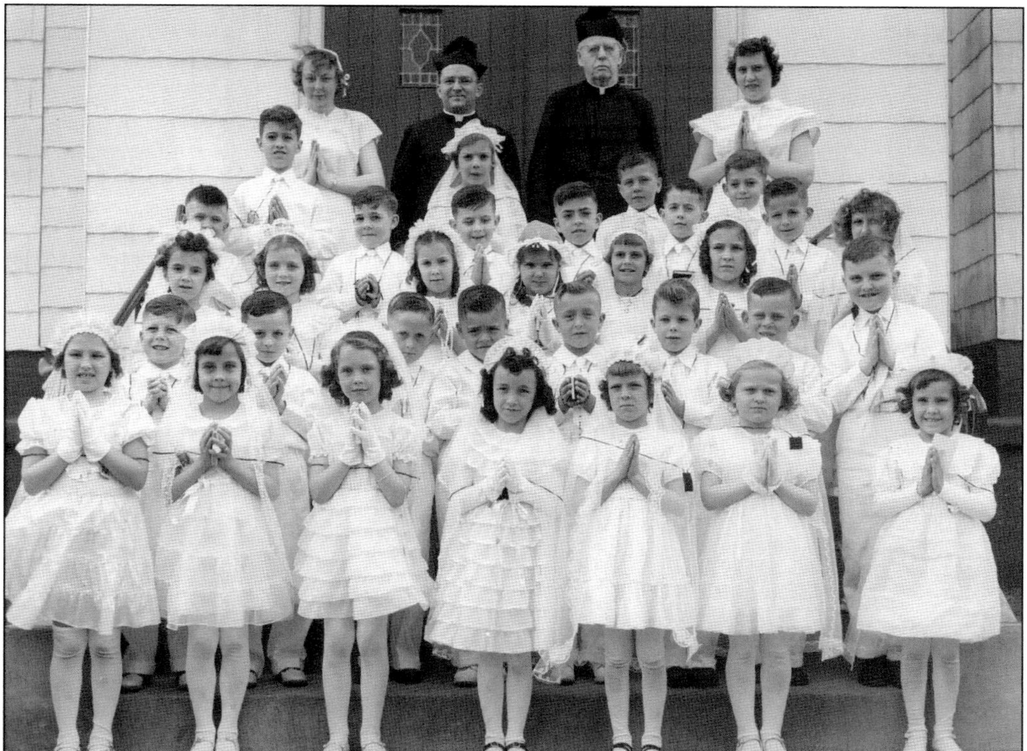

In 1948, Fr. Louis Charron (left) and Fr. William Lucey (right) pose on the steps of the newly rebuilt St. James Church behind the First Communion class. At St. James Church, both French-speaking and Polish-speaking priests ministered to the needs of the community.

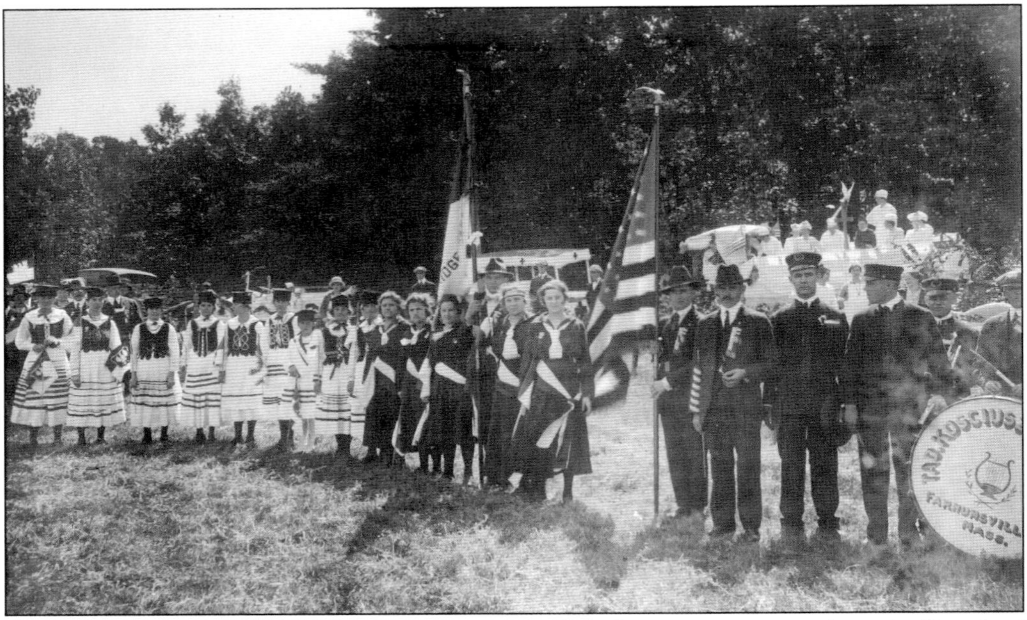

The Town of Grafton invited the South Grafton Polish Community to march in the Fourth of July parade for the first time in 1919. The Tadeusz Kosciuszko Band was followed by young women in traditional Polish dress. (Courtesy of the Rawinski family.)

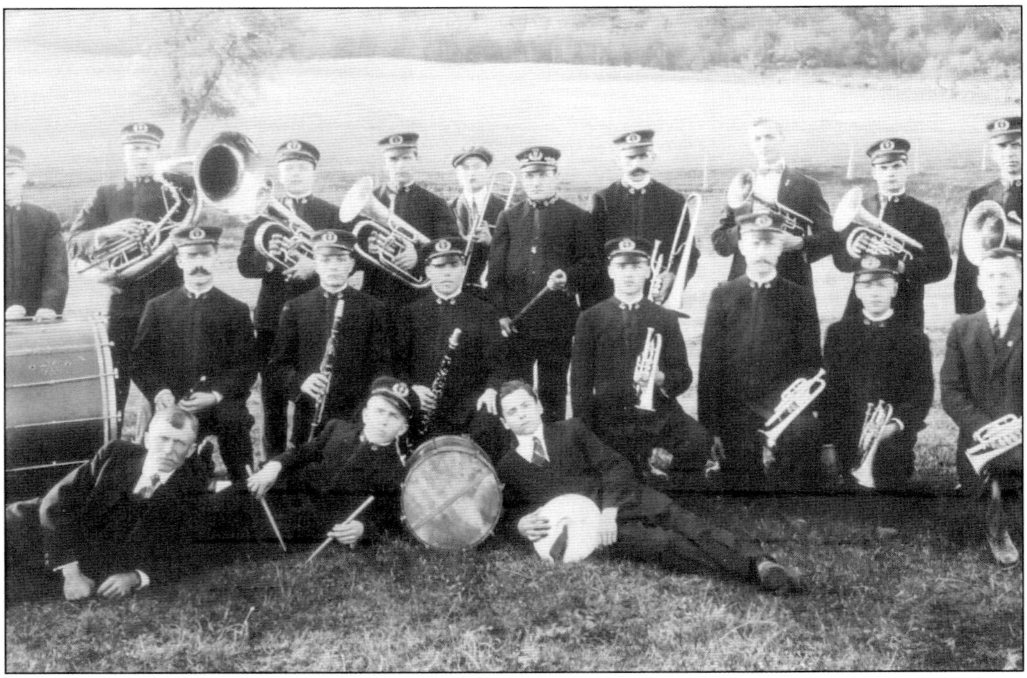

The Tadeusz Kosciuszko Band played for Polish picnics and parades in South Grafton. The band members are, from left to right, (first row) unidentified, Joseph Swidrak, and Joseph Polak; (second row) Albert Kuras, Thomas Obara, Stanley Stopyra, Stanley Matuszek, Frank Satlawa, Joseph Kozil, and Vincent Obara; (third row) Sobestyan Matuszek, Peter Teczar, Wladyslaw Prejsnar, J. Cyganiewicz, Joseph Gniade, a Mr. Korlacki (leader), Joseph Sabicki, Anthony Szarek, Frank Teczar, and Joseph Mika.

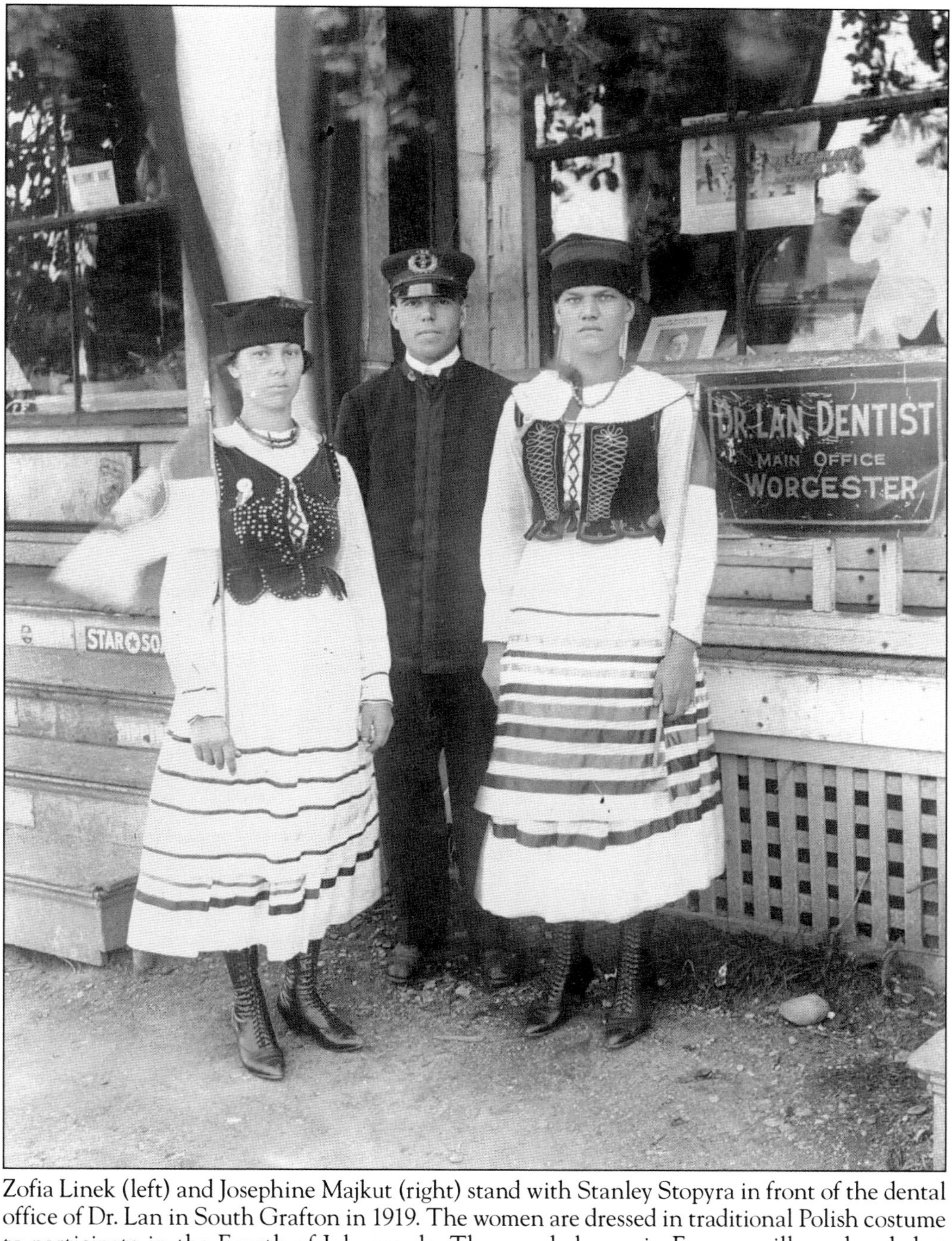

Zofia Linek (left) and Josephine Majkut (right) stand with Stanley Stopyra in front of the dental office of Dr. Lan in South Grafton in 1919. The women are dressed in traditional Polish costume to participate in the Fourth of July parade. The parade began in Farnumsville and ended at Fisherville Ball Park. (Courtesy of the Rawinski family.)

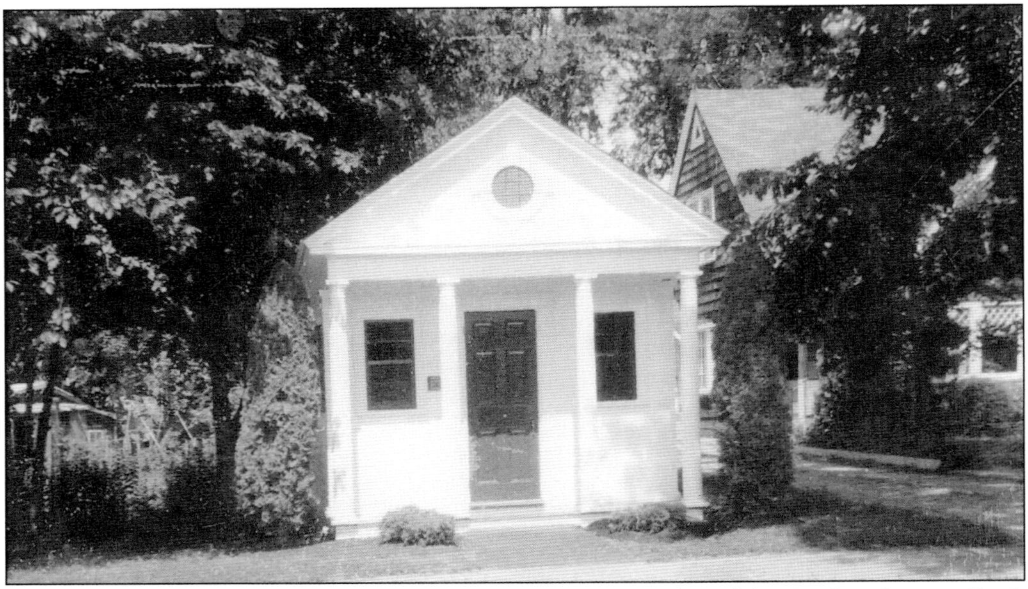

Built in the 1930s between Cross and Collette Streets, this replica of the Grafton Savings Bank served as a branch facility for the mill workers of South Grafton. When it was no longer needed as a branch bank, it was purchased by the Grafton Historical Society, moved to Upton Road, and used as the society's headquarters. In 2012, it was moved to the South Grafton Mills Park.

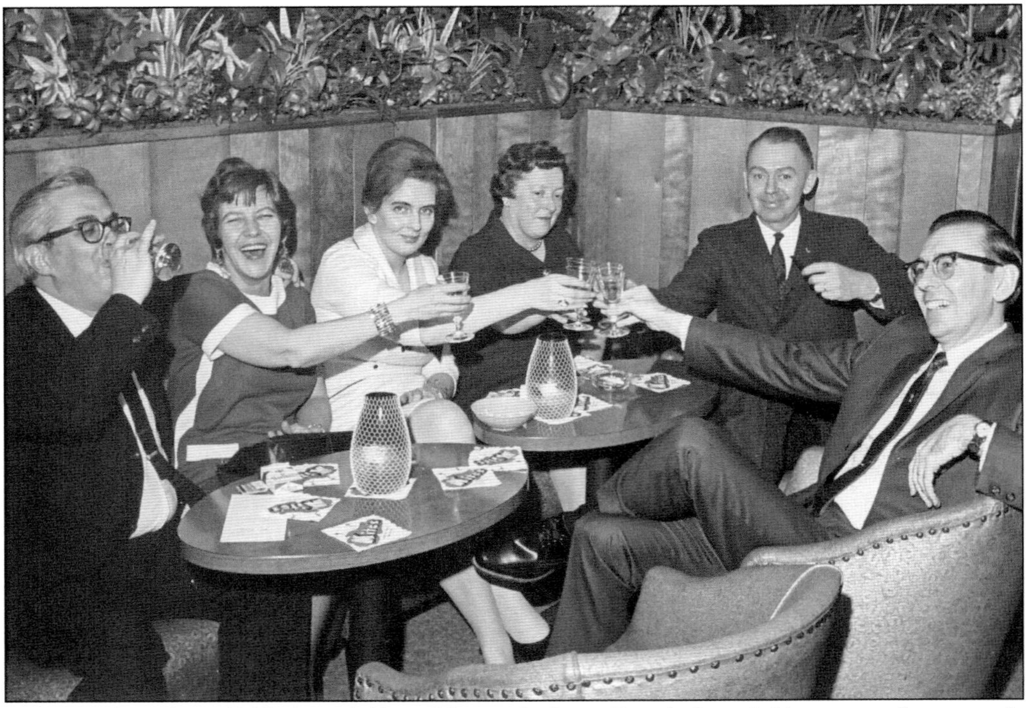

Writer Bob Wilson (fifth from left) and his wife, Jane (fourth from left), enjoy a dinner with friends at Kite's Steakhouse on Ferry Street. The restaurant, opened in 1938 by Lucien S. "Kite" Morin, featured lobsters, steaks on hot skillets, and flaming desserts, all served by waiters in red jackets. It also boasted a mural painted by noted Grafton artist Bernard Corey. The restaurant burned in 1975 and was never rebuilt.

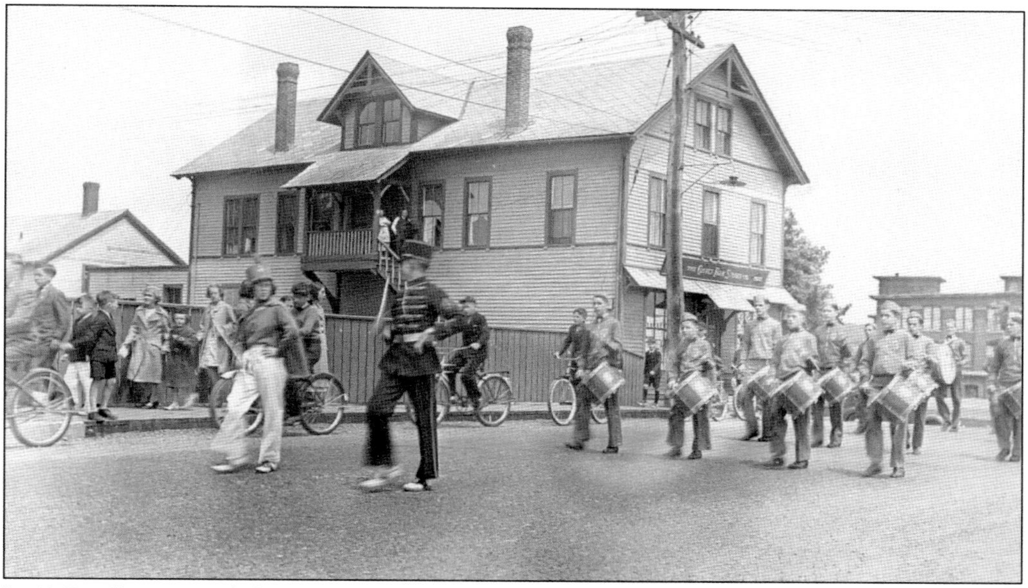

In 1945, villagers watch from the sidewalks as a parade marches past Clover Farms Market, operated by the Guilmette brothers. The building was originally the A.L. Fisher store.

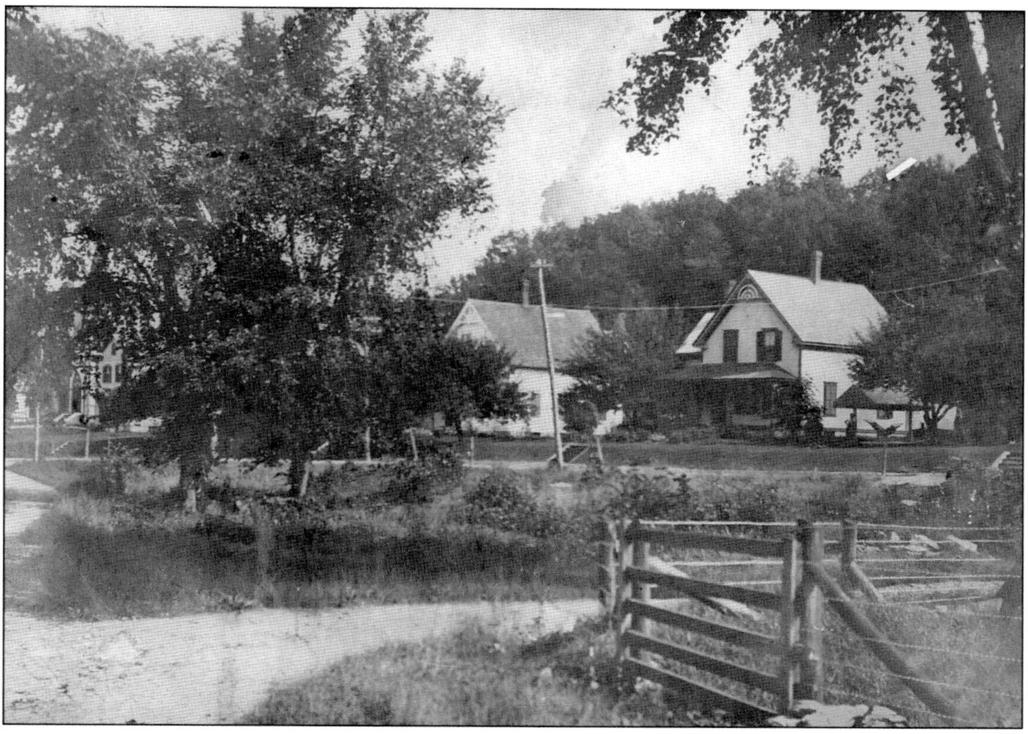

Sampson Park is shown here as it looked in 1910. The house seen across the street is 101 Main Street. In 1922, the town developed the park and placed there an oval granite monument to Grafton servicemen who died in World War I. Joseph Sampson (1893–1918) is one of those honored, and the park was named for him. (Courtesy of Carolynne Grimley.)

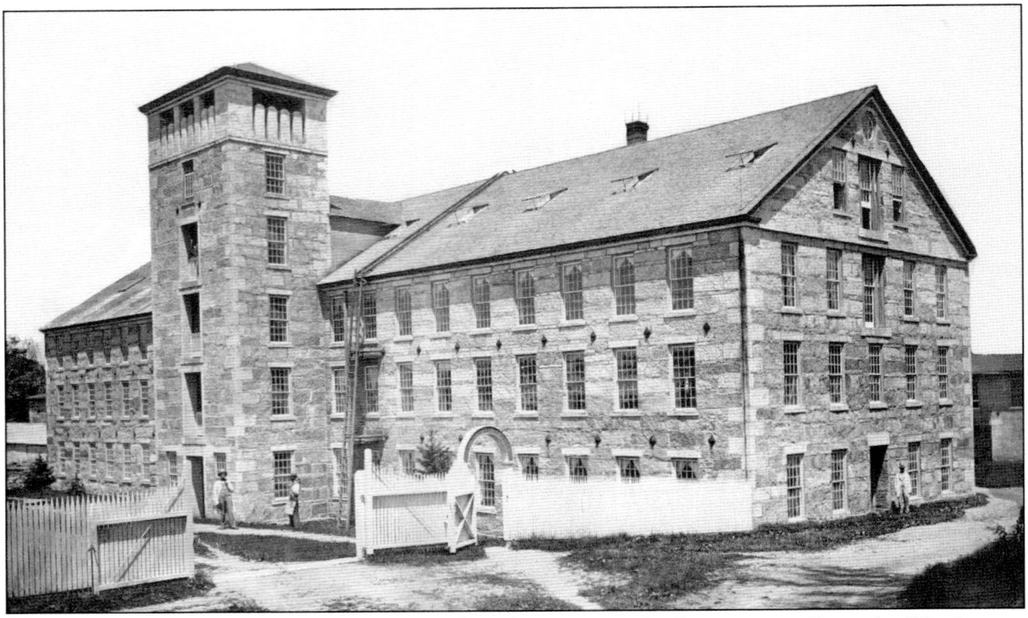

In 1835, the Saunders brothers, Esek, Israel, and Benjamin, built a stone mill on the Blackstone River. By 1880, the Saunders Cotton Mill Company employed over 200 workers, mostly Irish and French. The village that grew up around the mill had 50 houses, a gristmill, a blacksmith shop, a wheelwright shop, a school, a store, a library, and a church. The mill also owned two private residences and a 200-acre farm.

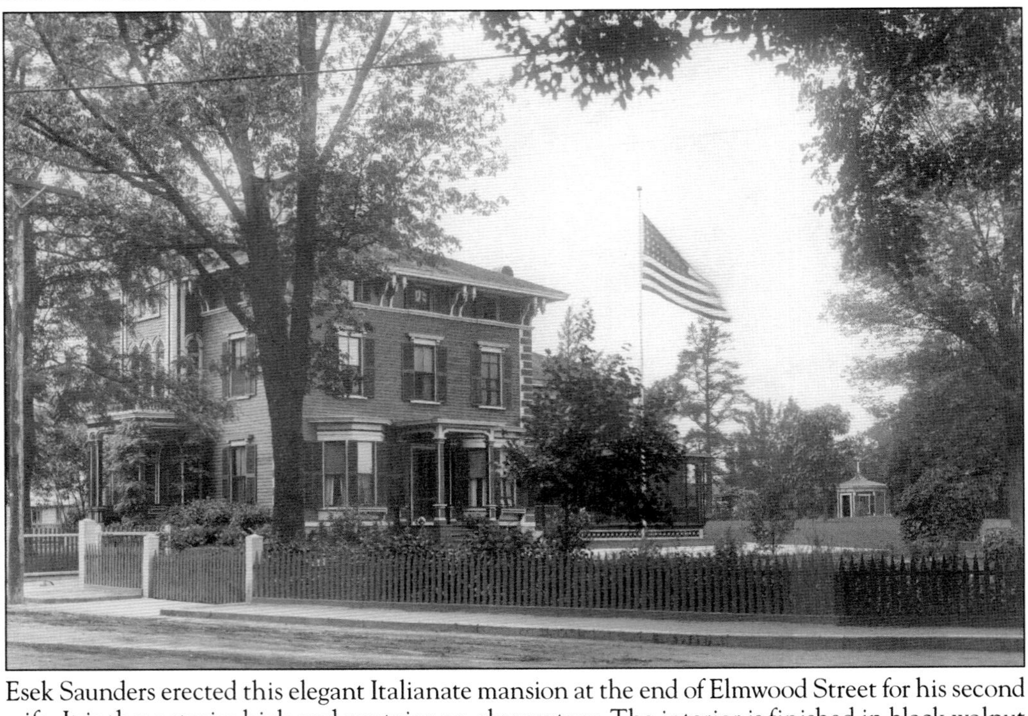

Esek Saunders erected this elegant Italianate mansion at the end of Elmwood Street for his second wife. It is three stories high and contains an observatory. The interior is finished in black walnut and chestnut. To pay for this extravagance, Saunders was forced to sell his shares in the mill. In the 20th century, the mansion served as the Carroll R. Gochie Funeral Home.

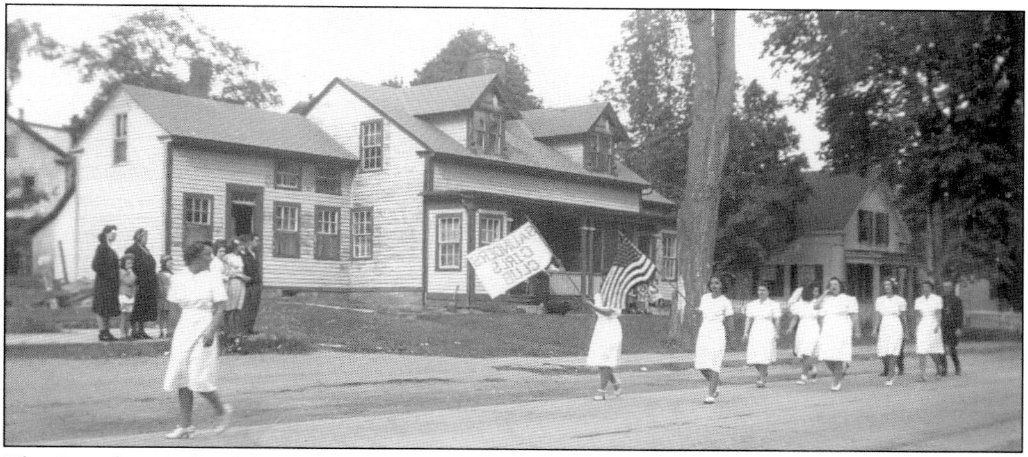

The Saunders Girls Club marches along Main Street in the 1942 Fourth of July parade. Patriotism was very high at this time.

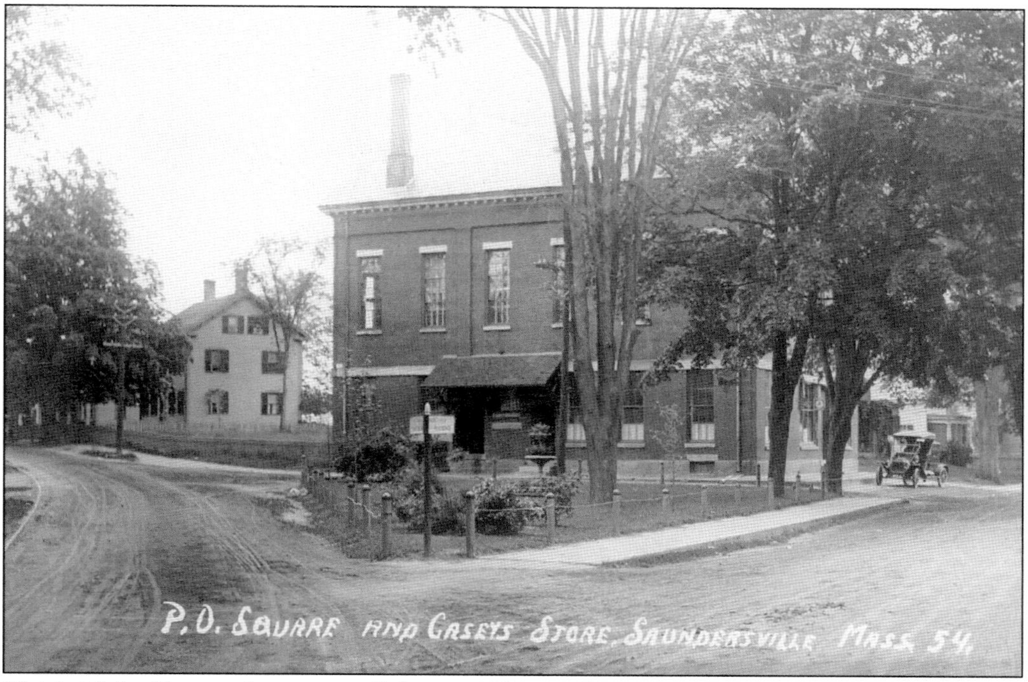

This brick building at the corner of Main and Elmwood Streets was constructed in 1857. In 1891, Maurice Casey bought the building and established a general store. In 1893, when he became postmaster of Saundersville, the store served as the post office as well. The building was destroyed in the hurricane of 1938.

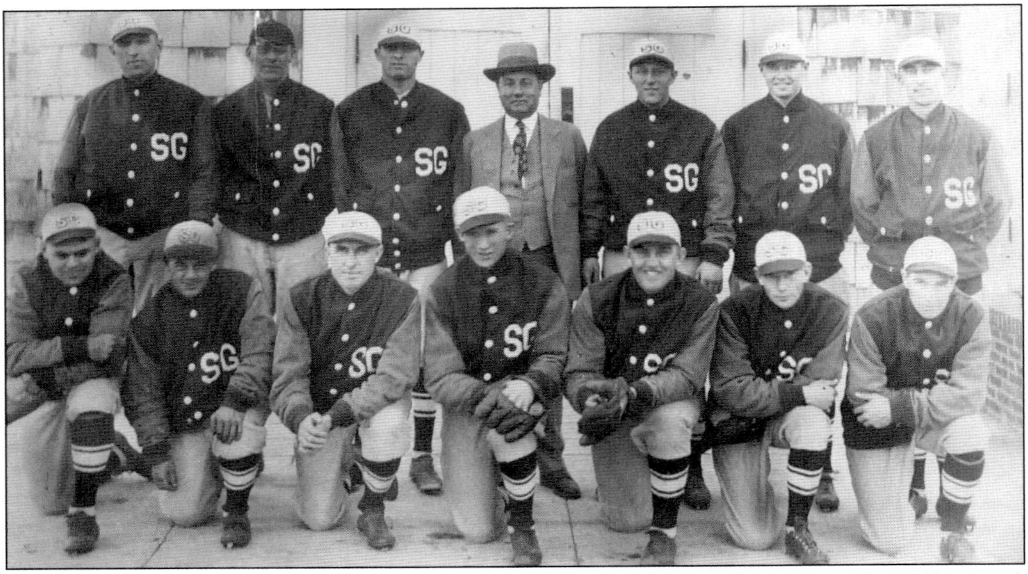

The 1927 South Grafton baseball team poses with their coach. From left to right are (first row) G. Daoust, H. Tessier, A. White, J. Wheelden, C. Carroll, E. Hinchcliffe, and I. Bigler; (second row) U. Courlard, J. Jowett, W. Ruggario, H.H. Daw, E. Desautels, A. Clarke, and H. Kearnan. Games were held at Fisherville Ball Park, where local residents would fill most of the grandstand.

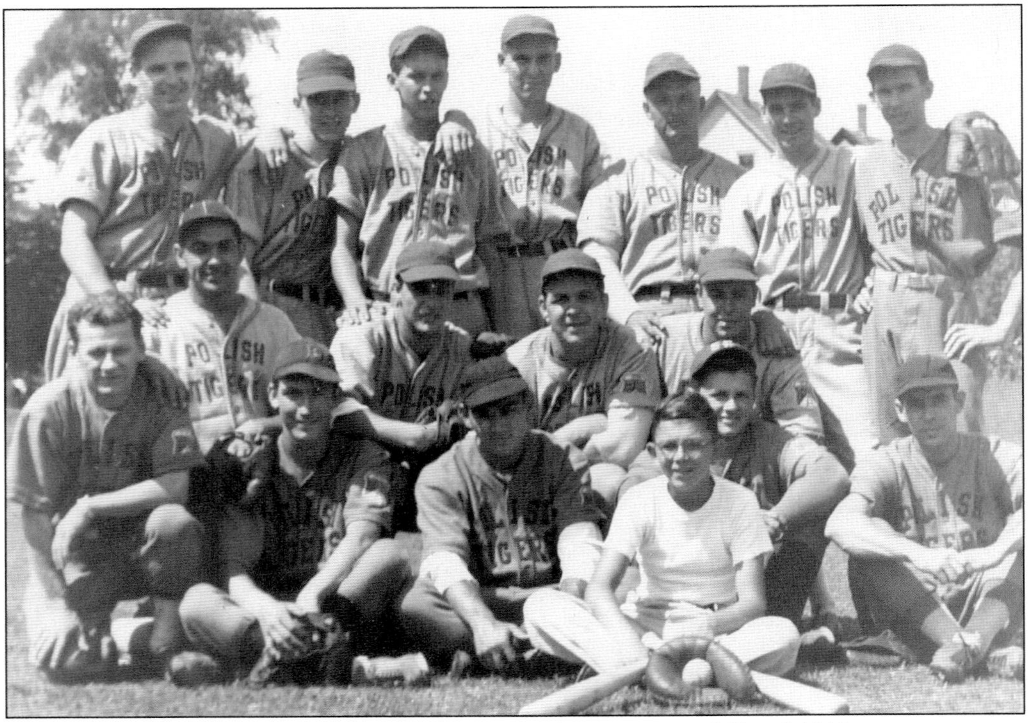

The South Grafton Polish Tigers, MacBen League champions in 1947 and 1948, was an amateur baseball team formed by Walter Such in 1927. From left to right are (first row) coach Joe Pastor, George Kuras, Ed Duda, Noel Lebeau (batboy), Leo Cadrin, and Larry Labrie; (second row) Joe Valente, assistant coach John Matuszek, Russell Dumas, and John Farrell; (third row) Stanley Baker, two unidentified, Louis Alexander, Frank Silum, Gagne Gribauskas, and Vincent Gribauskas.

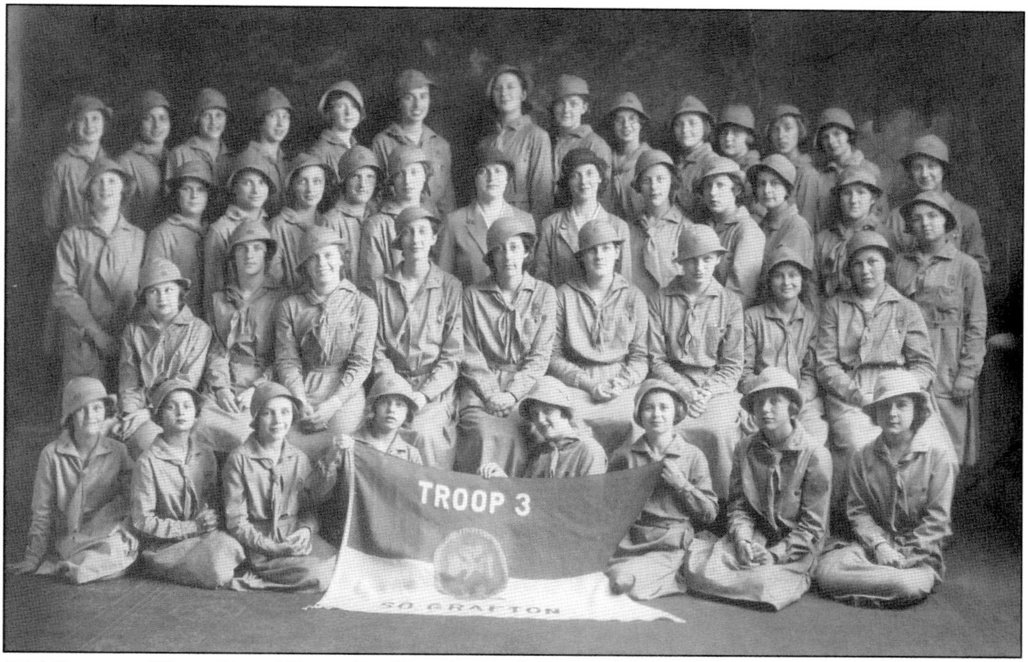

Girl Scouts of Pine Cone Troop 3 of South Grafton are shown in this 1934 photograph. Lillian Boutiettte Dziembowski was a member of this troop and is seen in the third row, third from the right. (Courtesy of Lillian Boutiette Dziembowski.)

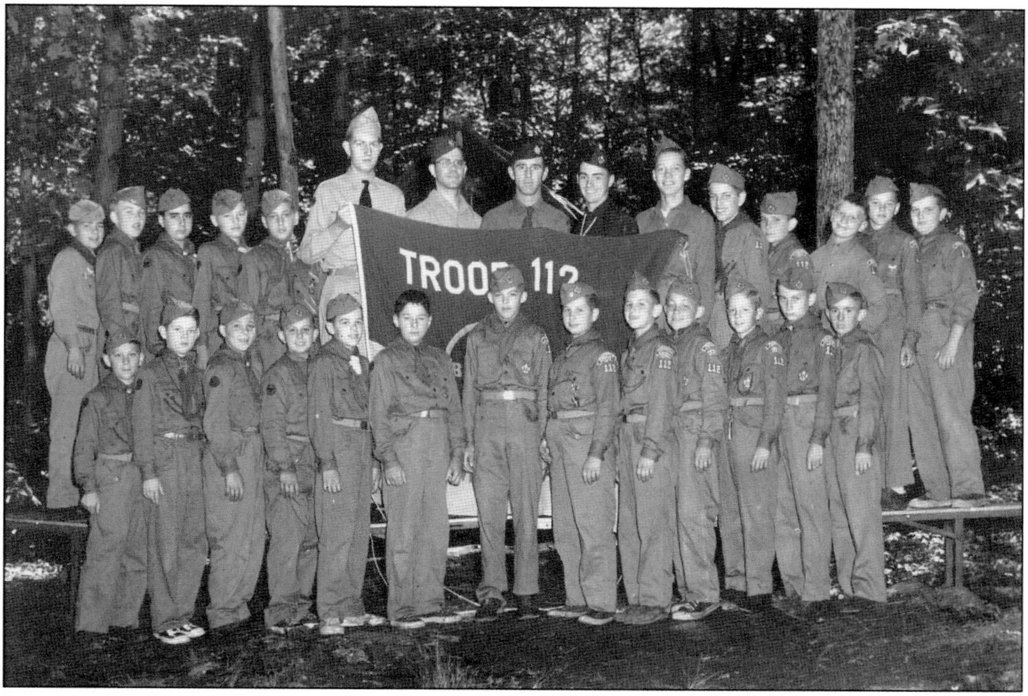

Boy Scout troops served Grafton for many years in all three sections of town. Here, Troop 112 from South Grafton poses for a photograph. The Scouts were involved in many community service activities. Clarence Gendron is in the first row at far left; Abbott Mongeau is fourth from the right in the first row, and Edward Casey is at far right in the second row.

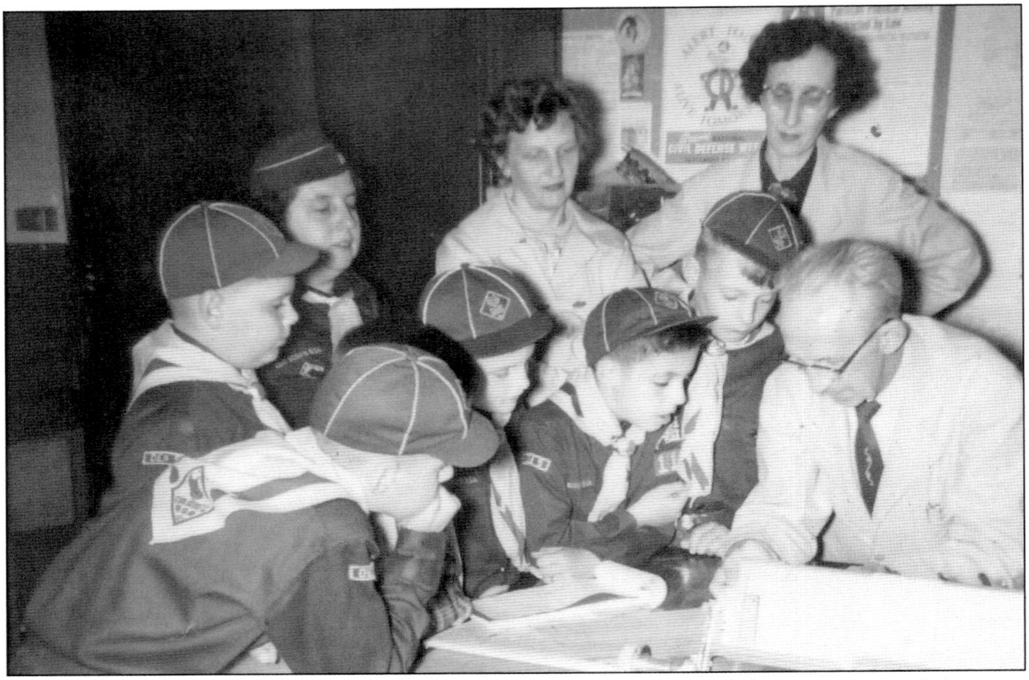

Arthur Boutiette and Lillian Boutiette Dziembowski (upper right) give a tour of the post office to a group of Cub Scouts. Before 1960, each South Grafton village had its own post office. In 1960, they were merged into one post office located in the old Fisherville Mill office building. In 1961, Boutiette was appointed postmaster and Dziembowski was appointed assistant postmaster. In 1963, Dziembowski became Grafton's first female postmaster. (Courtesy of Lillian Boutiette Dziembowski.)

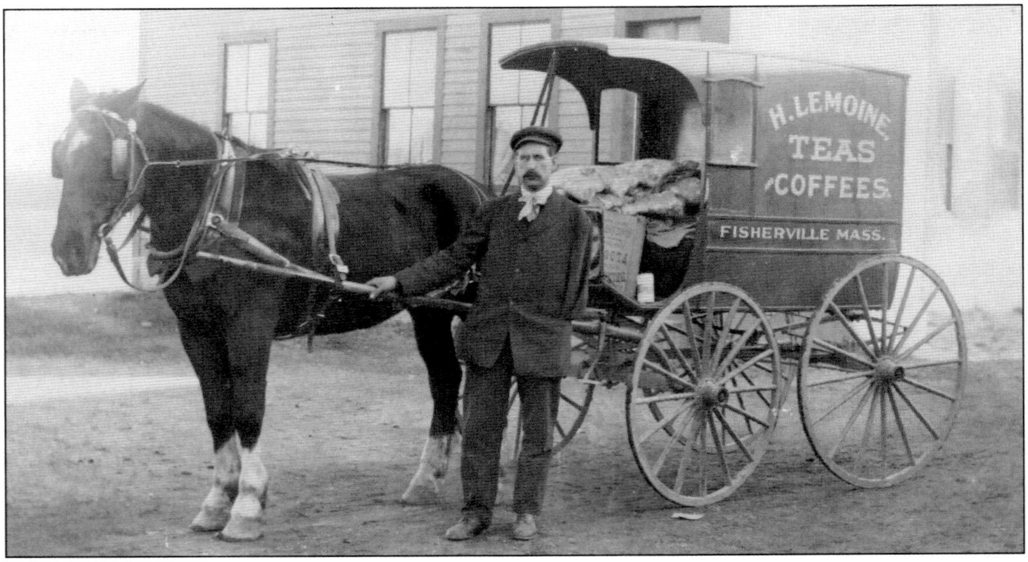

Hormidas Lemoine Sr. (1878–1928) emigrated from Canada as a child and lived in Grafton from 1900 until 1920. He was a day laborer at the Wilkinson Mill but lost his left arm in a mill accident around 1901. Between 1903 and 1918, he was a tea and coffee agent, selling his products from this delivery wagon. In the 1950s, the Lemoine family ran Lemoine's Variety Store in Farnumsville. (Courtesy of Joseph Lemoine.)

Six

SCHOOLS

Grafton's first schoolhouse was built in 1731 near the common to accommodate children of the first settlers, as well as the local natives. By the 1840s, there were 11 one-room schoolhouses scattered throughout the town. Roads being of poor quality and transportation slow, schools needed to be close to the students. Each school district maintained its own school building on donated land. Initially, each district funded its own school. All grades were taught together with one teacher. There was little training for teachers, discipline was a big problem, and many teachers quit in defeat. In 1869, the town took over the running of the schools and bought all the school buildings for $16,000.

In the early 1800s, the mills employed large numbers of children, preventing them from attending school. In 1873, when a state law was passed requiring school attendance for children aged 7 to 15, school participation increased. To accommodate more students, elementary schools were built in each village: Norcross School on North Street in the Center, Perry Hill School in North Grafton, Saundersville School on Pleasant Street, and Farnumsville and Fisherville schools on Main Street. Most students attended school only until they reached age 15.

The first high school was established in 1838 in the basement of the Congregational Church. Fourteen students attended. In 1850, Grafton Academy was opened at 8 Worcester Street as a public high school. By 1900, enrollment had increased, and the town erected a new building at 35 Worcester Street. The old building became the Grange Hall. After 1900, Grafton High School introduced courses in practical arts: accounting, secretarial skills, drafting, metalwork, woodwork, mechanics, and the household arts of cooking and sewing. The high school building at 35 Worcester Street served the community until 1952 when a new Memorial Junior Senior High School was constructed on Providence Road. It is now the Grafton Municipal Center.

Grafton High School, attended by students from all sections of town, played a major role in unifying the town. Children in Grafton attended neighborhood schools until eighth grade and most had never met students from other sections of Grafton until they reached high school. Attending classes, playing sports, and going to school dances with students from other villages were all experiences that helped to break down barriers between sections of town.

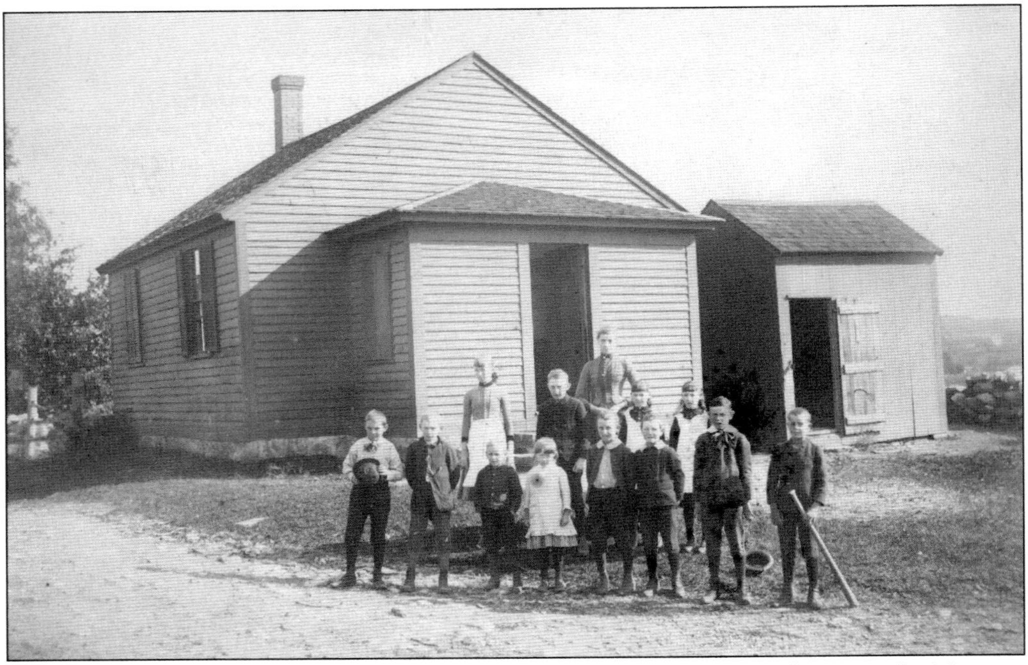

Catherine Worcester poses in 1889 with her pupils at the one-room schoolhouse in the Merriam District. A privy can be seen beside it. There were 11 schoolhouses established in Grafton by the 1840s. Schoolhouses were built close to student homes because most children walked to school. Sanitation was a constant problem in these schools.

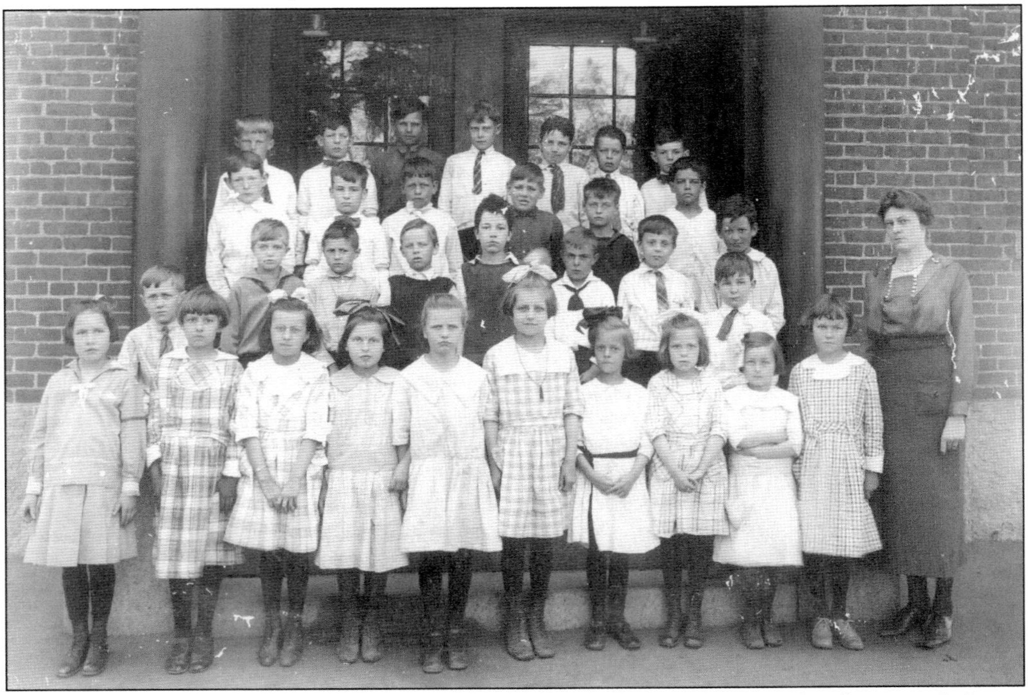

Teacher Jeanette Struthers poses with her second grade class at Norcross School on North Street in 1922. In 1896, the state police ordered better ventilation at the brick school, and a new wing was added, as well as modern toilets, in the basement.

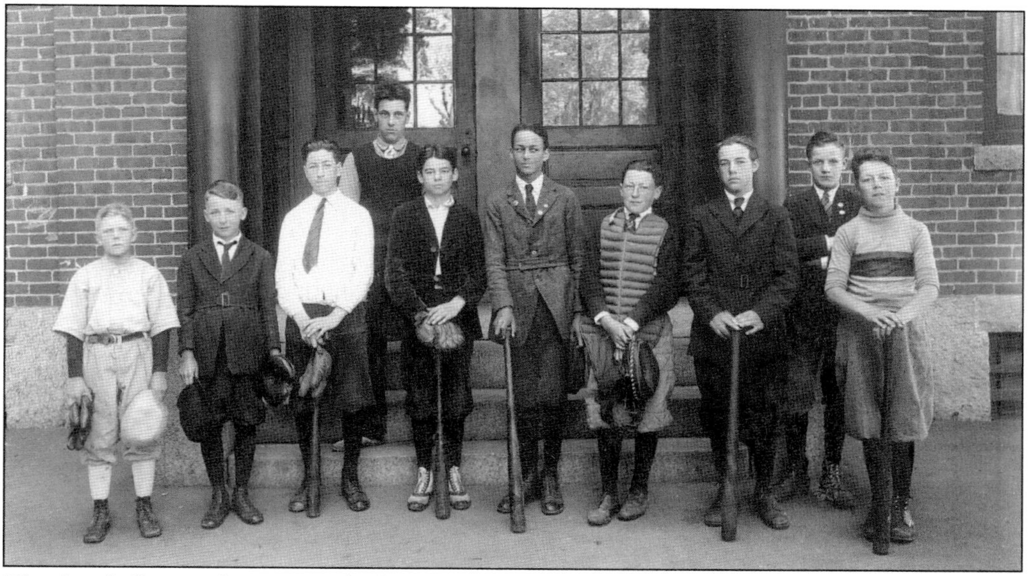

This baseball team lines up with their coach in front of the school for a photograph in 1920. The boys are seventh and eighth grade students at Norcross School. The school was named for D. Webster Norcross, who served on the school committee for 33 years (1869–1904) and who initiated major improvements to the Grafton educational system.

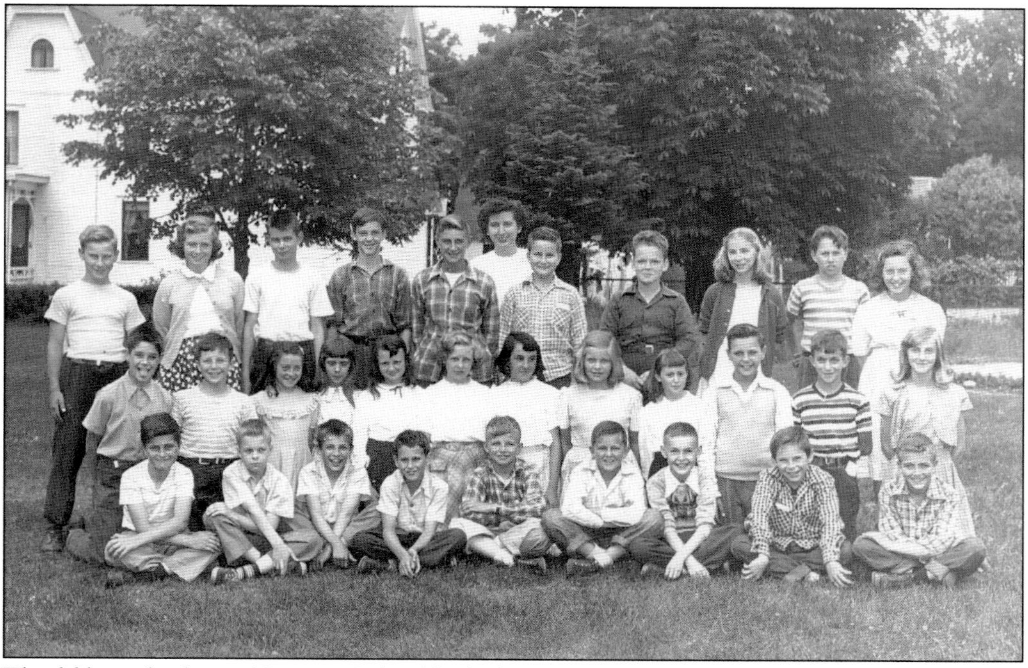

The fifth grade class at Norcross School looks happy as they pose on the side lawn of the school. This photograph was taken in 1946. (Courtesy of William Fiske.)

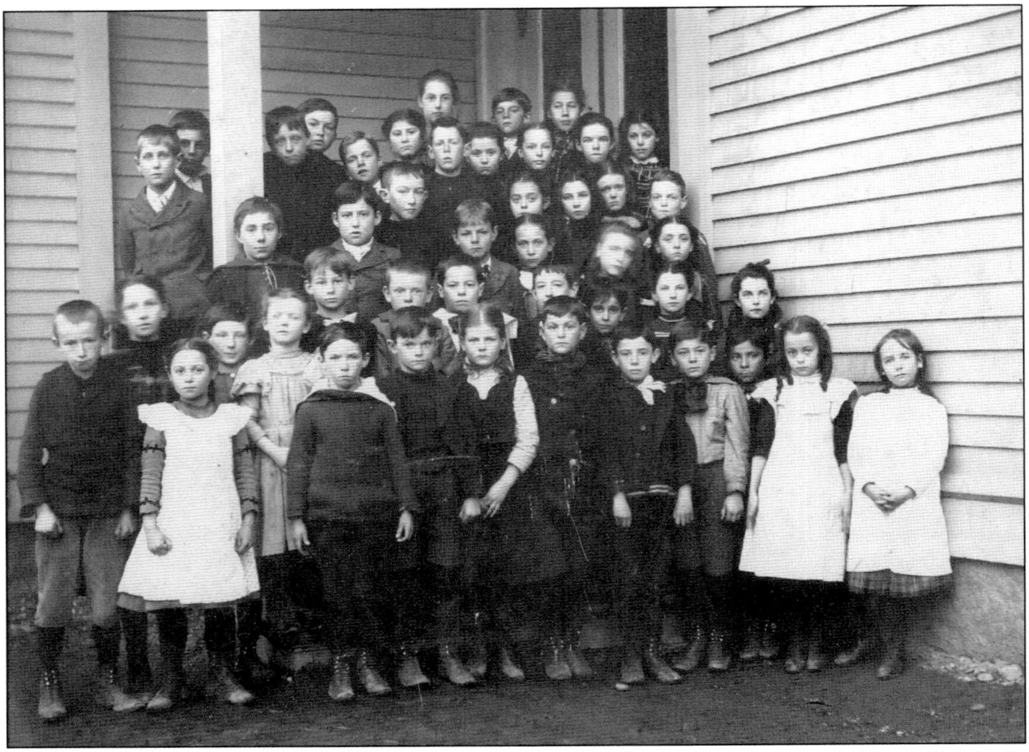

This first grade class at Perry Hill School in 1898 included many immigrant children. Elizabeth Dickson (first row, far right) came with her family from Scotland in 1892 to join relatives working in the mills and businesses of North Grafton. (Courtesy of Elizabeth Stinson.)

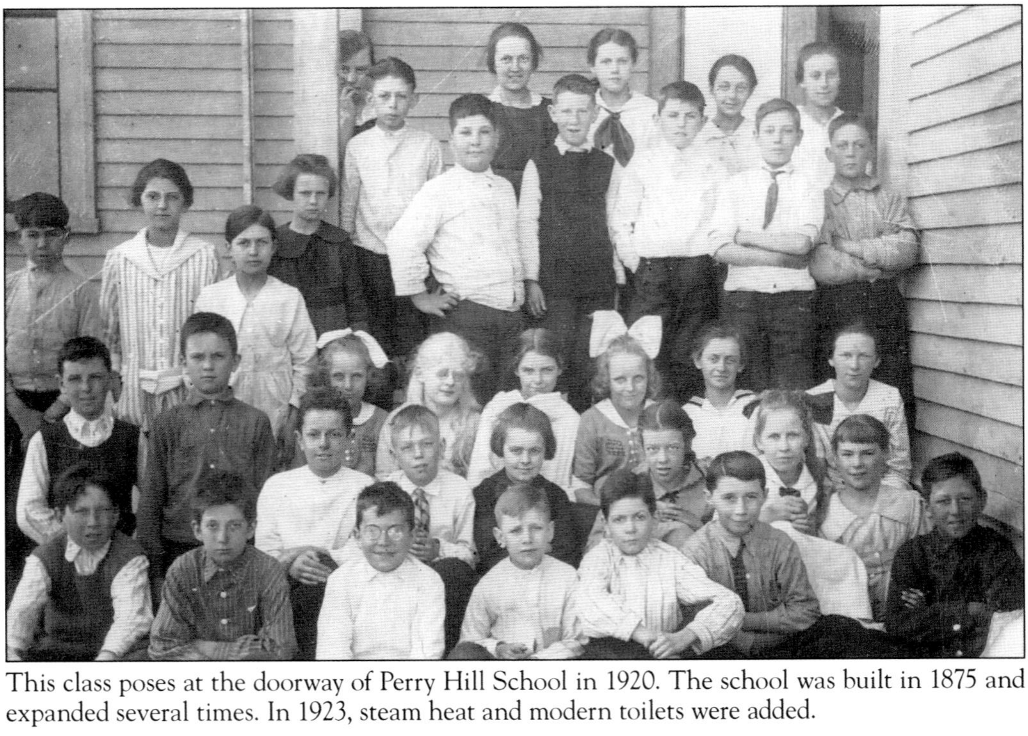

This class poses at the doorway of Perry Hill School in 1920. The school was built in 1875 and expanded several times. In 1923, steam heat and modern toilets were added.

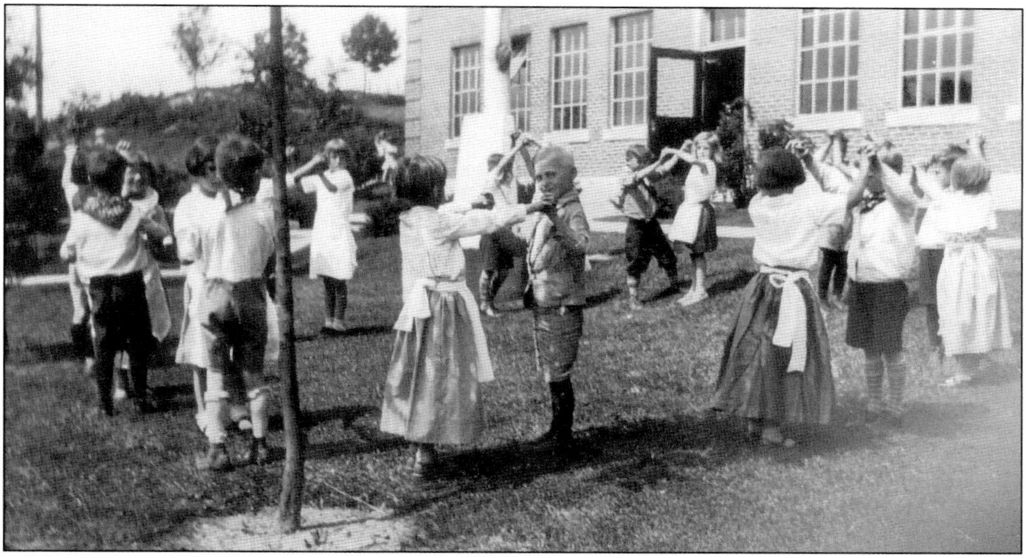

Children at Harding Street School in Farnumsville play London Bridge on the playground. This photograph dates from the 1940s.

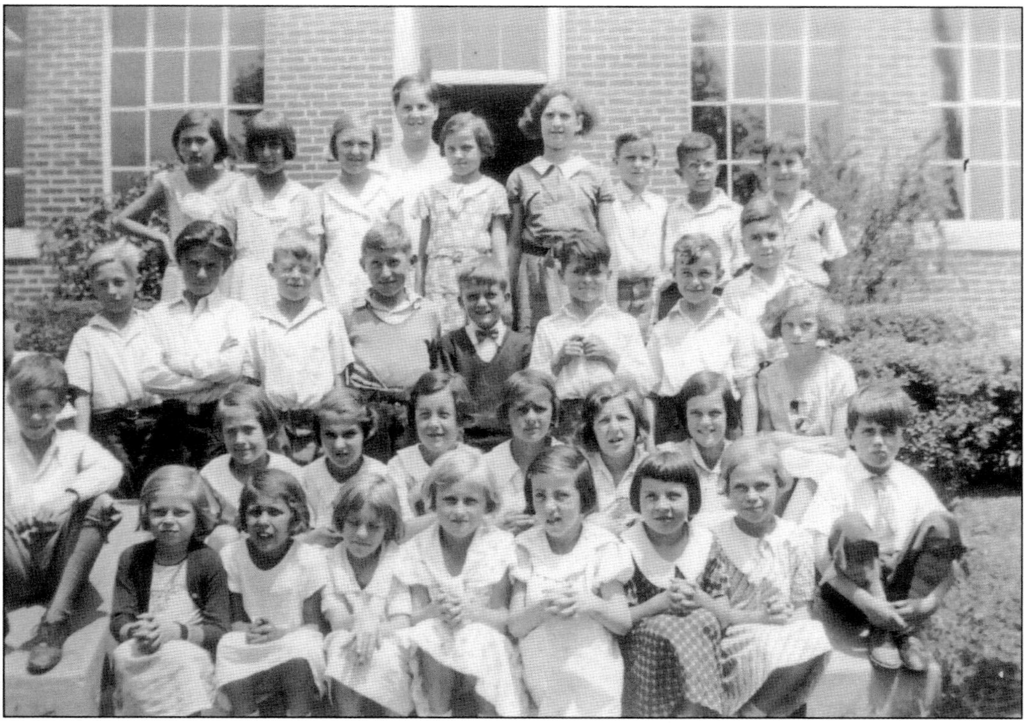

Students at Harding Street School pose for a photograph in front of the school in the 1950s. The school was later converted into an apartment complex.

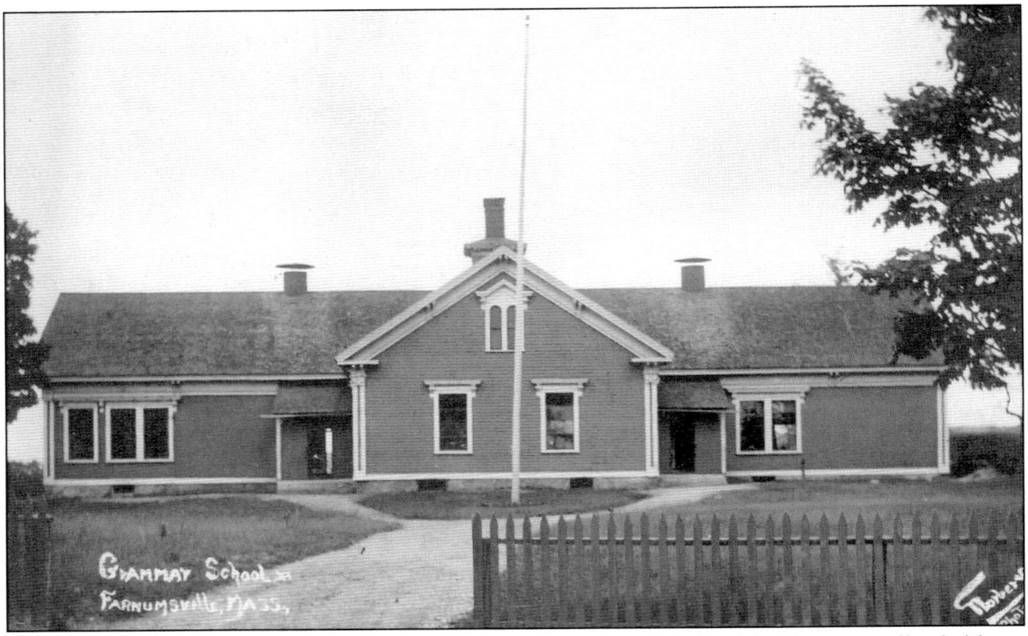

This building, constructed before 1884, served as the grammar school for Farnumsville children. It was shaped like a Maltese cross and had separate entrances for boys and girls. In 1922, toilets were installed in the basement, and a skylight was added to the center of the building to let in more light. In 1936, the school was closed. It is now the South Grafton Community House.

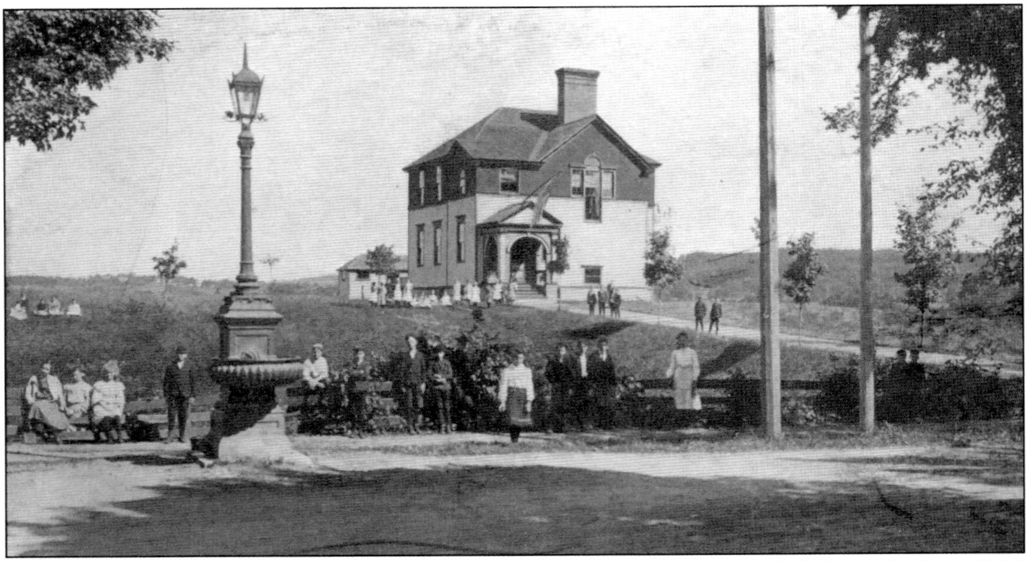

This postcard of Fisherville School shows the school before it was expanded. It was built in 1900 as a two-room structure. In 1908, two rooms were added, and in 1921 four additional rooms were added, as well as stairwells, steam heat, and modern toilets. Immigrants attended evening classes here to learn the English language and to work toward their American citizenship status.

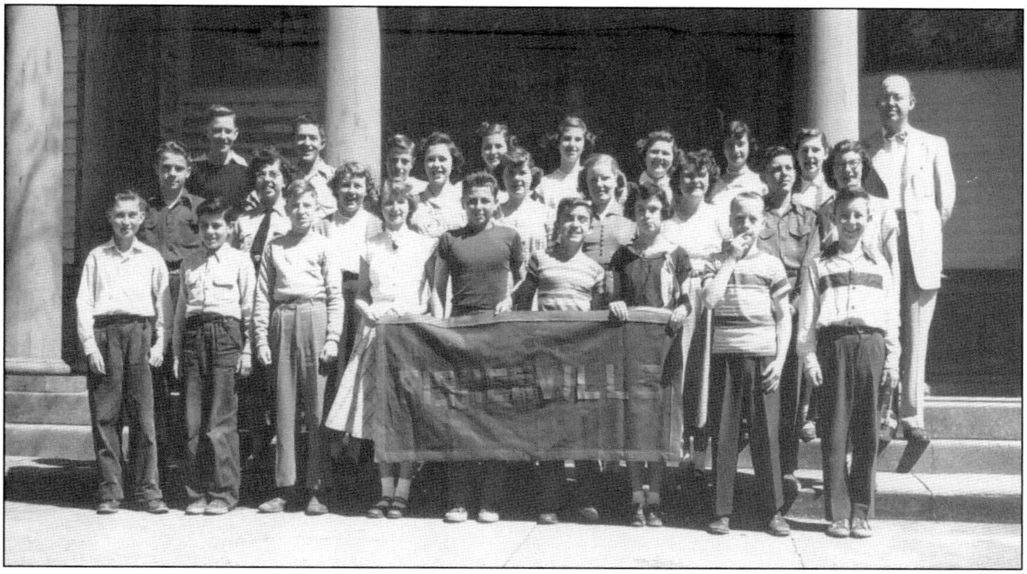

The students in grade eight at Fisherville School in 1951 pose for a photograph. John Russell is the teacher.

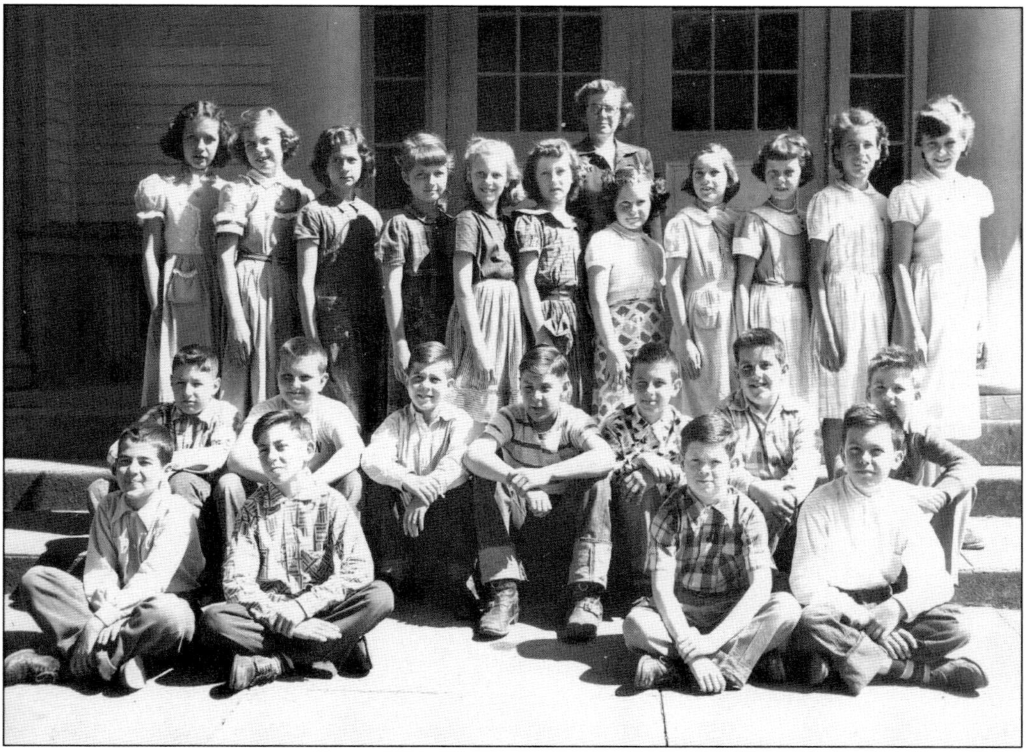

Julia Cota's fifth grade class at Fisherville School poses for a class picture in 1953. From left to right are (first row) James May, Carl Vincent, William Dowd, and Peter Millette; (second row): Richard Gosselin, Edward Casey, William Rose, Albert Miranda, Robert Girouard, Edward Parent, and Bruce Tessier; (third row) Loretta Benoit, Nancy Hospod, Genevieve Hisoire, Carole Amour, Rita Jones, Marilyn Wenc, Barbara Beaudoin, Lorraine Leger, Judy Barnes, Lorraine May, and Charlotte Hefferman.

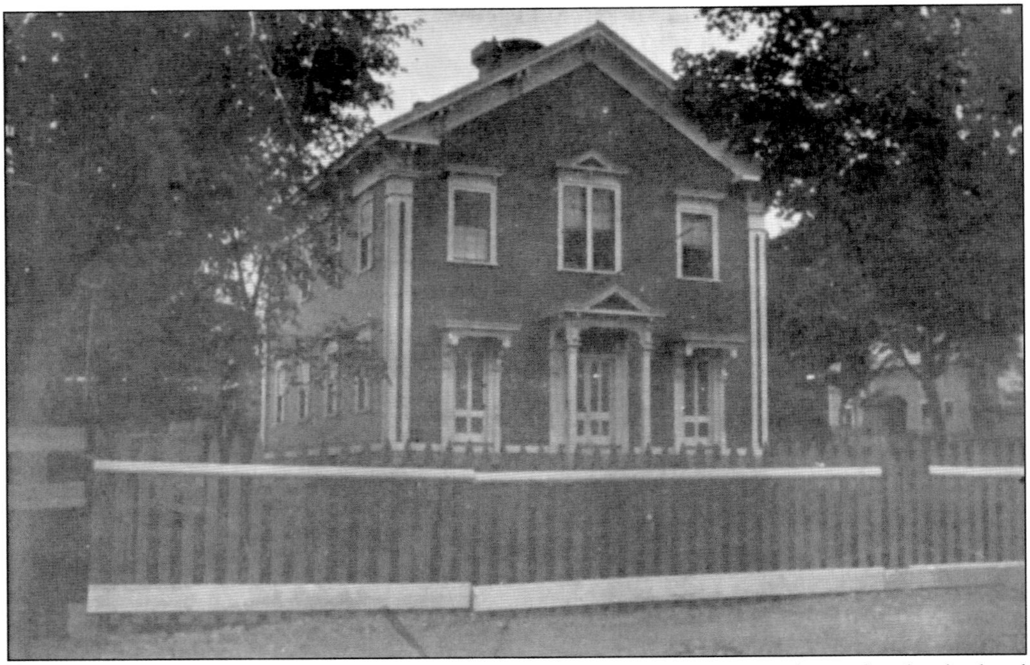

The Saundersville schoolhouse is believed to have been built in 1869 and was the third school for that village. It replaced an earlier structure on Elmwood Street built by Esek Saunders in 1837. The first schoolhouse was bought, moved, and converted to tenements by Saunders and is now a residence at the corner of Gristmill Road. In 1895, the Saundersville School had an enrollment of 67 students.

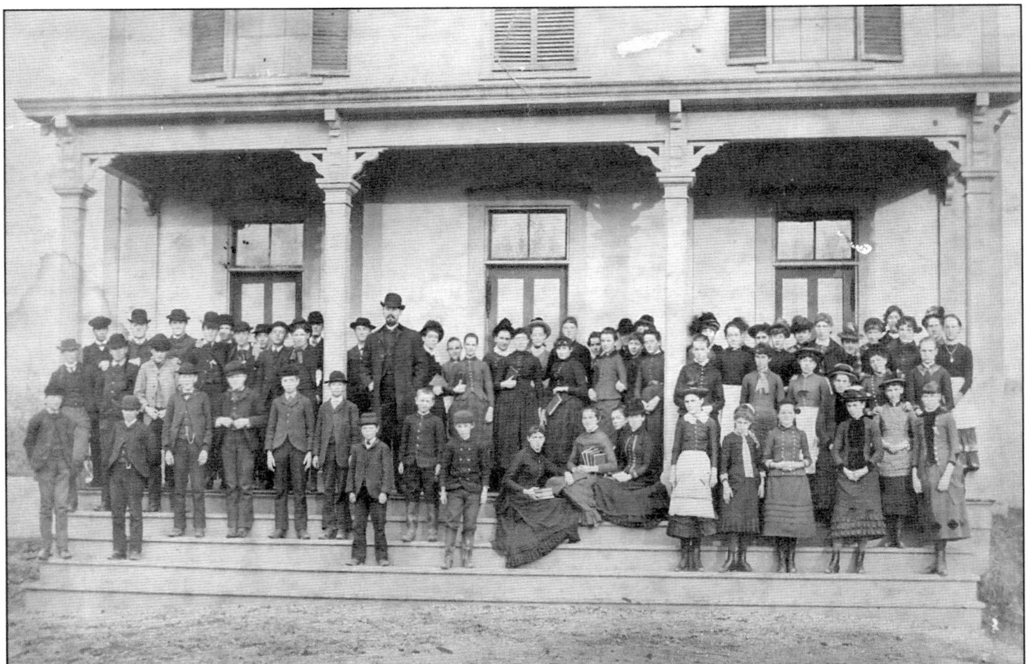

A group of high school students stands on the porch of Grafton High School with principal John B. Scott in 1885. Several of the girls are holding textbooks.

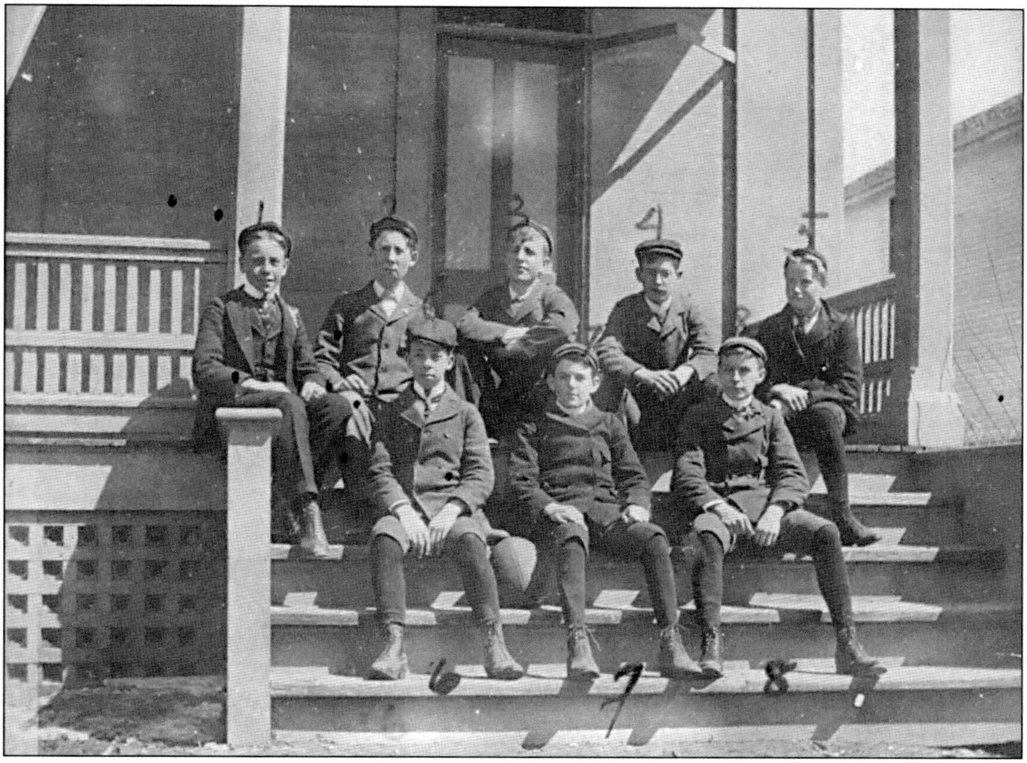

These boys sit on the steps of the first Grafton High School building in 1897. In 1900, when the town built a new high school at 32 Worcester Street, this structure was sold to the Grafton Grange.

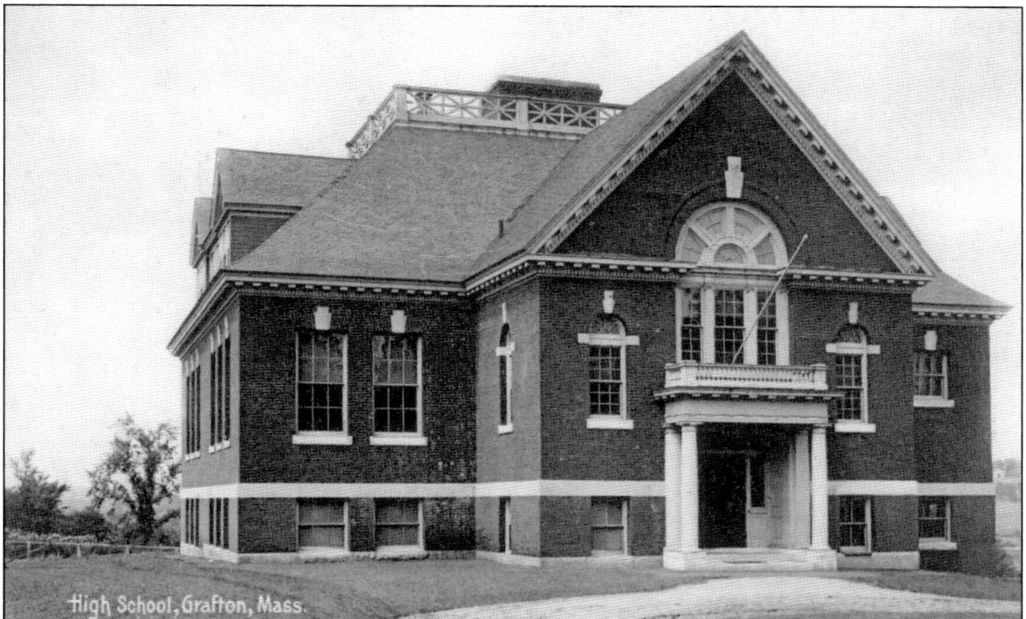

In 1900, this building was constructed on a site on Worcester Street. It served as Grafton High School for 50 years until a new school for grades 7 through 12 was built on Providence Road in 1952. This building was then used for a variety of classes from Norcross School.

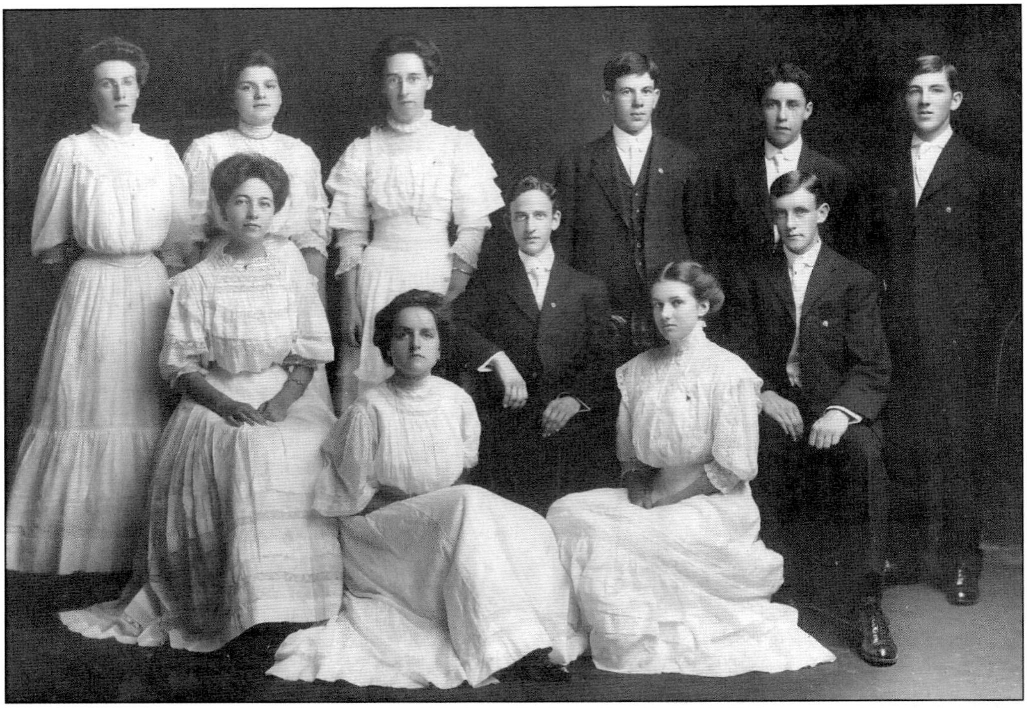

The Grafton High School class of 1908 sits for their graduation photograph. Included in this group (in no particular order) are Nina MacKenzie, Lucy Adams, Florence Small, Edith Webster, Sylvia Hutchinson, Caro Fletcher, David Fleming, James Fleming, Raymond Johnson, George Martin, and Irving Woodcock.

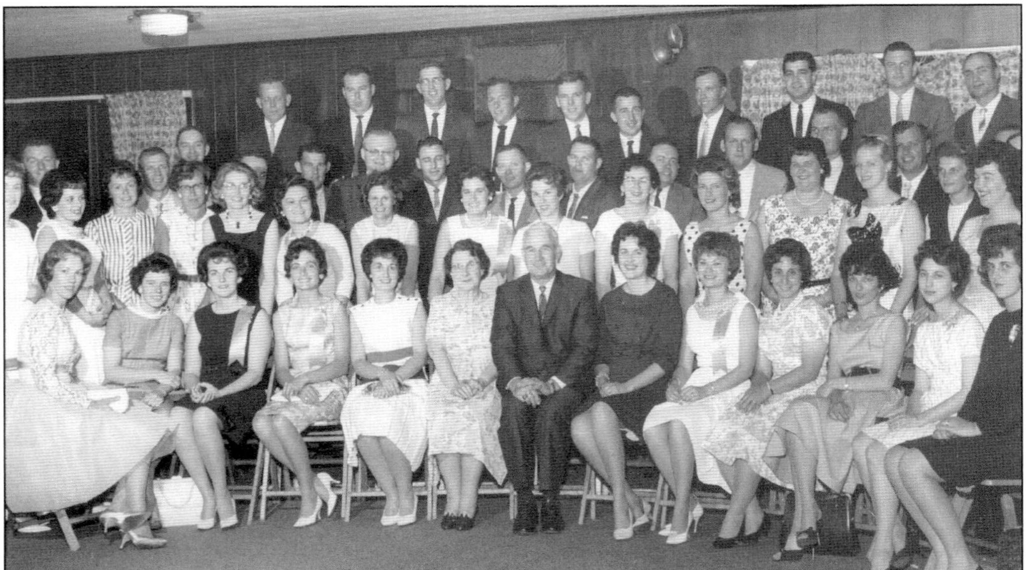

The Grafton High School class of 1953 is gathered at the Driftwood Restaurant for their 10th reunion. Ruth Gordon, a teacher for many years at the high school, and school principal James Dorsey were class advisors and are seated sixth and seventh from left in the first row.

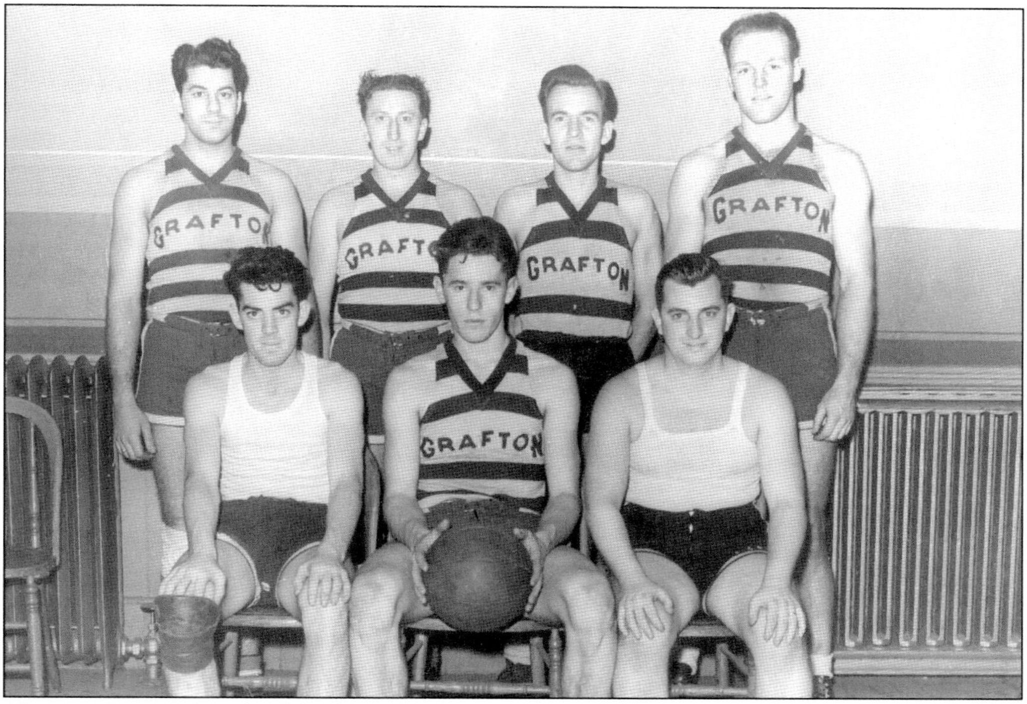

The Grafton High School basketball team of 1938 is shown here. From left to right are (first row) Charles Wade, Emmet Ludy, and ? Gadbois; (second row) Clayton Holland, Albert Banks, Charles Fulton, and George Kuck.

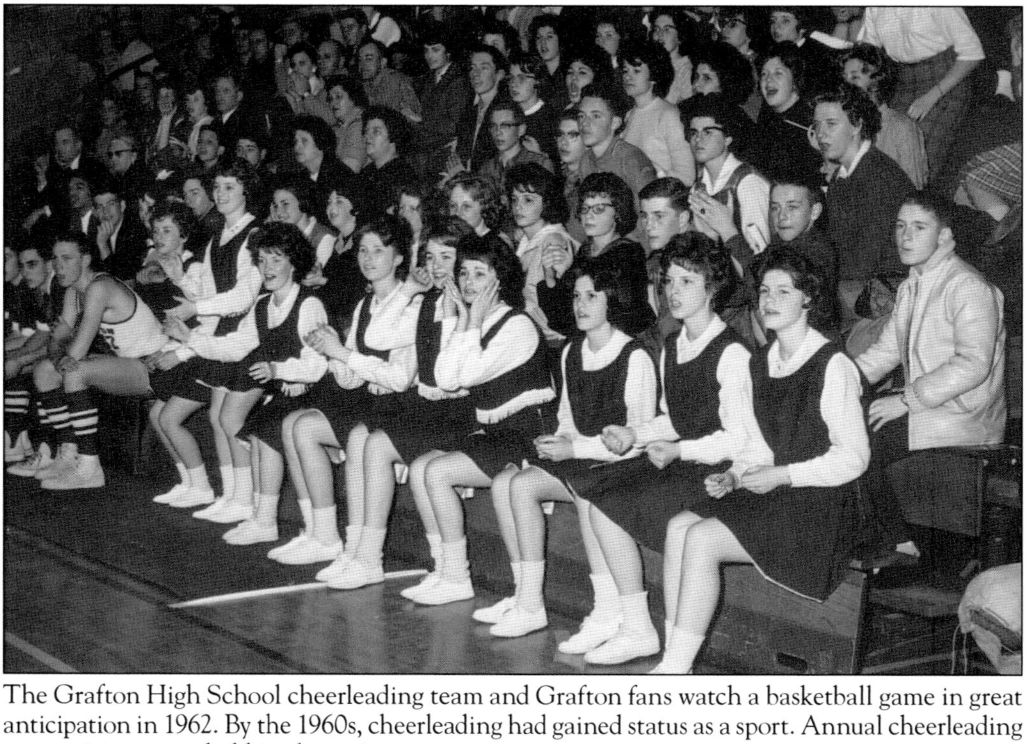

The Grafton High School cheerleading team and Grafton fans watch a basketball game in great anticipation in 1962. By the 1960s, cheerleading had gained status as a sport. Annual cheerleading competitions were held in the region.

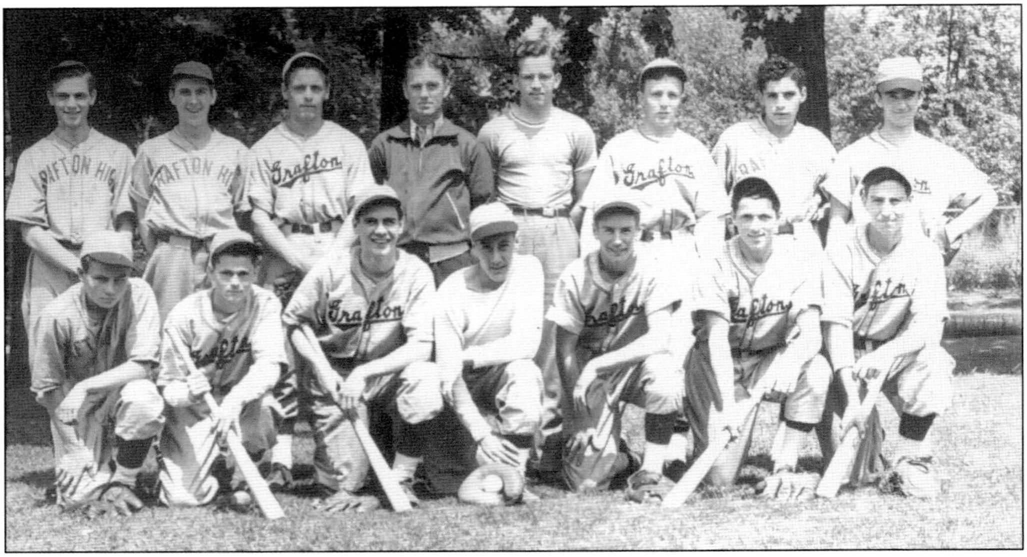

The Grafton High School baseball team is shown here in 1940. The coach, Leon Hamil, was a teacher at the high school.

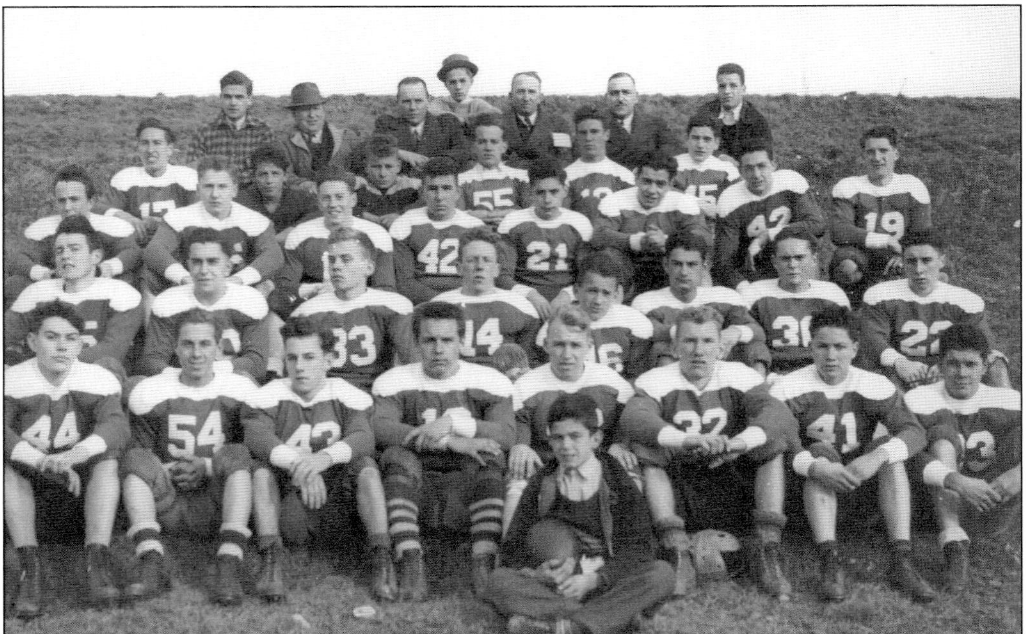

The Grafton High School football team is pictured in 1940. Matthew Smith (third from left) and George Jordan Jr. (fourth from left) are seated in the second row. George Jordan Sr. is in the back row with the other coaches.

Seven

Coming Together

From the early days of settlement, local residents maintained a deep loyalty to their villages. By mid-20th century, however, the community began to see itself as one town. A single high school had a unifying effect. Civic organizations brought Grafton residents together, encouraging them to work in unison for charitable purposes. Celebrations, wars, and natural disasters provided opportunities for cooperation and unity.

The residents of Grafton came together to celebrate town anniversaries and other happy occasions. Celebrating Grafton's founding has always been very special. These events included historic pageants, parades, plays, firemen musters, orations, ceremonies, banquets, balls, and dances. Residents from all the villages participated, helping to promote town unity.

World War II transformed the country and Grafton with it. Enlisted men and women traveled to far countries. The folks at home, too, saw a larger world as they followed war events playing out around the globe. As Grafton united behind the local men and women serving in the war, village loyalties faded. A bronze plaque with the names of all Grafton's World War II participants was placed in the new Grafton Memorial Junior Senior High School in 1952.

Civic organizations played a key role in building a more cohesive community. The Kiwanis, the Masons, the King's Daughters, the Odd Fellows, and many others called upon residents to work together toward economic, compassionate, or charitable goals. The Grafton District Nursing Association cared for those in need no matter where they lived.

When disasters struck, residents helped and consoled each other. The hurricane that hit Grafton in 1938 did considerable damage to all sections of town. The roof of the Fisherville Mill was blown off, trees around Grafton Common were uprooted, the steeple of the Evangelical Congregational Church was blown off and fell into the sanctuary, greenhouses were shattered, many homes were damaged, and two men were killed. Folks from all sections of town worked together to put things right.

Unity did not come easily. Village loyalties were very strong. However, in 280 years, Grafton has evolved from a cluster of small villages scattered along its waterways to become a cohesive community where its residents think of themselves as "from Grafton."

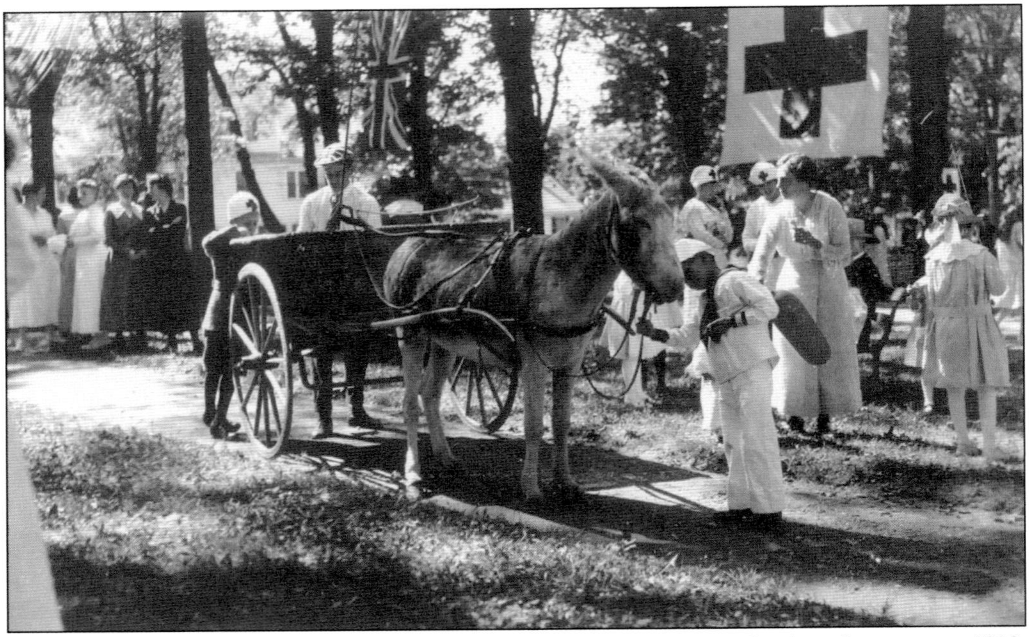

A donkey cart is the center of attention at the Red Cross Auction on Grafton Common in 1918. The auction was held to raise money for the American Red Cross.

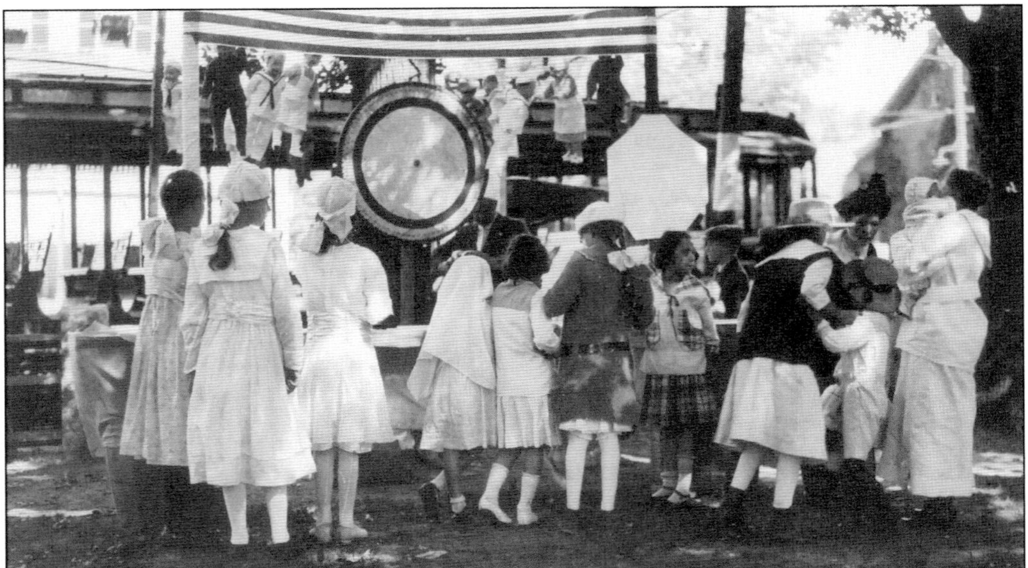

At the Red Cross Auction, games of chance offering prizes were very popular. This vendor offered dolls as prizes but had so many winners that he ran out. He began buying back dolls from former winners, offering $1 for each doll, a very good price in those days.

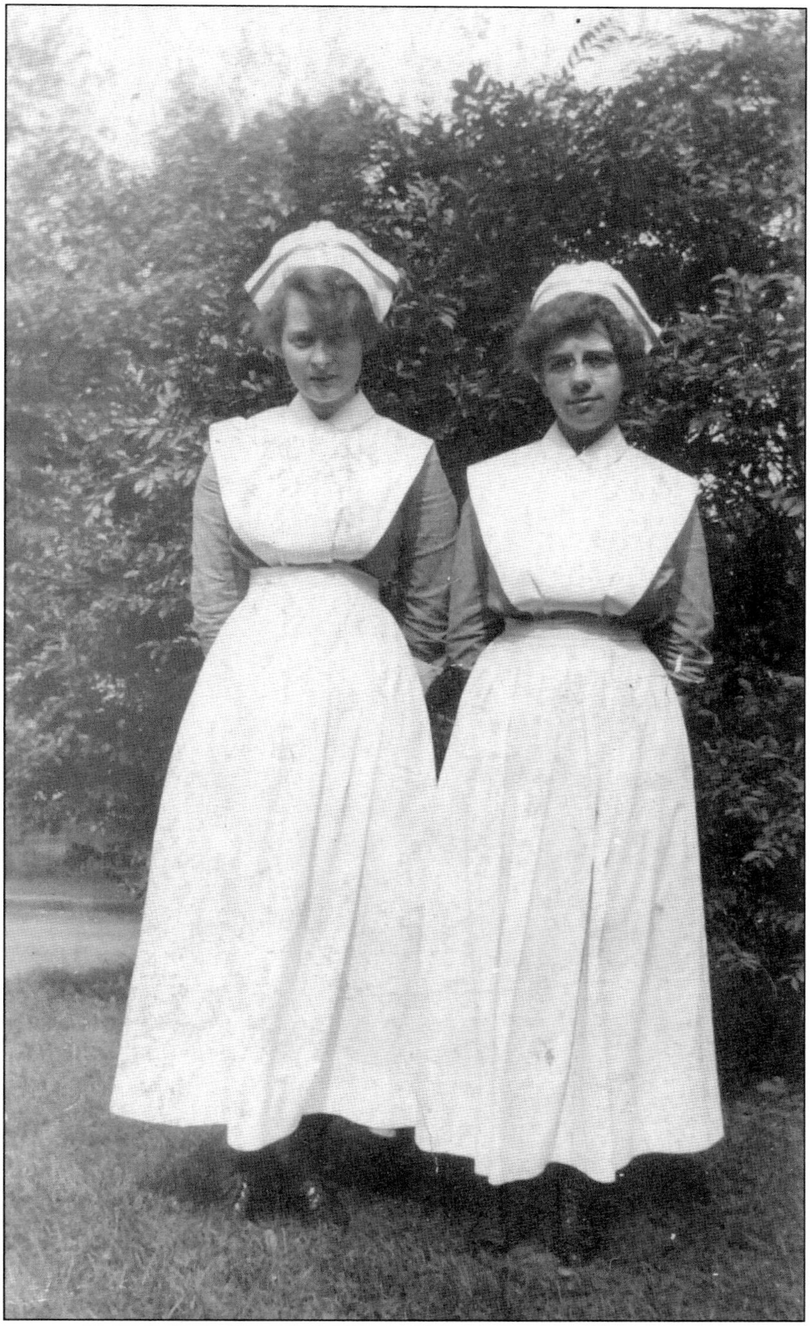

After graduating from Grafton High School in 1914, Edith Axtell Hayden trained as a nurse at Worcester City Hospital. In 1927, she was hired as the school and district nurse for the Grafton-North Grafton area and served in this position for 30 years. Her position as district nurse involved home visits where she tended the ill, comforted the bereaved, chopped wood, cooked meals, tended babies, cleaned houses, washed clothes, ran errands, and settled family disputes. She was frequently "on call" 24 hours a day. As the school's nurse, she knew several generations of Grafton families and was well loved and highly respected. Hayden (right) is seen here with a friend during her nursing training around 1916.

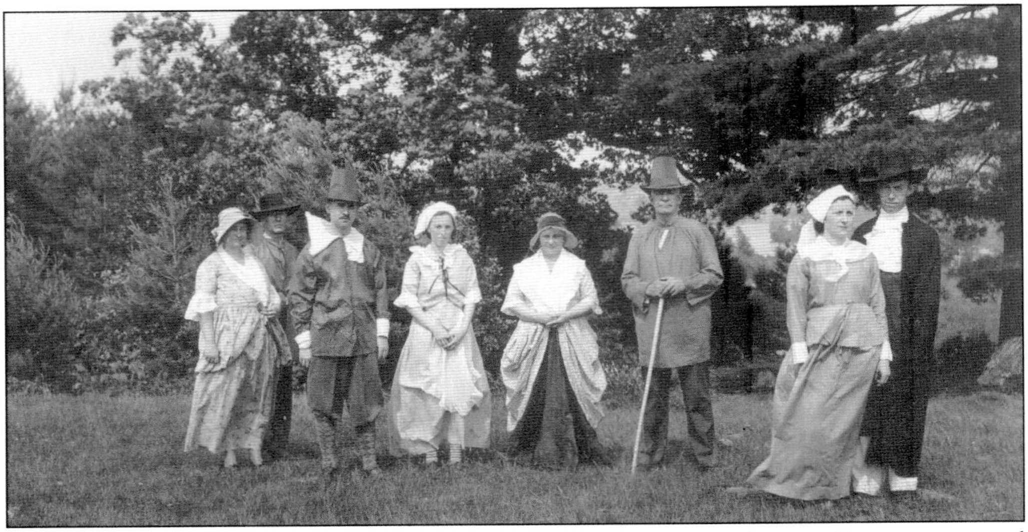

In 1935, on the 200th anniversary of the town's incorporation, Catherine Warren wrote and directed a pageant held at Carlson's Grove on Upton Road. Albert Smith (third from left) played Simon Willard, Margaret Gillespie (fourth from left) played Martha Willard, and Rev. Roger Pecke Cleveland (far right) played the Reverend John Eliot.

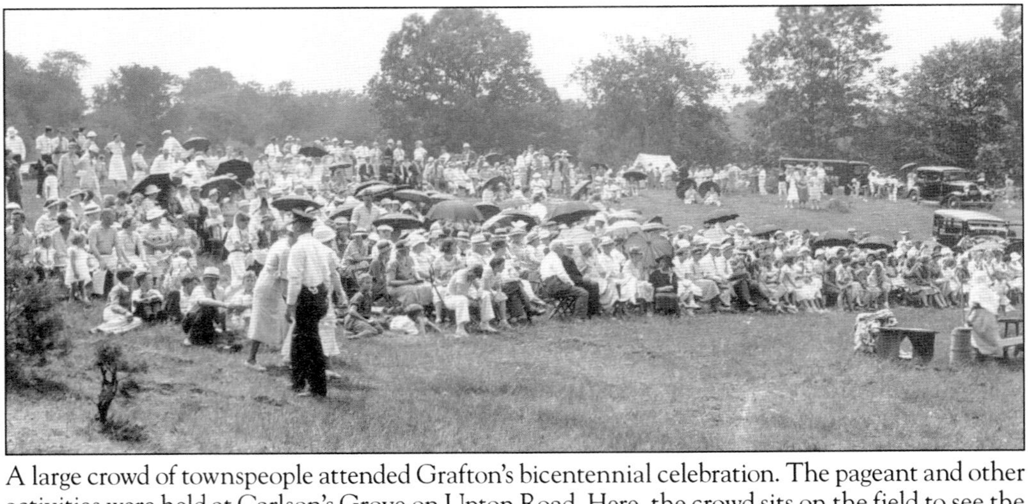

A large crowd of townspeople attended Grafton's bicentennial celebration. The pageant and other activities were held at Carlson's Grove on Upton Road. Here, the crowd sits on the field to see the pageant on a very hot July day in 1935. The Grafton Flea Market occupies that site today.

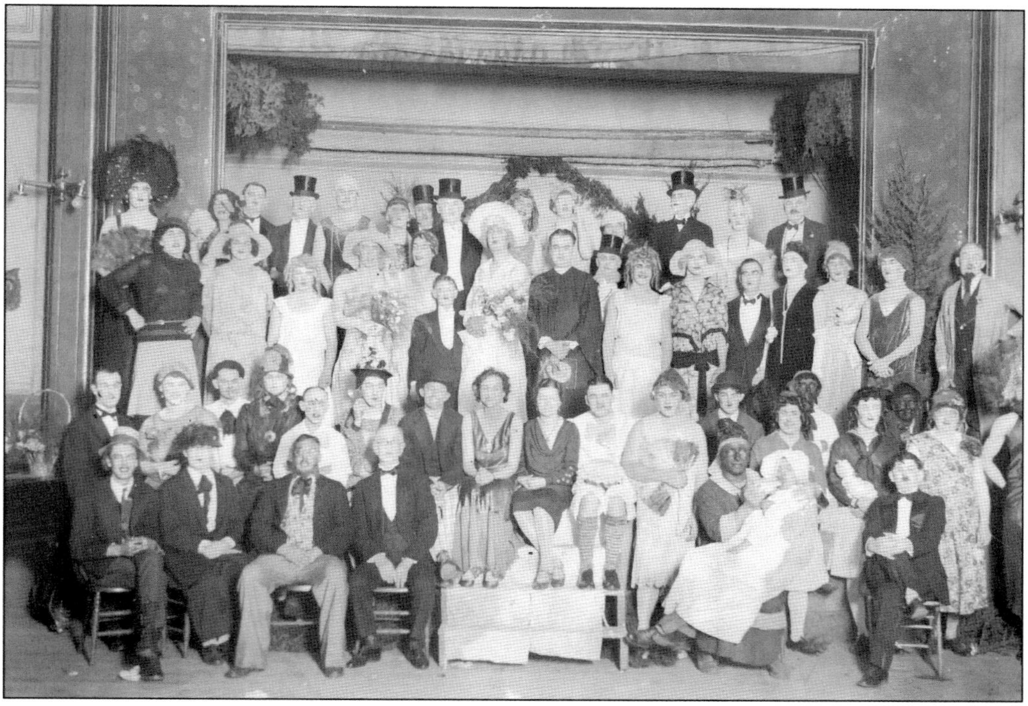

During the first half of the 20th century, most entertainment was homegrown. Local talent was invested in plays and shows of many kinds. This play was called *The Covered Wagon* and starred Isabel and Charlie Tebo, Forbush Anderson, Florence Clapp, Stanley McGarry, John Ingerson, and Joseph Goddard. It was performed in the Unitarian Church in 1920.

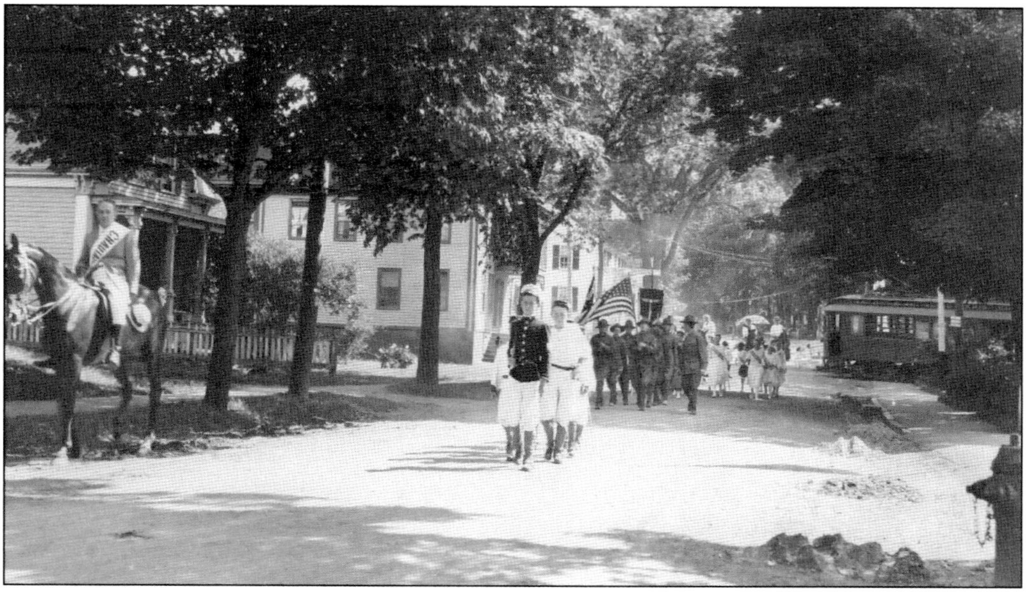

Boy Scouts, nurses, and horseback riders march down North Street in a Chautauqua parade in the 1920s. Grafton Common and the trolley can be seen behind them. A Chautauqua was a popular adult education movement in the early 20th century. Named after a lake in New York where it originated, a Chautauqua Assembly brought entertainment and culture for the whole community through teachers, preachers, musicians, and entertainers.

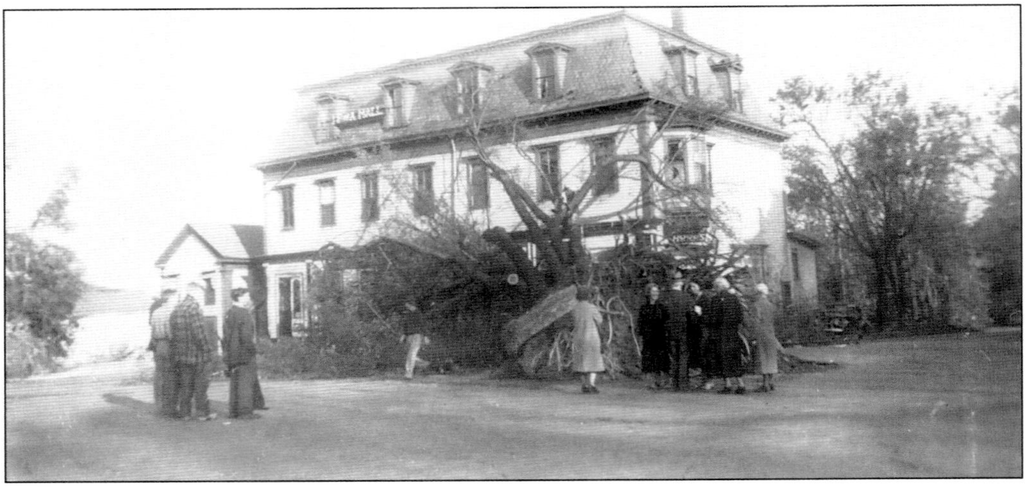

In 1938, a powerful and destructive hurricane struck Grafton. Trees in all parts of town were badly damaged. Heavy rains preceded the storm, saturating the ground. Many trees, such as this one, were uprooted. Every available man was pressed into service to clear the highways. Candles and oil lamps were the only means of light, and telephone service was crippled.

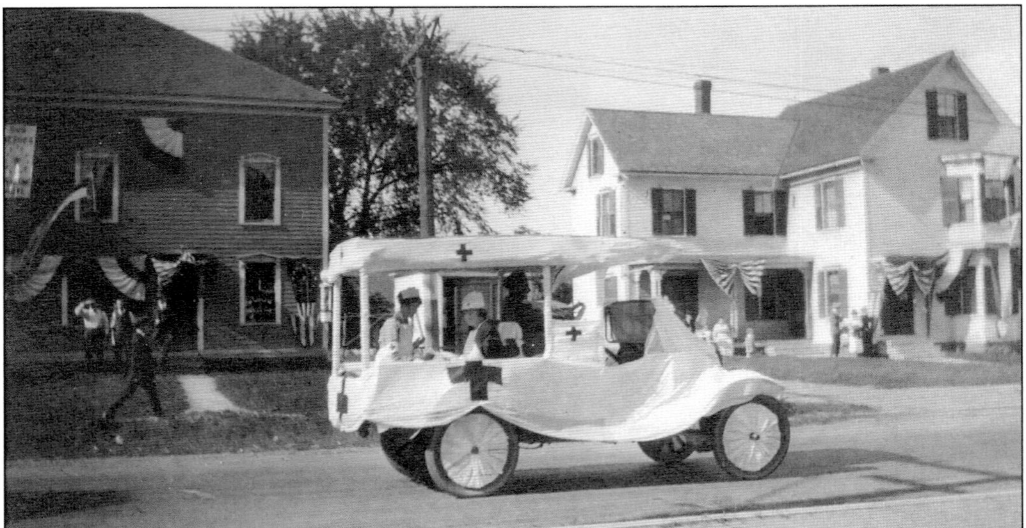

In 1918, a parade was held to welcome home the men who had fought in World War I. A float celebrating the efforts of the American Red Cross moves down Providence Road in South Grafton. A sign on a nearby building reads, "Our Heroes, Welcome Home."

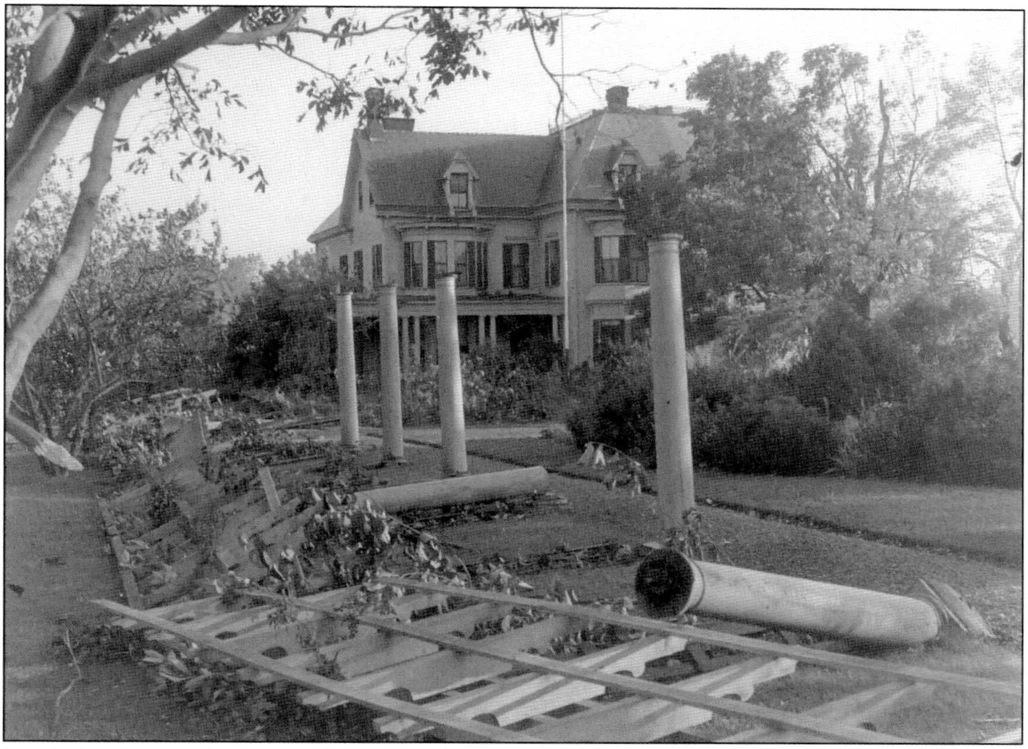

North Grafton was hit especially hard by the hurricane of 1938. Trees lie uprooted near the pergola of the Nelson Mansion. Orchards suffered heavy damage as high winds stripped the fruit off trees. Two North Grafton men died in the storm. Hiram F. Flansburg was killed when he was blown from the roof of a building he was repairing. George Howe died after being hit by a falling branch.

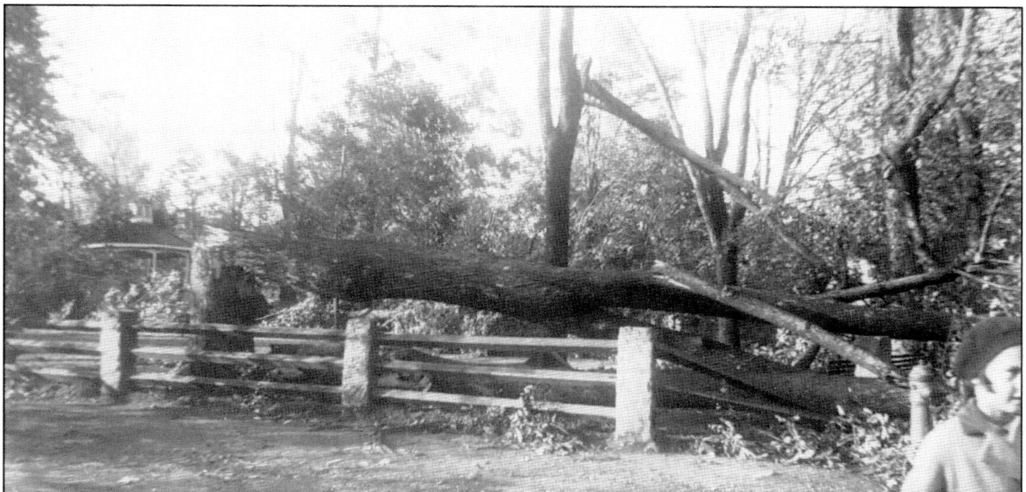

Trees on Grafton Common show extensive damage from the hurricane of 1938. The steeple of the Congregational Church was toppled and fell through the roof into the sanctuary. The roof of the stable owned by J. Frank Donahue was blown off. Prout's greenhouse on Meadowbrook Road was destroyed. The mill chimneys at Centerville and at the Linen Thread Co. were damaged. The town suffered $300,000 in damage.

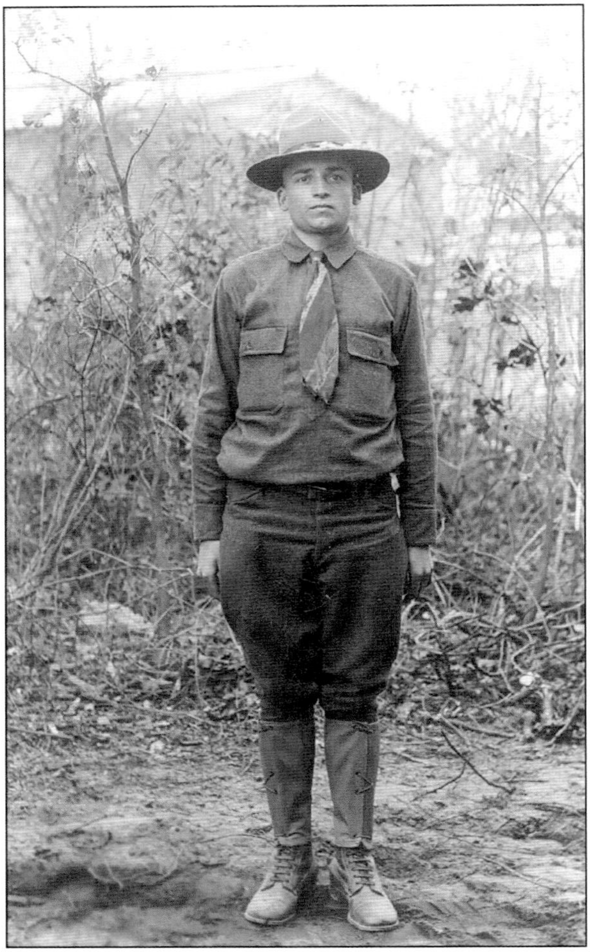

Stanley Popek, a barber, was one of many men from Grafton who enlisted in the Army to participate in World War I. He later married Mary Kostka from Fisherville. Stanley's sister Mary Kupiec ran the Cabot Inn on Sampson Street. His brother Anthony was a cobbler and lived in Farnumsville.

Soldiers and sailors of the North Grafton Depot neighborhood enjoy a sunny afternoon with family before being shipped out during World War II. From left to right are (first row) Charles Nason and Alden Bull; (second row) Aubrey Bull, Carol Bull, Clayton Fowler, and Doris Fowler. (Courtesy of Jacqueline Davison.)

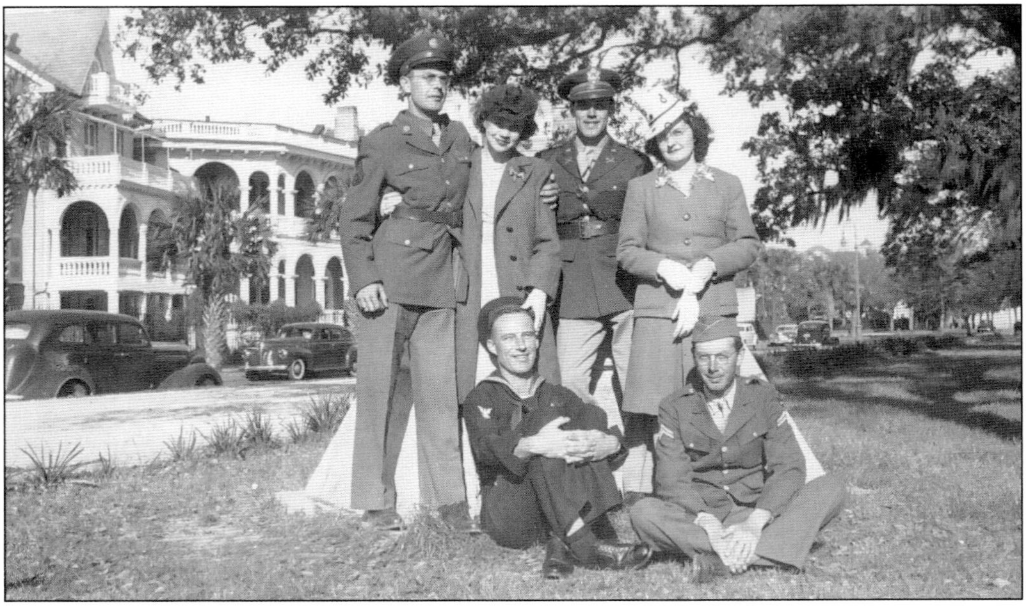

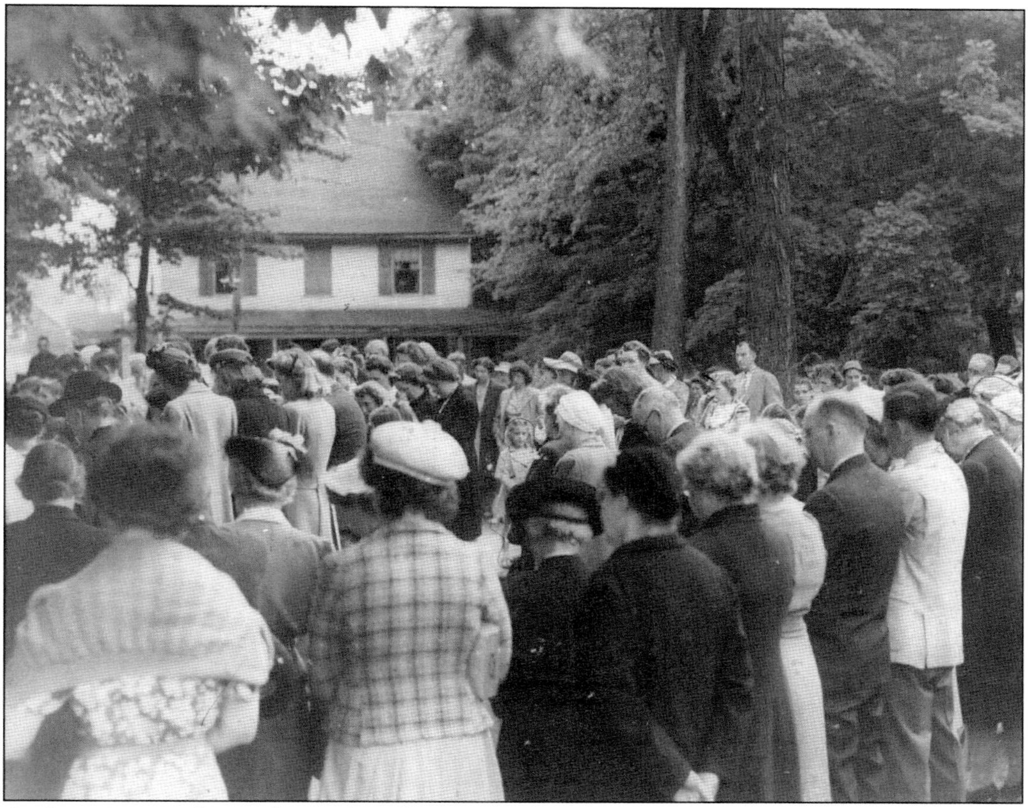

On June 6, 1944, the residents of Grafton came together on Grafton Common to observe D-day. Sirens were sounded, and people gathered quickly for the service. Prayers were led by local clergy, including Rev. Roger Pecke Cleveland, minister of the Evangelical Congregational Church, and Rev. Chester Drummond, minister of the Unitarian church. The Congregational church was opened, and people went there to offer their silent prayers.

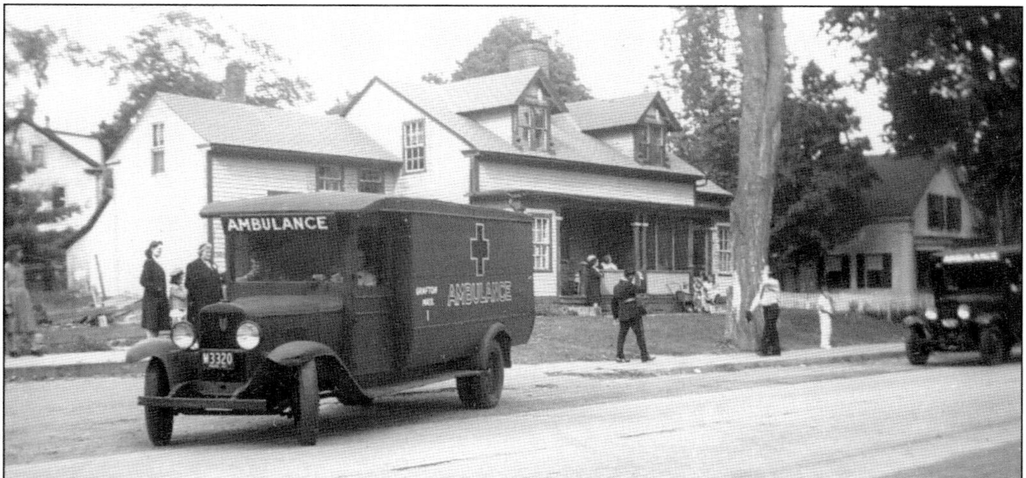

This ambulance was on display in a Grafton parade in 1942. With ambulances needed for the war effort, hometown ambulances were in short supply. Ruth Prout Jordan convinced her husband, George, to convert his school buses to ambulances for local use during the war.

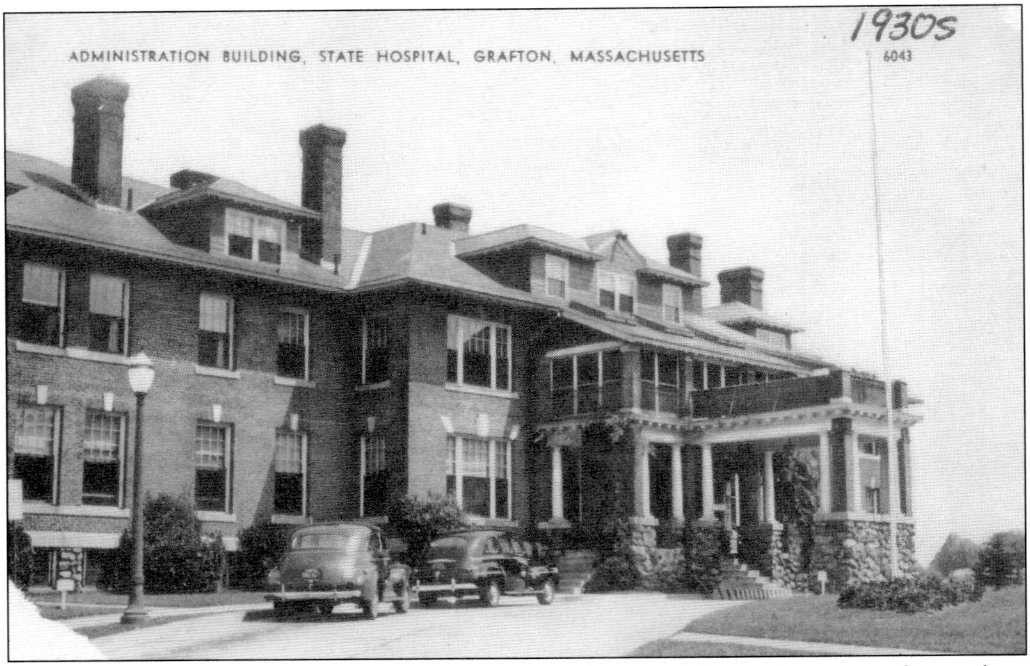

Grafton State Hospital was established in North Grafton in 1901 as a therapeutic farm colony for "chronic insane patients." In 1945, the hospital housed 1,730 patients. Many Grafton residents from all sections of town found employment here. The hospital was closed in 1973 when the state deinstitutionalized the psychiatric patient population. In the 1980s, the town united in an effort to bring New England's only veterinary school to the deserted property. The campus is now occupied by the Tufts University Cummings School of Veterinary Medicine and the Federal Job Corps Program. The photograph above shows the administration building as it looked in 1930. The photograph below shows construction of a dormitory in 1913.

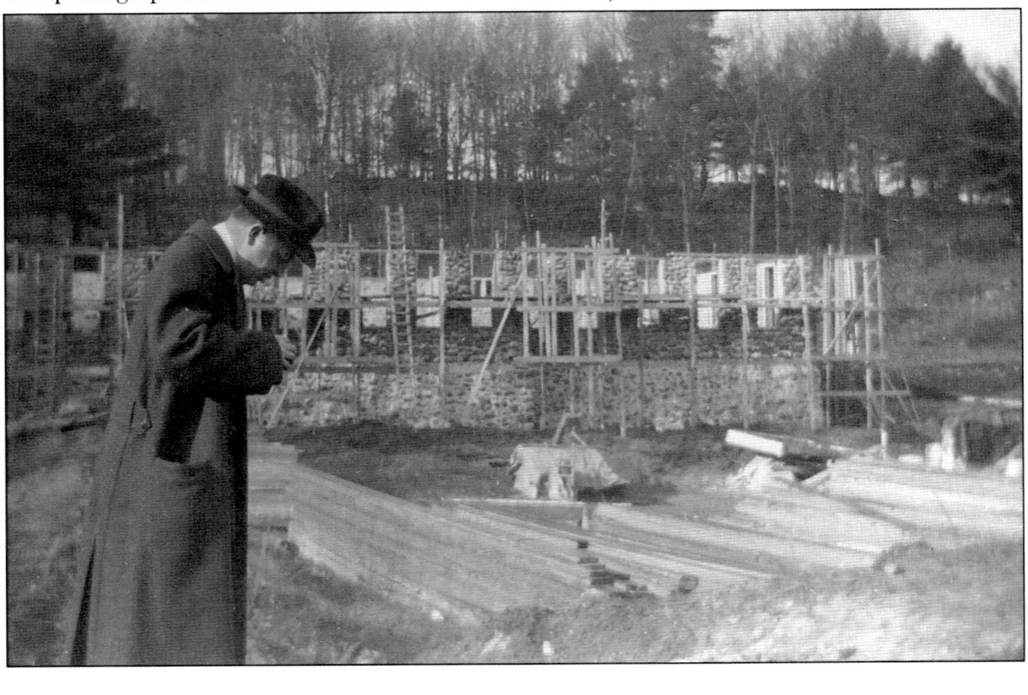

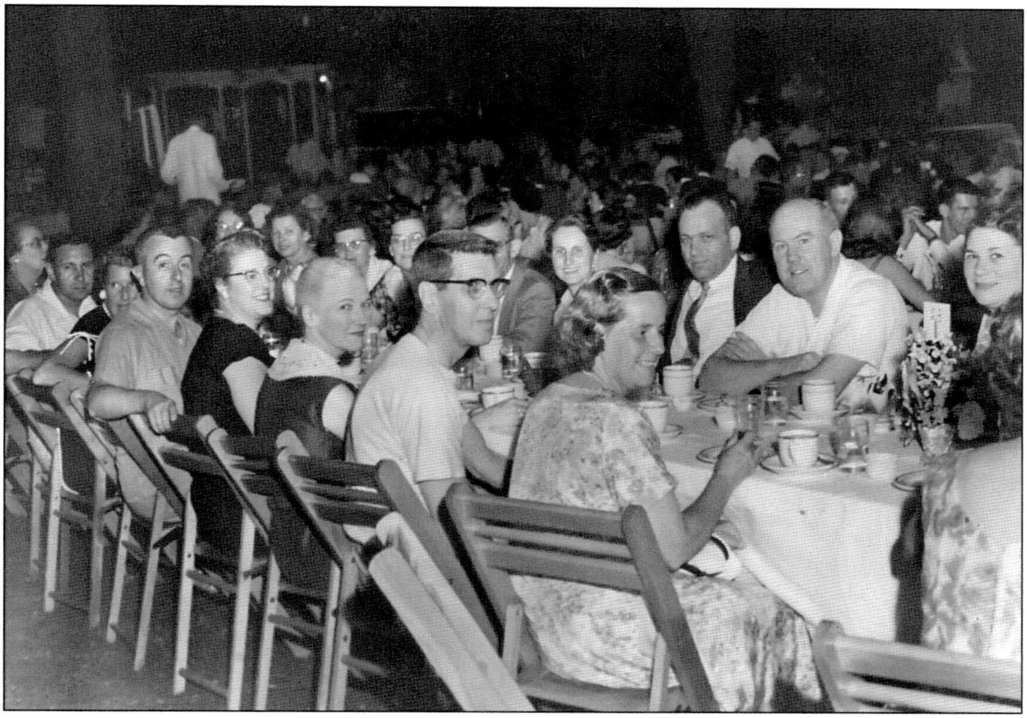

In 1949, the Grafton Alumni Association organized a high school reunion that attracted 540 guests. The event was held on a clear summer evening on Grafton Common with long banquet tables arranged in a fan shape around the bandstand. Dr. William B. Clapp was master of ceremonies and Nora Garner Riggs, class of 1942, was vocalist. William Woodburn, a local musician and music instructor, is seen on the right, facing the camera.

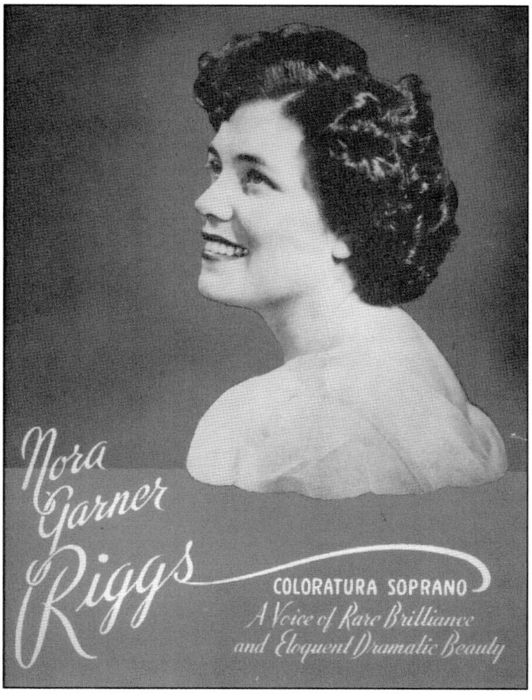

Nora Garner Riggs Belfay is a coloratura soprano who provided local entertainment during the 1940s and who achieved fame well beyond Grafton. She was born in South Dakota but moved to North Grafton when she was 14. Her musical talent was recognized early, and she was awarded scholarships to the Boston University College of Music. She was soloist for many orchestras, including the Boston Symphony Pops Orchestra.

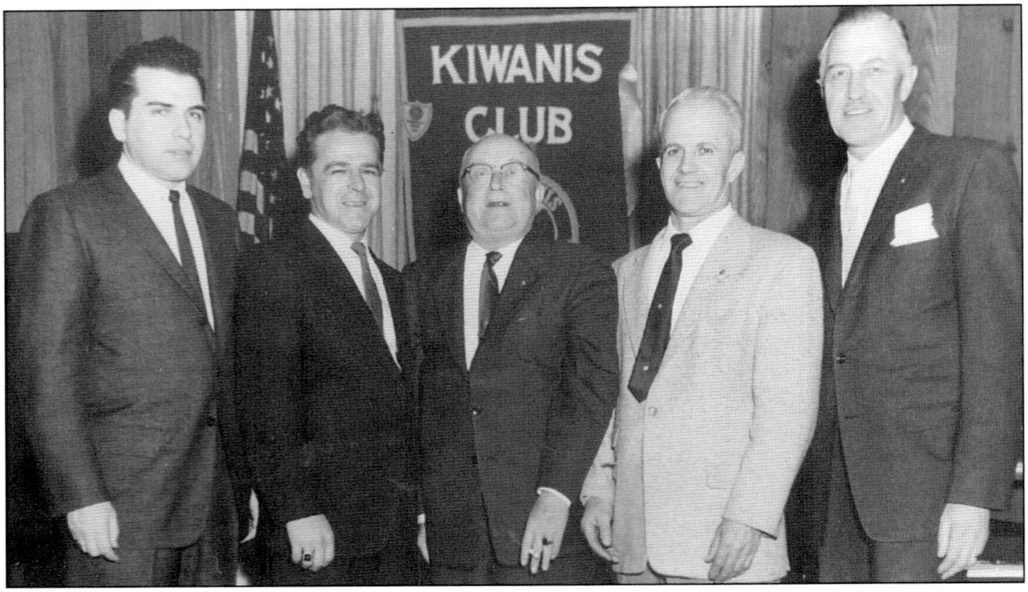

The Kiwanis Club, a philanthropic organization, met regularly at the Grafton Inn during the 1940s and 1950s. Pictured from left to right are local Kiwanis members Barry Hodes, owner of Hodes Market; Ray Fontaine, local barber; unidentified; Aldo Leofanti, owner of Leofanti's Restaurant; and Dr. Lannigan, local optometrist.

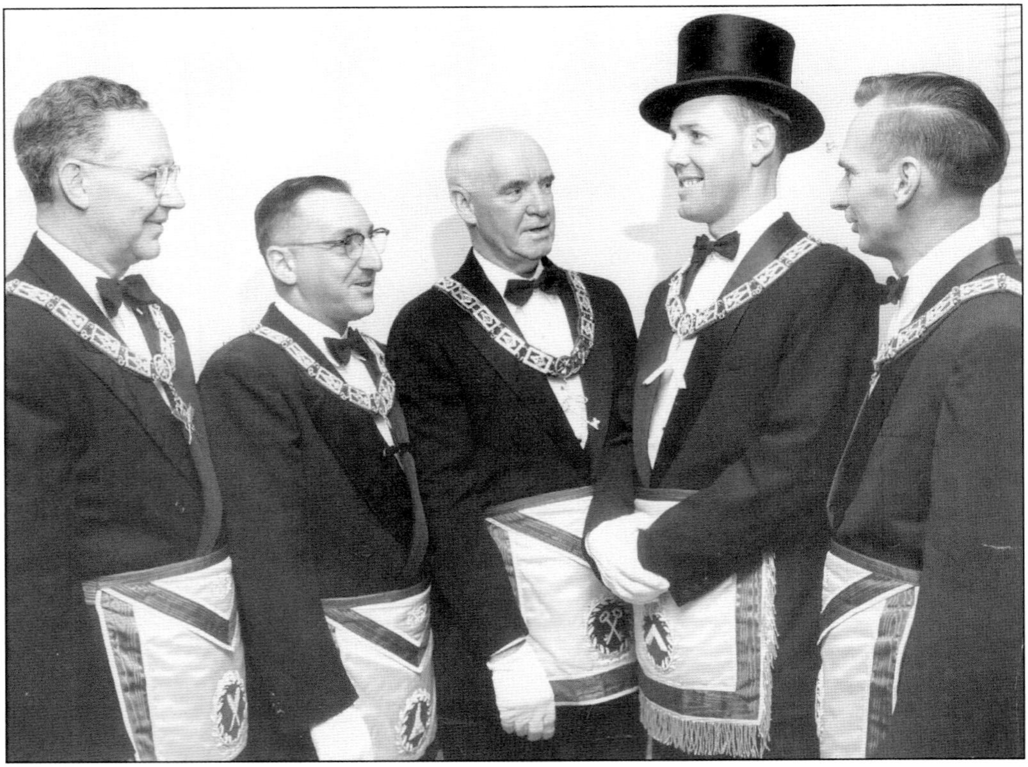

The Franklin Lodge of the Masons was constituted in 1852 as a community-based fraternal organization. In this 1950s photograph, from left to right are unidentified, Robert Roney, unidentified, Clayton Fowler, and Raymond Allen. (Courtesy of Jacqueline Davison.)

Bernard Corey (1914–2000) was born in South Grafton and lived there for most of his life. Although he had no formal training, he taught himself to paint in oils and watercolors. For 25 years, he worked painting houses and hanging wallpaper before dedicating himself to his art. He achieved national recognition and is considered one of the best New England plein air artists of the 20th century.

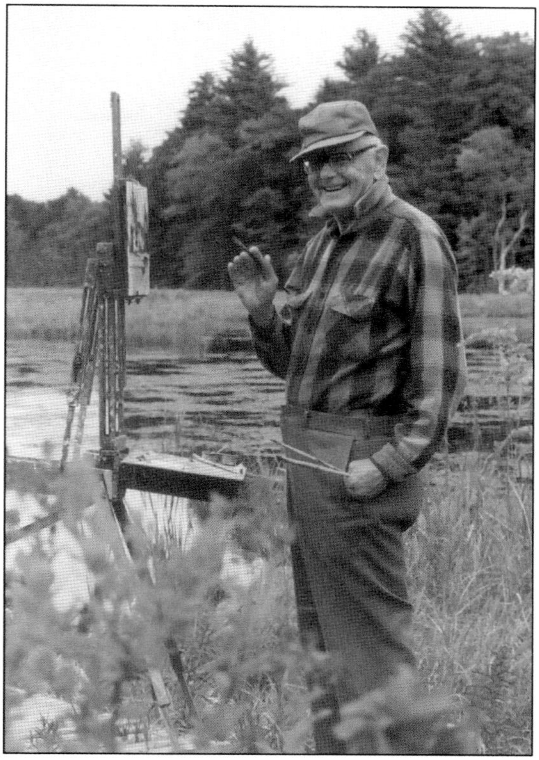

In 1962, Edward "Ted" Kennedy, who was running for US Senate for the first time, was a guest of the Grafton Democrats at Leofanti's Restaurant in North Grafton. Posing with him are, from left to right, (first row) William Roche, Thomas Quinn, Lorraine LeBlanc, Joan Kennedy, Minnie Briand, and Walter Baran; (second row) Joseph Knych, William Fields, Kennedy, Henry McNamara Sr., Henry McNamara Jr., and Chester Hospod. (Courtesy of Nancy Lemoine.)

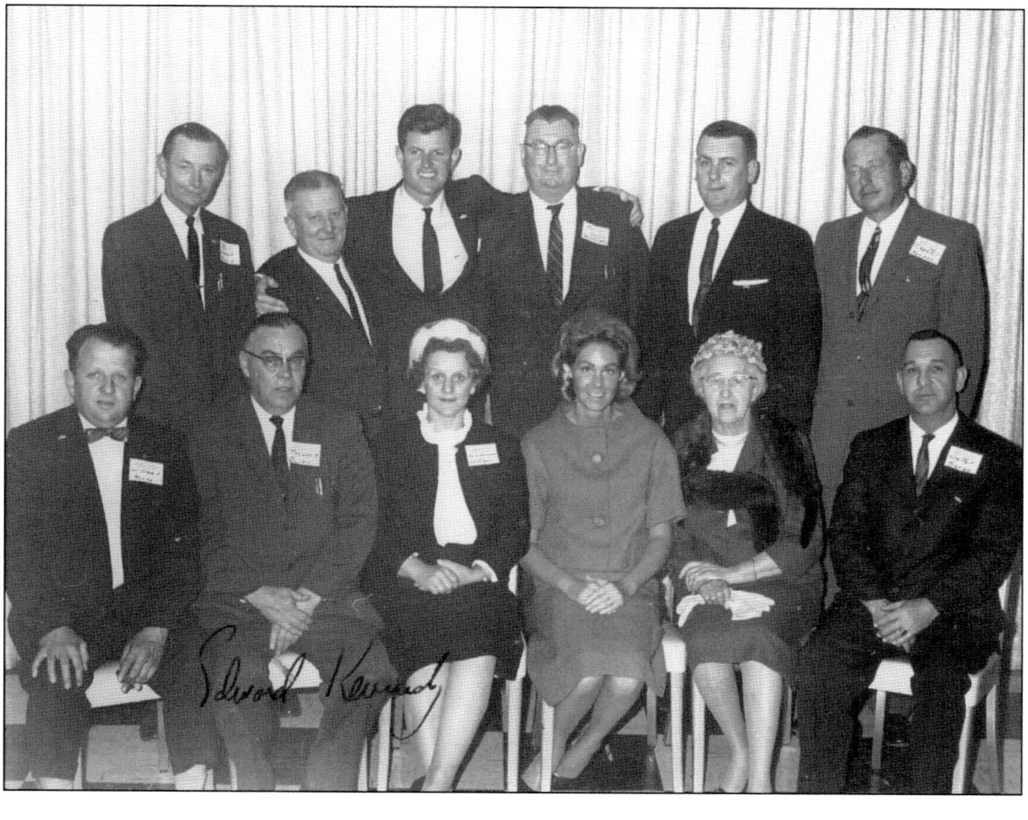